Legions of Boom

REFIGURING AMERICAN MUSIC / A SERIES EDITED BY RONALD RADANO AND JOSH KUN / CHARLES MCGOVERN, CONTRIBUTING EDITOR

Legions of Boom / Filipino American Mobile DJ Crews in the San Francisco Bay Area / Oliver Wang

Duke University Press / Durham and London / 2015

© 2015 Duke University Press / All rights reserved / Designed by Natalie F. Smith / Typeset in Chaparral Pro by Copperline

Library of Congress Cataloging-in-Publication Data / Wang, Oliver, 1972– / Legions of boom : Filipino American mobile DJ crews in the San Francisco Bay Area / Oliver Wang. / pages cm —(Refiguring American music) / Includes bibliographical references and index. / ISBN 978-0-8223-5904-3 (hardcover) / ISBN 978-0-8223-5890-9 (pbk.) / ISBN 978-0-8223-7548-7 (e-book) / 1. Filipino American youth—California—San Francisco Bay Area—Music—History—20th century. 2. Filipino Americans—California—San Francisco Bay Area—Ethnic identity. 3. Disc jockeys—California—
San Francisco Bay Area—History—20th century. I. Title. II. Series: Refiguring American music. / F870.F4W364 20115 / 305.235089'92107307946—dc23   2014041941

Frontispiece: Newspaper ad for a 1988 party in Union City hosted by the Legion of Boom, an alliance (cooperative) between several different Bay Area crews. Courtesy of Francisco Pardorla. / Cover art: Illustration using a photo of Arnie Espinosa (Images Inc., Fremont) by Francisco Pardorla, c. 1986. Photo courtesy of Francisco Pardorla.

This goes out to Sharon, Ella, and all Bay Area crew.

Contents

ACKNOWLEDGMENTS (ix)

PROLOGUE / THE GIG (1)

INTRODUCTION / A LEGION OF BOOM (7)

1 / CUE IT UP / SOCIAL PRECONDITIONS FOR THE MOBILE SCENE (29)

2 / TEAM BUILDING / MOBILE CREW FORMATIONS (49)

3 / UNLIMITED CREATIONS / THE MOBILE SCENE TAKES OFF (79)

4 / IMAGININGS / BUILDING COMMUNITY IN THE SHOWCASE ERA (95)

5 / TAKE ME OUT WITH THE FADER / THE DECLINE OF THE MOBILE SCENE (125)

CONCLUSION / ECHO EFFECTS (151)

APPENDIX 1 / CAPTAINS OF THE FIELD / SAN FRANCISCO DRILL TEAMS (163)

APPENDIX 2 / BORN VERSUS SWORN / FILIPINO AMERICAN YOUTH GANGS (167)

NOTES (173)

REFERENCES (203)

INDEX (213)

Acknowledgments

This book has been such a long time in coming that I feel obligated to open with both a "thank you" and an apology, especially to all the respondents who generously shared their stories with me over the years. As I hope is clear in the book, I have tremendous awe of and admiration for the kind of fully realized cultural scene (or, as Jeff Chang keeps insisting, movement) they created—and as teenagers no less. To be able, in any small and modest way, to retell or share even a sliver of that history is a remarkable honor. Therefore, I first have to thank the many respondents who sat down with me over the years (oftentimes in Starbucks, as it were), including those whose voices I ultimately couldn't include in the text.

There are a few people from the scene who deserve special recognition for going above and beyond in assisting me with testimonials and artwork: Daphnie Gambol Anies (the Go-Go's), Rene Anies (Electric Sounds), Royce Anies, Paul Canson (Second To None), Jon "Shortkut" Cruz (Just 2 Hype), Jay dela Cruz (Spintronix), John Francisco (Expressions), Henry Geronimo (Unique Musique), Gary "Genie G" Millare (Ultimate Creations), "DJ Apollo" Novicio (Unlimited Sounds), Francisco Pardorla (Images Inc.), Richard "Q-Bert" Quitevis (Live Style), Suzie Racho (Cosmix

Sounds), Dave "Dynamix" Refuerzo (3-Style Attractions), Rafael Restauro (Sound Explosion), Dino Rivera (Spintronix), Liza Dizon Vargas (the Go-Go's), and Ricky Viray (A Touch of Class).

Extra special thanks to Burton Kong (Sound Sequence) for giving his blessing for me to use the Legion of Boom name and especially to Melanie Caganot Kong for mounting her seminal 2001–2002 *Tales of the Turntable* exhibit at the San Mateo County History Museum and giving me a starting point for my research. I also want to acknowledge the importance of music writer Neva Chonin at the *San Francisco Bay Guardian*, from whom I first learned about the Filipino American scratch DJ scene, as well as journalist-DJ-organizer David "Davey D" Cook, who was perhaps the first journalist from outside the mobile scene to write about its history.

I especially want to thank Michael Omi, my graduate school advisor at the University of California, Berkeley. He convinced me to take what had been a proposed dissertation chapter and turn it into the entire project. This book, in no small way, came about because of his insights as a mentor. Likewise, the first time I met Josh Kun was when I guest-lectured on Asian American music for a class he was a teaching assistant in. After I finished, he walked up to me, introduced himself, and said, "You need to write a book." Fast-forward about eighteen years and this book appears in the series that Josh edits; funny how that works out.

And of course, this book would literally not exist without the unflagging support of Duke's Ken Wissoker. He believed in the worthiness of this project back before I had even completed the research on it as a dissertation. Ever since, he has shepherded it through its various revisions and tweaks with enthusiasm (and patience). I am incredibly honored to have the book appear on the Duke imprint and under his guidance.

I owe much gratitude for all the editorial help I was given by Laura Helper-Ferris, Amy Rasmussen, Lis Pisares, and Loren Kajikawa, all of whom helped review preliminary draft chapters and provided crucial feedback. That goes double for both Josh Kun and Mark Anthony Neal, both of whom "outed" themselves to me as the manuscript's early reviewers. Given my immense respect for their work, I feel remarkably fortunate to have had their feedback to guide my early revisions. Likewise, Jeff Chang came in during the eleventh hour with integral suggestions on streamlining the book's prose and narrative choices. Throughout our long friendship, Jeff has always been one of my most hard-to-please editors, but I feel like my work has always benefited for it. Most of all, I need to thank Joe Schloss, who served as the book's primary outside editor and always made himself available to lend substantive feedback, not to mention moral support.

Especially because my research was so intensely interview-based, Melissa Padua, Roseli Ilano, Margaret Cakir, Jordan Chalifoux, and Gary Powell were all crucial in providing transcription services. Likewise, my research assistants at California State University, Long Beach—Matt Nailat, Jason Chung, and Alissa Puccio—helped in organizing much of my loose data into more manageable forms.

Throughout the years, I've enjoyed the privilege of discussing and writing about this research for the likes of Christine Balance, Ta-Nehisi Coates, Loren Kajikawa, Mark Katz, Matthew Ledesma, Jan Lin, Mark Anthony Neal, Varisa Patraporn, and Mark Villegas (and his *Empire of Funk* coeditors, Kuttin' Kandi and Rob Labrador). Appreciation also goes out to the program committees in the Association for Asian American Studies, American Studies Association, and especially everyone associated with the Experience Music Project's Pop Conference. I'd also like to thank everyone connected with the USC Vectors program for helping me develop the digital repository for the book's research (see http://legionsofboom.com for more information).

Writing and editing can often be solitary, isolating experiences by necessity, so I've always been thankful for opportunities to interact with people during that process, dating all the way back to when Tony Tiongson and I used to run into one another at Gaylord Cafe on Piedmont, both of us working on dissertations about Filipino DJs. This goes out to just a few of the informal writing partners I've had over the years, including, but not limited to, Stewart Chang, Christina Chin, Robert Ito, Jordan Smith, and Patricia Wakida. Shout out to all the coffee shops in Los Angeles where I wrote or revised most of this book, especially Bobatime (West LA), Xokolatl (El Sereno), La Monarca and Charlie's (South Pasadena), and Honey Badger (Alhambra).

I began writing about Bay Area DJs as a journalist before I ever took the topic on as a scholar. Throughout the years, my writing opportunities have improved my overall quality of life and contributed to my skills as a scholar and teacher (and vice versa). The list of outlets who've given me those opportunities is far too long to list here, but a few special shout-outs go to Tommy Tompkins at the *San Francisco Bay Guardian*, Kathryn McGuire and James Tai at URB, Tom Cole at NPR, Brian Digenti at *Wax Poetics*, Drew Tewksbury at KCET's Artbound, and KPCC's Jacob Margolis. Similarly, as a DJ who still (occasionally) practices the craft, I'm very appreciative to DJ Phatrick, Terril Johnson, Wilson Bethel, Vinnie Esparza, Michael Barnes, Radio Sombra, the entire KALX family, and all the promoters and wedding clients who've let me get my spin on.

I've enjoyed great professional support over the years from my colleagues at CSULB, including Gordon Abra, Sabrina Alimohamed, Carole Campbell, Norma Chinchilla, Kim Glick, Larry Hashima, Linda Maram, Nancy Martin, Brett Mizelle, Lily Monji, Varisa Patraporn, Amy Rasmussen, Sarah Schrank, Jacqueline Southern, Jake Wilson, Kerry Woodward, and Kris Zentgraf. Similar thanks go to the *Journal of Popular Music Studies* team: Meghan Drury, Anastasia Nikolis, Gus Stadler, all the associate editors, and especially Karen Tongson and my coeditor Gayle Wald, both of whom have been inspiring mentors and colleagues to boot.

Over the long years, my endeavors have been buoyed by the unflagging enthusiasm of many friends and colleagues (many of whom have already been mentioned), including also Daphne Brooks, Jon Caramanica, Dan Charnas, Colleen Chien, Moe Choi, Theo Gonzalvez, Mimi Ho, Patrick Huang, Todd Inoue, Gaye Theresa Johnson, David Leonard, Maxwell Leung, Robin Li, Harry Lin, Cynthia Liu, Kai Ma, Dawn Mabalon, Adam Mansbach, Ernest Mark, Susette Min, Rani Neutill, Mimi Nguyen, Joseph Patel, Lisa Persky, Oiyan Poon, Chris Portugal, Ann Powers, Joy Press, Simon Reynolds, Morgan Rhodes, Ikuko Sato, Junichi Semitsu, Nitasha Sharma, Leonard Shek, Sean Slusser, RJ Smith, Jay Smooth, Chris Veltri, Eric Weisbard, Deborah Wong, Phil Yu, and Andy Zax. A deep dedication goes to the late Matthew Africa, a friend, mentor, and a stalwart Bay Area DJ if ever there was one.

Deepest appreciations to those who've left an indelible impact on my work and life over the course of this book (and beyond): To the "Three Js"—Jeff, Josh, and Joe—over the years, all three of you have inspired my own "lightbulb moments" when I realized what was possible because you led by example. Those have been gifts I can only hope to pay back by hopefully paying forward. To Loren Kajikawa and his family: we may never live in the same city again, but our families will always be close in spirit. To my parents, Richard and Tamie, for all the support (and prodding) that have shaped my life in incalculable ways. To Diane Mizota and Irene Yamamoto, for having taken such good care of my family since our arrival in Los Angeles. To Jess Wang, for being the best ally and mediator a brother could ask for. As for Hua Hsu: thank you for being a most remarkable sounding board, confidant, conspirator, counselor, et al. My appreciation for our daily correspondence is boundless.

Lastly, to Sharon Mizota, thank you for being my partner in so many meanings of the word. For your affection, patience, and enthusiasm. For being my favorite everything (over the age of ten). I love you and I like you. And to Ella, thank you for being my favorite everything (ten and under). For being one of the most interesting and entertaining people I've ever met. It is such a profound privilege to be your dad. I dedicate this book especially to you and all the children of my respondents, who may yet become the next generation of spin doctors.

Prologue / The Gig

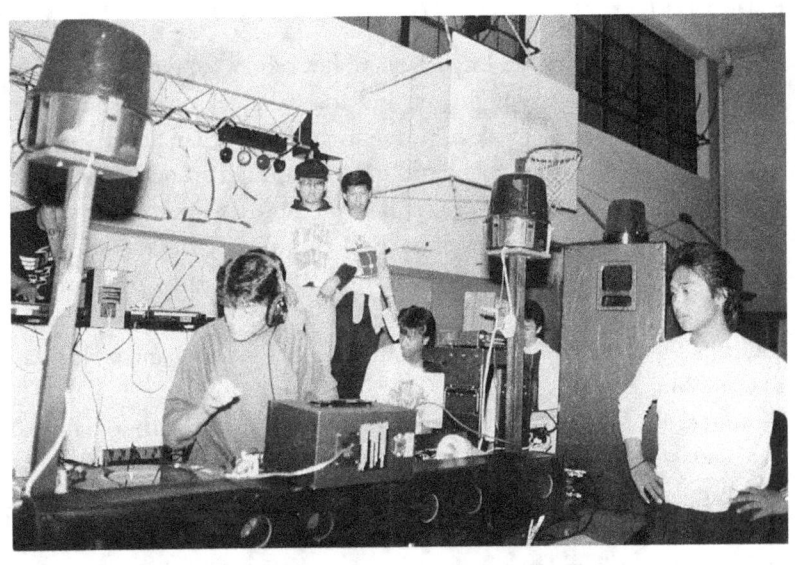

P.1 / Spintronix (Daly City) in 1986, performing at Philip Burton Middle School (San Francisco). Spintronix is one of the longest lasting mobile crews and is still active today. Left to right: Dino Rivera, Chris Miguel, Kormann Roque, Noel Laxamana, Larry Alfonso, Ron Mananquil, Robert Cristobal. Photo courtesy of Ray Portugal.

Friday, 3 p.m. / Westmoor High School / Daly City

Dino Rivera sits quietly in English class, but school isn't on his mind at the moment. Tomorrow night, he and the members of his Spintronix crew will be throwing a party at St. Augustine's Church in South City. All week long, friends and family have dropped by high schools, malls, and other parties around the Bay Area to help promote the event, and now, on the eve of the big night, Rivera runs through a mental checklist of what's left to do. There's still a few places to drop off flyers, there's equipment to rent, and a motley crew of folks need to be assigned different responsibilities. Once the school bell rings, Rivera's out the door and on his way to Chris Miguel's house.

    Miguel is a fellow Westmoor student and Spintronix's other main DJ. His house is the crew's de facto headquarters; it helps that he has the best garage where they can store all their DJing and lighting equipment. Within an hour after school, half-a-dozen or so Spintronix members gather at Miguel's and pore over the last-minute details. First step is figuring out how much equipment they'll need for the gig: do they have enough speakers? Amps? Lights? Maybe they'll need to make a quick trip down to Pacifica to rent extra equipment from Manor Music, or maybe they can just borrow a loaner from one of the other Daly City crews they're friendly with. They'll also need transportation to move everything, and for that, they can count on Chris's father, Luciano "Lou" Miguel. He used to drive Chris to every gig when he was too young to have a license, and the rest of the crew consider Lou to be the godfather of Spintronix.

The crew have their plan in order, and everyone except for Rivera and Miguel leaves. As the crew's main DJs, they stay behind to practice the mix they have planned for the next night. Spintronix has a reputation to hold up, not just for the quality of their mixes, not just in terms of song selection, but in how well Miguel and Rivera work together as a pair. Rivera's gift is in "blending," that is, creating a seamless transition from song to song, not just in tempo but also in melodic key. In contrast, Miguel is better known as a "quick mixer"; he specializes in throwing down song after song, in quick succession, but always done in tempo so the dancers don't get thrown off. Especially for bigger parties, such as this St. Augustine's gig, the two DJs want to prepare their sets well beforehand so they can pull it off without a hitch when the moment arrives.

Rivera could practice at his own home, but the crew consolidate all their records at Miguel's in order to keep them better organized. It's part of their philosophy as a crew: focus on the needs of the collective rather than any single individual. Especially in Spintronix, the core members foster a family dynamic; Rivera is practically an unofficial member of Miguel's clan, and he comes over so many times a week to practice that he has "in and out" privileges, even if Miguel isn't home. After a few hours, the two DJs feel satisfied that they have their mix down pat. They call it a night; tomorrow will be a far busier day.

Saturday, Early Afternoon / Chris Miguel's

Back at their respective homes, the Spintronix members prepare for the evening with some key sartorial decisions. These parties are as much about socializing as entertaining, and everyone wants to make sure they are "dressed to impress." Tight-fitting Levi's or fresh-pressed Lee jeans are always in fashion, and thanks to Run DMC's burgeoning popularity, Adidas shell-toes are now in (though British Knights are still in vogue).

The party starts at 8 p.m., which means the crew need to gather at Miguel's house by 4 p.m. The rental truck pulls into the driveway, and immediately the crew begin to load equipment from the garage into the back of the truck. When they first started, the process was more disorganized, with various cables and equipment tangled or jumbled on the garage floor. Over time, though, they've gotten loading and unloading down to a science; members know exactly where and how to pack things efficiently and quickly. In less than half an hour, they are ready to roll.

Ordinarily, for a smaller gig, such as a garage party, Spintronix would bring a more compact setup: a pair of speakers, subwoofers, amplifiers, and a basic light array of "helicopters," oscillators, and truss.[1] For bigger parties, that trip to Manor Music might be warranted, but tonight the crew decided to compromise. Rather than rent more lights, they will build a bigger truss and then space the lights out over them, forming an illusion of having a bigger setup than actually exists.

Saturday, 6 p.m. / St. Augustine's

The sponsors of tonight's party are the Young Adult Group at St. Augustine's. For several years now, the Young Adult Group has been active in booking local DJ crews to throw dances for neighborhood teens. Its members are finishing with decorations as the Spintronix truck pulls up, and they watch as a swarm of people begin pulling equipment out. Spintronix rolls with an auxiliary "staff" of friends willing to help as roadies. Kormann Roque, one of the crew founders and their lighting expert, directs people in assembling everything together.

It takes a little over an hour to set up the truss, stage, and equipment properly—at this point, Spintronix has mastered the process with clocklike efficiency—and once the turntables are in place, Miguel and Rivera begin pulling records out of their sleeves and stacking them on either side of the turntables; this will allow them to mix between records more quickly once the party is in full gear. A few records are marked with masking tape with each song's tempo and pitch information written on it; this too helps with mixing more cleanly.

Saturday, 8 p.m. / St. Augustine's

The gig begins, and Rivera is the first to man the tables. He always opens the evening, while Miguel is the designated closer, and in between they trade off thirty- to forty-minute sets. Rivera's challenge is in building the floor, trying to coax dancers off the wall. He finds that Latin freestyle often does the trick and mixes in songs by the Cover Girls, Sweet Sensation, TKA, and others. As a blend mixer, Rivera's skill lies in making sure each song mixes fluidly into the next, creating a "nonstop" flow of music that gradually pulls people to the floor and, more important, keeps them there.

By 10:30 p.m., the party begins to reach critical mass, with a couple hundred people in attendance. Miguel shifts the sound from freestyle into an R&B and hip-hop set, dropping 2 Live Crew and MC Shy D, then Run DMC and LL Cool J. It's a church dance with high school students in attendance, so he needs to be wary of excessive profanity, but as a quick mixer, he's adept at moving records in and out with dizzying speed. He keeps pushing the tempo up; 110 bpm (beats per minute) jumps to 120, then gradually builds again to 130 as the dance floor locks in with a frenzy. The coup de grace? When the DJs drop Spintronix's unofficial anthem, "Boogie Down Bronx" by Man Parrish. The crew's fans know to expect it at some point, and when it finally slips into the mix, they roar with appreciation.

Midnight / St. Augustine's

School dances usually have to end by 10:30 or 11 p.m., but the Young Adult Group lets the party go until midnight. By the very end, the crowd has faded off the peak, but patches of people are still hanging out. Once the music ends, Spintronix members clamber on the stage to begin breaking everything down and repacking it into the truck. They drive the equipment back to Miguel's house and store it quickly but carefully—the crew may have back-to-back gigs on weekends, so leaving everything in a mess will only hurt them that second night.

The after-gig ritual is always the same: crew members are treated to a late-night meal at the Denny's in Westborough. They are hardly alone—Denny's is *the* hangout spot, and as Rivera walks in, he recognizes a bevy of friends and peers, including members from other mobile crews. Spintronix's business manager and cofounder, Jay dela Cruz, quickly counts out the evening's proceeds, subtracting the money they'll want to reinvest for new equipment or records. Whatever is left is for this Denny's run. The crew socialize, talking and joking about who they saw and what they did that night. Rivera joins in, but somewhere, in the back of his mind, he is also thinking about the next gig, when they'll do this all over again.

Dedicated to the memory of Lou Miguel

Introduction / A Legion of Boom

I.1 / Various Bay Area mobile crew business cards. Courtesy of Dino Rivera.

What is it about a turntable that invites our touch? Some seem incredulous that they even still exist and they reach toward them as if touching an exotic animal previously thought to be extinct. For others, turntables at a nightclub or bar seem like an invitation for people—often inebriated— to play amateur DJ for a moment, usually to the ire of the actual working DJ. Still others—namely, my then-toddler daughter—like to jab the "Start/Stop" button just to see the platter spin around.

For me—and I suspect many others as well—touch is how we literally and figuratively connect to a record player's purpose and powers. Everything about DJing with turntables is tactile: you pull a vinyl record out of a sleeve, place it on the platter, lift the stylus, and drop it in a groove. In watching the DJ, seeing how she or he grazes the platter or pinches the spindle, we learn how important touch is to the act and art of DJing, how that physical interaction is not incidental but essential. A turntable may be a remarkable conduit for music's pleasures, but it requires human hands to unlock that potential.

My own fascination with turntables began in the summer of 1988, at a garage party thrown by a high school classmate, Sanjeev Ravipudi. Like many an amateur DJ before him, Ravipudi had raided whatever home stereo equipment he found in his parents' living room and assembled a setup in their garage. In that space, all cold and concrete, I watched Ravipudi mix records, my first time observing a DJ in action. I have no recollection if he was actually any good or not—he is now a successful cardiovascular surgeon, so apparently he had deft hands—but Ravipudi took the time to explain how "beat-matching" worked, how he would slow down or speed up each turntable to get the tempos to match one another in order to seamlessly mix between them.

Beat-matching, when done right, facilitates an endless flow of music. These days, we take that experience for granted, but imagine what dancing would be like with a not-so seamless flow. What beat-matching, among other techniques, helps achieve is a way to bring people together on a parquet and keep them there, nurturing an ephemeral community of dancers. Ravipudi was the first person to teach me how DJing could influence social bonding; in the years to come, I would understand how those forces could work beyond the dance floor and impact an entire region.

Beginning in the late 1970s and through the mid-1990s, on any given weekend in the San Francisco Bay Area, there were dozens, if not hundreds, of parties jumping off. That included garage and house parties, church hall dances, school gym dances, weddings, debuts, and christening and birthday parties, to say nothing of large-scale performances ("showcases") and competitions ("battles"). Mobile DJs—DJs who provide audio and lighting services—ran these parties, organizing themselves into different groups, aka *crews*.

Mobile crews could range from small and modest, a few friends sharing a mix-and-match sound system and a strobe light, to large and elaborate—an organization of a dozen-plus members, boasting high-end professional speakers, amps, turntables, and concert-quality trussing installed with helicopters, oscillators, and a spotlight trained on a disco ball. The early mobile DJs were "blend-mixers," skilled at overlapping two (or more) records over long, seamless segues. Later, "quick-mixers" came into vogue, capable of whittling through literal stacks of records in rapid order. At the scene's tail end, scratch DJs arose, manipulating vinyl and styli to create new sounds and rhythms.[1] All mobile crews shared one core mission: to keep people dancing, whether through their mixing techniques, song selections, lighting displays, or enthused exhortations from the DJs themselves, urging crowds to get on up, then get on down.

If this was a party being hosted by one of the tens of thousands of Filipino Americans living in Bay Area cities like San Francisco, Daly City,

Fremont, Vallejo, San Jose, and so on, it was quite likely that the DJ or DJs at this party would be someone you knew from the neighborhood, from school, from church. They may even have been your cousin (or at least your cousin's cousin). These DJs, their crews, their audiences, and the friends, families, and organizations that hired their services all constituted the Bay Area's *Filipino American mobile disc jockey scene*.[2] From the late 1970s through the early to mid-1990s, the scene was a dominant part of the recreational life of Filipino American youth in the Bay Area; even among those who did not actively participate in the parties, most would have known of them and the people involved with them.

The mobile DJ crew phenomenon in the Bay Area was hardly an exclusively Filipino American affair. Other communities, including Latino Americans, African Americans, and Chinese Americans, also boasted mobile crews, and many Filipino American–led crews included non-Filipino members (Cook 1995). However, in terms of size, scope, and longevity, the Filipino American mobile scene was unrivaled, partially thanks to the extensive support given to them by families and community groups.

Moreover, *teenagers*—most of them in high school and overwhelmingly middle-class young men—dominated. Many began so young that they could not yet apply for a driver's license. Yet these same youth could install a performance stage, spin for a crowd of hundreds, earn thousands of dollars, and still be ready for Sunday Mass in the morning, plotting next weekend's party while waiting for Communion.

If you did *not* grow up in or around this scene, chances are you have never heard of it until now. Even at its height, in the mid- to late 1980s, the mobile parties slipped past the attention of local media, to say nothing of regional or national outlets.[3] In addition, unlike other DJ-oriented scenes such as hip-hop, house, techno, and reggae, Filipino American mobile DJs never made a successful jump from record-playing to record-*making*.[4] In other words, they had little physical media to leave behind. The mobile crews may have created a thriving party scene, but even at the best parties, once the house lights go up and everyone leaves, all that remains are the memories.

This was when I discovered the legacy of the mobile scene; after its end. In the mid-1990s, I began to write about arts and music for local Bay Area ethnic press and alternative weeklies. I was also an aspiring DJ. For professional and personal reasons, I was drawn to the rise of the Bay Area's Filipino American scratch DJs and ended up interviewing the likes of Richard "Q-Bert" Quitevis and Jonathan "Shortkut" Cruz, members of the renowned turntablist crew the Invisibl Skratch Piklz. A common thread began to emerge in my conversations with them: they all began their careers as members of different mobile crews. Q-Bert was part of Live Style Productions, Shortkut was in Just 2 Hype; Invisibl Skratch Piklz's cofounders, "Mixmaster Mike" Schwartz and "DJ Apollo" Novicio, came from Hi-Tech and Unlimited Sounds, respectively.[5]

The mobile scene was already well past its prime, but these scratch DJs eagerly reminisced about the hall parties they used to attend or spin at, about all the different mobile crews they ran across as kids. As ascendant as turntablism had become in the Bay Area, it was clear that the scratch scene's roots grew in soil first tilled by the mobile crews. As both a journalist and a scholar, I recognized a good story when I heard one. This book is a direct product of the impulse to chase down that story, to learn the history of the mobile scene, to understand how it came to be, and more important, to learn what it meant to those on both sides of the DJ booth.

Broadly speaking, my research into the mobile crews spun off from a larger interest in studying the role of popular music in the lives of ethnic and racialized communities. Previously, I had interviewed everyone from rappers to jazz artists to folk musicians, exploring the motivations and rewards behind musical performance and production. I was especially interested in how music intersected with identity and community formation, how it mediated cross-cultural relations, how it provided people—especially youth of color—with a platform for creative expression.[6]

Those remain guiding research interests, but one important change I underwent concerned my thinking on the relationship between music and identity. I once thought of music as mostly a *reflection* of a community's identities, values, and histories; one of my favorite quotes came from George C. Wolfe (1996), producer of the Broadway musical *Bring In 'da Noise, Bring In 'da Funk*: "If you actively unearth popular culture and look inside it, you can find all kinds of secrets and truths and rhythms of a time period, much more than you find in written history." I still believe in that concept, but I could have been faulted for treating music and culture too much as fixed, static objects, as if I were studying pieces of amber under a jeweler's loupe.

What broadened my thinking was Simon Frith's (1996a: 111) essay "Music and Identity," where he explicitly challenges the "music-as-reflection" model and instead argues that "[social groups] only get to know themselves as *groups* (as a particular organization of individual and social interests, of sameness and difference) *through* cultural activity.... Making music isn't a way of expressing ideas; it is a way of living them." In other words, the act of performing and listening to music produces, maintains, and transforms relationships that shape group identity, not as some fixed "end" product but as a *process*. Frith's idea that "identity is mobile" has since become conventional wisdom in cultural studies, but at that point in the late 1990s, at least for me, I found these ideas to be revelatory. (I still do.) This was especially true as I began to dig deeper into mobile DJ culture; I saw those ideas playing out within this particular community in powerful ways. The relationships between performers and audience, space and place, and especially identity and community were not as straightforward as I had originally assumed. DJing is an inherently social act, where "building community" is not accidental but deliberate and necessary. The mobile scene may have emerged out of a larger Filipino American community, but in turn the DJ crews also helped produce and define a community of their own in its wake. That process began humbly on the dance floor.

Building the Floor / DJs Mediating Community

There is this moment, a pause really, that hangs in the air when a DJ drops a new song into a set.[7] It is a mix of anticipation, hope, and a healthy dash of fear, since any new song can either enhance or disrupt the delicate chemistry of a dance floor. What you hope for is a spontaneous burst of enthusiasm as people recognize and respond to the song positively, more colloquially known by the cheer "That's my jam!"

"That's my jam!" acknowledges our personal connection to songs—it is a claiming, a way of expressing that these songs somehow "belong" to us individually. However, that ownership can also be collective. When we hear other people proclaim "That's my jam (too)!" that both affirms our tastes and connects us to those fellow fans, even if they are complete strangers.

Frith writes about how "the experience of pop music is an experience of identity: in responding to a song, we are drawn, haphazardly, into emotional alliances with performers and with the performers' other fans" (1996a: 121).[8] The DJ—in clubs, on the radio, at parties—mediates that "emotional alliance," providing the musical lubricant *and* glue to facilitate social contact, interaction, and identification. When "That's *my* jam!" turns into "That's *our jam!*" the dance space becomes more than just an assemblage of random bodies. It goes from being "a floor" to becoming "*the* floor," that is, a communal entity with a life of its own, and the DJ is the caretaker.

This is what DJs mean by "building" or "working the floor."[9] Whether in a spartan school gymnasium or a baroquely designed discotheque, the basic interaction between a DJ and an audience is essentially the same. In a delicate and symbiotic relationship, DJs and dancers nurture a "vibe," by which I mean a mix of forces, both tangible and invisible, that can either create a pleasurable, memorable experience or bring down the mood of an entire crowd. Dance music journalist Simon Reynolds describes the concept of a vibe as "a meaningful and *feeling*-full mood" that "materially embodies a certain kind of worldview and life stance" (1999: 372). The vibe, in other words, mediates the emotional qualities of a dance floor experience, which in turn helps create and reinforce shared group identities and values in those moments.

In building a floor, the DJ is nominally in control. As Daly City's Anthony Carrion, founder of Unlimited Sounds, put it, "depending on what kind of music you play, you can hype up the crowd or you can kill the crowd. . . . It is kind of a power thing where you control the crowd and you control the tempo of the party, the way it goes."

However, control is never one-way; the crowd is hardly powerless here. The DJ spins at the crowd's pleasure. If a DJ's decisions please the crowd, they dance, helping maintain the vibe and build the floor. If they disapprove, they withdraw from the floor, destroying the vibe, and thus repudiate the DJ. When a floor dies, no one blames the dancers; we hold the DJ at fault. Every song, therefore, represents a step in an evolving relationship of mutual trust between the DJ and the dancers.[10] Each needs the other to fulfill their respective desires—DJs want to be in control, dancers want to lose control.

The first goal is to get everyone "locked in," that is, enthused and committed. From there, it is a matter of pushing the vibe along a trajectory that eventually attains climax (or several of them). The sexual/spiritual metaphor is deliberately chosen: when the energy of a floor peaks, there can be both a physical and an emotional rush and release, not just individually but *communally*, resembling what Emile Durkheim described as "collective effervescence," by which he meant those moments of emotional intensity when a gathered crowd becomes overtaken by a sense of ecstatic connectivity (Olaveson 2004). Durkheim never lived to make it to a modern discotheque, but it is striking how this passage from him sounds almost identical to an ethnographic description of a dance floor at full climax:

> Once the individuals are gathered together, a sort of electricity is generated from their closeness and quickly launches them to an extraordinary height of exaltation. Every emotion expressed resonates without interference in consciousnesses that are wide open to external impressions, each one echoing the others. The initial impulse is thereby amplified each time it is echoed, like an avalanche that grows as it goes along. And since passions so heated and so free from all control cannot help but spill over, from every side there are nothing but wild movements, shouts, downright howls, and deafening noises of all kinds that further intensify the state they are expressing. (Durkheim 2003: 109–10)

Interestingly, Durkheim goes on to say that "probably because a collective emotion cannot be expressed collectively without some order that permits harmony and unison of movement, these gestures and cries tend to fall into rhythm and regularity, and from there into songs and dances" (110). It would seem, in this formulation, that dance music both produces and is a product of a different form of collective effervescence, one that manifests within temples of rhythm.

That transcendent, climactic moment is ephemeral, but the rush of emotion and empathy is one of the compelling forces that beckon people to dance floors on monthly, weekly, even daily occasions; think of it as a pleasure-centered form of devoted pilgrimage. For Durkheim, it was a shaman-like figure who initiated the religious ritual; in the metaphor of nightclub-as-church, that shaman would unquestionably be the DJ.[11]

That notion became part of the cult of the DJ from at least the late 1960s. As Tim Lawrence chronicles of New York City in that era, "what had emerged . . . was a social and egalitarian model of making music in which the DJ played in relation to the crowd, leading and following in roughly equal measure. . . . As a result the relationship between the DJ and the crowd resembled a dynamic conversation between separate agents that, when combined, had a greater total effect than the sum of their individual parts" (2004: 38). To put it another way, Sarah Thornton suggests, "it is as orchestrators of this 'living' communal experience that DJs are most important to music culture" (1996: 65).

Bringing this back to the mobile DJs, what makes them particularly remarkable is their ability to adjust to myriad dance situations, where

I.2 / Cosmix Sounds (San Jose), c. 1985. The San Jose–South Bay area was one key hub in the larger mobile scene. Left to right: Richard Ignacio, Benjy Santos, Romel Pagaduan, Suzie Racho, Ron Valenzuela, Joey Santos. Photo courtesy of Suzie Racho.

conditions are not always optimal. Expensive discotheques can boast state-of-the-art sound and lighting systems, and their exclusivity can produce a self-selected group of dancers who have gone through considerable time and expense to "have a good time." A mobile DJ, however, has to be prepared to adjust to any number of different spatial and social environments and build the floor accordingly. How one approaches a middle school dance filled with twelve-year-old wallflowers is different from your cousin's three-hundred-person wedding is different from a battle where half the crowd is ostensibly there to back your competitor's crew. In DJing parlance, on those able to effectively work with practically any crowd, in any space, is bestowed the honorific "party rocker." It is a skill set that mobile DJs ideally must master, especially to become an effective mediator of community-building on the dance floor. Within the mobile scene, party-rocking was a responsibility shouldered not just by individual DJs but by the entire crew.

A Legion of Boom / 15

Back of the Club (My Crew's behind Me) / DJing as Collective Practice

In the summer of 2012, I DJed a wedding alongside a friend, Patrick "Phatrick" Huang. It was about an hour into dancing, the floor was locked in, and I decided to throw on David Bowie and Queen's "Under Pressure." For anyone under the age of forty, "Under Pressure" is a bit of a tease, since its signature opening bass line usually makes people think of Vanilla Ice's massive 1990 rap hit "Ice Ice Baby," which interpolates that bass line.

"Under Pressure" is a fantastic dance song in its own right, with a hard, driving backbeat, not to mention stellar vocals from both Bowie and Queen's Freddie Mercury. However, it is not a particularly long song—less than three minutes—and I was brainstorming what to mix in next when Phatrick tapped me on the shoulder, indicating he had something in mind. Within seconds, he prepped "Ice Ice Baby" on the other turntable and scratched in *that* song's bass line to synch with an isolated bass line passage on "Under Pressure." He created a mix between the two songs that was so seamless that the delighted crowd did not even realize he had dropped in Vanilla Ice until they heard the rapper's voice kick in: "alright stop / collaborate and listen."

It was the perfect song at the perfect time, but on my own that moment would not have happened. Not only did I not have "Ice Ice Baby" with me but I would not have known to "catch the break" where Phatrick did, conceivably the *only* point in the song where his specific mix could have worked.[12] It was only by working as a collective unit that we were able to create that perfect moment for the floor. Collaborate and listen, indeed.

I offer this anecdote because so many contemporary depictions of DJs fixate on them as solitary figures. Flip through popular culture and advertising images of DJs and you will find them standing alone, one hand cupping headphones to an ear, the other hand manipulating a turntable, maybe with a thronging crowd dancing in front of them.[13] That image may invoke a sense of power and play, but the DJ is almost always depicted as a *lone* figure. Nothing about those images suggests that DJing might also be a *collective* or communal activity.[14]

In contrast, I have always found DJing to be an intensely social activity, not just between DJ and audience but *among DJs themselves*. More experienced DJs mentor the beginners, they share record recommendations, they practice and rehearse their craft together in bedrooms and basements. Mobile crews take things a step further, out of practicality if not also desire: vinyl records and audio and lighting equipment are heavy and bulky; it helps to have extra people around to divvy up the work of moving and assemblage. However, though division of labor provides a basic raison d'être behind how mobile DJ groups form, that is hardly their only or most important draw.

The best mobile crews worked as a collective unit, where individual abilities operated in concert with those of other members. The crew model does not require the erasure or dilution of individual identity but rather draws on those personal talents (and/or talented personalities) for the betterment of the crew as a collective unit. In other words, mobile crews embody what ethnomusicologist Mark Slobin—writing about musical performance—describes as "both the assertion of pride, even ambition, and the simultaneous disappearance of ego" (1993: 41; though some of my respondents would likely debate to what extent "ego" truly disappears).

For my respondents, mobile outfits served many important communal functions. They became informal families, fraternal organizations, cliques of like-minded peers; these nuances are what separate "groups" from "crews."[15] As graffiti historian Joe Austin put it, crews are "a kind of social hybrid, combining the informal organization of a peer group, the shared-goal orientation of a sports team, and the collective identity and protective functions of a gang" (2001: 64).[16] In other words, all crews are technically groups, but not all groups are crews; the difference lies in the degree of social bonds between members. The fundamental thing that makes a crew "a crew" is that collective all-for-one, one-for-all identity. For that reason, the DJ groups I discuss herein were first and foremost crews, regardless of whether they ever self-described themselves using the term.[17]

The collective nature of crews is important for several reasons. First, as I noted earlier, it challenges the perception of DJing as an individual activity by highlighting the inherently social nature of the craft. Second, it helps explain how crews drew young people (and predominantly men) by offering a sense of camaraderie, a sense of belonging, built around a shared mission. In that sense, working together as DJs gave them a common purpose, but the crew model—as an organizational entity—was a draw unto itself. Third, the collective nature of crews also helps explain their relationship to a larger peer community. They functioned similarly to a school sports team or club, engendering a form of fan-based loyalty or identification that was tied, rather than to any individual, to the collective unit; that is, "I'm a fan of Ultimate Creations" (a respected San Francisco crew). Finally, I suggest that the collective nature of the mobile crews made it more likely that other members of the wider community—not just friends but relatives, school officials, community leaders and organizations—would be supportive of the activity as they saw its benefits extending across many youth and not just a select few. As I discuss later, that community support proved especially crucial in helping the Filipino American mobile scene flourish. More to the point, though, that interaction is also crucial to understanding the mobile scene *as a "Filipino scene."* In other words, as I suggested earlier, the Filipino American community in the Bay Area certainly shaped and influenced the contours of the mobile scene, but likewise, the scene itself shaped the contours of Filipino American identity in that particular time and place. Yet, despite that, surprisingly few DJs saw the mobile scene as having much to do with ethnicity at all.

Pleats on Your Pants / Filipino American Identity in the Mobile Scene

If you ever want to get a quick, visual sense of the mobile scene's creative diversity, hop onto Highway 1 from where it snakes off from Interstate 280 in Daly City and head toward the small, fog-shrouded, seaside town of Pacifica. In a few minutes, right off Highway 1, you will find Manor Music, a purveyor of audio and lighting equipment. For many San Francisco and Daly City crews during the 1980s, Manor was *the* store to patronize if you needed to buy or rent DJ gear. Walk up to the store's register and look down to find dozens upon dozens of business cards beneath the glass top. They come from all the different mobile crews—Filipino or otherwise—who have come through Manor over the last quarter century, with such fanciful names as Futuristic Sounds, Music Blasters, Spintronix, and one of my personal (alliterative) favorites: Chilltown Crush Crew.

Business cards were some of the first physical media I came across in my research—respondents kept binders of them, neatly arranged like baseball or Pokémon cards. Scanning across them, I was struck by the incredible diversity of creative expression contained within even something as small as a name and logo fit into a three-and-a-half- by two-inch card. Something as simple as a font or a piece of clip art went a long way—in addition to the crew's name itself—to give a crew character. Ultimate Creations, one of the most lauded crews out of San Francisco, had their cards made in silver and black—the Oakland Raiders' colors—which made them stand out for their simple elegance. Burt Kong, of South San Francisco's Sound Sequence, would hand-scrawl a picture of himself onto his cards. Daly City's Unique Musique—besides boasting an indelibly memorable name—fashioned their logo after the iconic Dave Bhang–designed logo for the rock band Van Halen.

However, in looking over these cards, I noted something else; an absence really: almost none of the crew names suggested an overt nod to race or ethnicity. Overwhelmingly, mobile crews chose names based around DJing and club nomenclature, but almost none of them seemed to signify anything that would identify them as being Filipino American.

This stood in stark contrast to a similar community of youthful performers I was familiar with: 1990s-era rappers.[18] For MCs, the simple act of naming oneself is a crucial act of signification. The Asian American rap artists and groups of the early 1990s whom I knew all chose ethnicity- or race-inspired names: Fists of Fury, Asiatic Apostles, Yellow Peril, Seoul Brothers (see Wang 2006, 2007).[19] More contemporary MCs, including Filipino American artists such as Bambu and the Pacifics, also chose monikers that signified, on some level, a relationship to Asia. And beyond their noms de plume, racial and ethnic awareness was often front and center in song lyrics (see Harrison 2009: 132–34; Viesca 2012).

This performance of identity via name was not just limited to MCs or hip-hop; in other areas of Filipino American cultural production, I knew of deliberate gestures to highlight or maintain ethnic identity and traditions, most famously via annual collegiate Pilipino Cultural Nights (in which DJing has played an important part since at least the 1990s; Gonzalves 2010). Mobile DJs, by comparison, barely acknowledged ethnicity or ethnic identity as being relevant to their craft or community. It was as if the scene's ethnic composition was so ordinary as to be unworthy of note or reflection, even though it could not be sheer coincidence that so many Filipino American teenagers formed into mobile crews *with one another*.

It was not that respondents lacked an ethnic consciousness *individually*. Some grew up feeling conflicted and confused over being Filipino. Others felt more at home identifying with black or Latino friends. Still others wore their ethnicity as a mark of honor and celebrated it through individual acts—painting the Philippines national flag on their sneakers, for example. These differences reflected a basic heterogeneity of identity among different individuals, but the point here is that these differences were not any more or less pronounced *because they were DJs*. Instead, their family and home environment, experiences in school with students of other ethnicities, and other life experiences seemed more important to their ethnic sense of self than anything consciously connected to the mobile scene. For example, during my interview with Ken Anolin of Daly City's Fusion, I asked:

> OW: Did you grow up exposed to Filipino culture as a child?
>
> KA: Oh yeah, my parents, aunties, uncles, grandma, grandpa, everybody. The dances that we went to. Traditional dances, dinner dances for my mom's women's club. All of those.
>
> OW: Did you have an identity as a Filipino as a youth?
>
> KA: Oh yeah. The baggy pants were in back then too. But it was baggy dress pants as they would be called now. The Converse All-Stars or the Nikes or whatever. The Members Only jackets, you got to tie those off. Your status was based on the number of pleats you had on your pants. You were really cool if you had the pleats on the back of your pants.
>
> OW: Did you see anything uniquely Filipino about the DJ scene?
>
> KA: Geez, not really.
>
> OW: Even though the scene was so heavily Filipino?
>
> KA: When we started, we didn't see it as that.

Anolin possessed a self-identity as a Pinoy, but when it came to the DJ scene, he did not connect the activity with that identity. Instead, signifying Pinoy-ness came through other gestures, especially in the clothing, even down to whether your pants were pleated or not. But DJing itself, to Anolin and many others, was not a gesture that came laden with those same meanings or significations.

As another example, DJ Apollo, who began his career in mobile crews before transitioning into scratch DJing, stated, "We were just some kids out here doing some DJ stuff and we happened to be Filipino. As I got older, I saw, 'Oh, there's a lot of Filipino DJs. Wow, that's pretty significant.' But we never went about it that way . . . it wasn't a conscious thing." Indeed, none of my respondents described DJing as a self-consciously *ethnic* form of expression. As with Apollo's testimony, the preponderance of Filipinos in the mobile crews was an obvious feature, but beyond that they did not actively perceive ethnicity as being related to their activities in the scene, at least not on the front end. It was only when I deliberately posed questions to them about that relationship that respondents began to theorize—seemingly on the spot—about how they thought ethnicity *might* have been a relevant dimension.

The "ethnicity question" held special resonance given the historical—and quite specifically racialized—marginalization of Filipino Americans within U.S. racial discourse. Filipinos constitute one of the largest ethnic groups in the Bay Area as well as the United States as a whole (U.S. Census Bureau 2007). However, their demographic presence has no equivalent in the realms of public media, popular culture, or political representation. As Elizabeth Pisares powerfully argues, "historical legacies of colonialism and the racial ideology of orientalism shut out Filipino Americans from the social processes that produce institutional knowledge about race and define their racial identity as an invisible, social one. Their exclusion from U.S. racial discourse sets the conditions for their social invisibility, and Filipino Americans are misrecognized as everything and anything but Filipino" (2011: 426–27).

Examples of this cropped up in my interviews; 3-Style Attractions' Dave "Dynamix" Refuerzo grew up in the Berryessa neighborhood of San Jose, and he related that when his family first moved there, "nobody knew what a Filipino was. People used to clown us." Likewise, Allyson Tintiangco-Cubales grew up in the Union City–Fremont scene, and she recalled white classmates calling her "bonsai" (presumably a Japanese reference being misapplied cross-ethnically). Clearly, there were those in the scene who possessed an acute awareness around ethnicity and race. As I have stressed, however, that awareness was highly individualized rather than a lens through which respondents read or understood the mobile scene.

As a way to try to unpack this dynamic, I chose a simple but significant inductive approach to my interviews, shifting my line of inquiry from "why?" toward "how?"[20] Rather than try to tackle the question "why did so many Filipino youth become DJs?" I shifted to asking instead "*how* did so many Filipino youth become DJs?" That difference is subtle but significant, as it avoids applying what might be otherwise spurious theories focused on "cultural motivations" (or even worse, pathologies) and instead focuses on the social processes through which the mobile scene came about: How did crews form? How did people learn how to DJ? How did they acquire gigs? How did families and community members play a role? In deploying this approach, I discovered that in addressing "how" I was also able to better explain "why"; the two "answers" were always linked, but it was only through pursuing the former that the latter became better illuminated.

If ethnicity was a concept "hidden in plain sight" for mobile crew members, my own blind spot, initially, was around gender. Going into the fieldwork, I assumed race/ethnicity would be the most obvious angle of analysis, but the scene's myriad gender dynamics were no less relevant to the story of the scene. Most obviously, the crews themselves were overwhelmingly male in composition. Their very formation as male, homosocial organizations was—if I may borrow from the idioms of the tech world—not a bug but a feature; it was part of their organizational appeal. Likewise, the absence of women from crew ranks was not random but deeply structured, including at the family level. At the same time, I also came to see how the scene as a whole was hardly bereft of women; they wielded tremendous influence as promoters, clients, audience members, objects of desire, and, in rare, exceptional instances, DJs too.[21]

To address all these complexities, I opted against a "dedicated chapter" approach in favor of working in discussions of ethnicity and gender (and class as well) across the book as a whole. I recognize that this decision risks diffusing the potency of any single theme by spreading it across several chapters, but it felt like the intuitive approach to take. Assembling this book was very much like planning a mix: one has to be selective with the content, sequence wisely, and hope the end product is coherent and compelling. And in the end, you can never be certain how well you put it all together until it is out of your hands and left for an audience to render judgment.

The Set List / Chapter Breakdown

As I just noted, one of the biggest challenges I experienced in writing this book was deciding between writing it as a linear, chronological history and focusing on specific issues and themes within that history. It was a classic balancing act between the needs of narrative and the needs of analysis, and there is a graveyard of discarded drafts that suggests how often I experimented with that balance. For me the narrative was always the initial draw, but I did not want to explore this history simply for history's sake; as I have already suggested, all kinds of other provocative issues and questions were raised in the process of exploring that history. In the end, I opted to organize the book in a very loose, chronological order but tackling a different set of themes in each chapter.

In chapter 1, I explore the scene's "social preconditions," in other words, the larger forces and phenomena happening in the 1960s through

1970s that created a social context in which the mobile scene could take root and grow. That includes both structural forces, such as large-scale immigration and settlement patterns of middle-class Filipino families in the Bay Area, as well as cultural trends, such as the brief but intense discotheque boom following the success of *Saturday Night Fever*. I also use this chapter to lay out class dimensions that become more pronounced as we move into the formal mobile era itself.

Chapters 2 and 3 delve into the early years of the mobile scene, examining two different sides to its establishment and growth. Chapter 2 focuses on the "internal" factors that drew young men to join or form crews, including the allure of social status, the aura of work as a DJ, and the appeal of homosociality. I also discuss how DJing lent itself to a (re)production of masculinity among the predominantly male participants. In particular, I discuss the metaphor of "mastery" as a DJing value and how this reinforces a particular ideal of masculinity. By that same token, I also discuss the relative absence of female DJs within the scene by examining some of the barriers women face to joining and forming mobile crews of their own.

Chapter 3 turns to the "external" factors that fueled the scene's overall growth, including the intertwined social networks connecting DJ crews, friends, peer-run student and church groups, middle-class parents and relatives, and Filipino community groups. Those networks formed what I describe as the "soft infrastructure" through which crews and clients could find one another, helping to circulate the necessary economic capital to help build the mobile scene over time.

Chapter 4 moves into the mid- to late 1980s with the large-scale mobile events known as "showcases" and the way these became massive magnets for DJs and audiences alike via common spaces for social contact. As a result, not only did these events provide an impetus for community formation by literally bringing people together but also the showcases and similar events became a common cultural experience that proved important to building a collective identity among all these youth. I end with an exploration of the subtle ways the mobile scene created the expectation that DJing and Filipino-ness were so "naturally" connected as to be taken for granted.

Chapter 5 focuses on the decline of the mobile scene by discussing a confluence of several different, discrete forces that gradually weakened the appeal of the crews. As the chapter details, after a decade of dominance, the mobile scene became, in a way, a victim of its own success, and

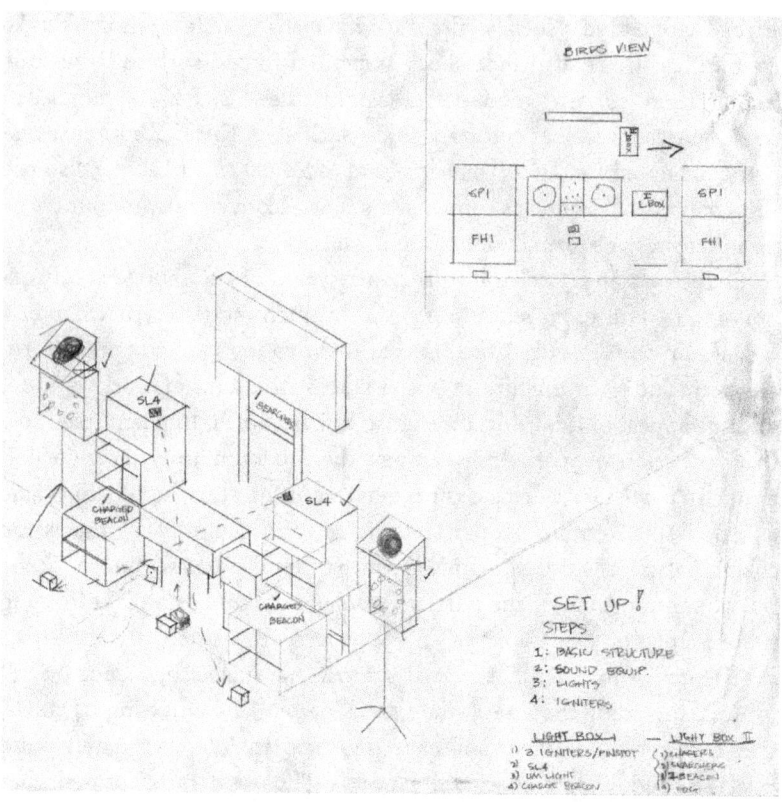

I.3 / Blueprint for a DJ stage setup for Unique Musique (Daly City). Elaborate staging designs for mobile events were influenced by both rock concerts and discotheques. Courtesy of Henry Geronimo.

as individual DJs enjoyed personal gains, the collective logic behind crews began to wither. Included in this chapter is a discussion of the rise of scratch DJing, not just an important factor behind the decline of the mobiles but also an important form of DJing performance and community-building itself.

I conclude the book with a brief discussion of how echoes of the 1980s mobile scene continue to reverberate within the contemporary Filipino American community in the Bay Area. I end with suggestions for future directions in scholarship around the mobile scene.

Check the Method / Research Design

As I noted earlier, the roots of this research began in the mid-1990s, when I was embarking on a freelance career as a music journalist. By this time, the dominance of Filipino American scratch DJs—not just in the Bay Area but globally—was reaching a zenith. In my conversations with these turntablists, what struck me was the way they treated DJing as a "natural" presence in their adolescence. To them, DJing was an expected cultural fixture in their youth, similar to the way Little League or Boy Scouts might function for other young men.

The scratch scene made them famous, but the mobile scene still held special importance. As successful as some of these turntablists had become, the mobile era was clearly a formative experience. Along with hip-hop, mobile DJing was the other youth culture they came of age in, alongside thousands of other Filipino Americans. However, despite the multitudes of people who lived through the mobile era, there was almost no collective history out there: no newspaper or magazine articles, let alone scholarly essays or books. What media did survive were rarely in the public realm.[22] The sole, and important, exception was Melanie Caganot's groundbreaking exhibit at the San Mateo County History Museum, *Tales of the Turntable*.

Caganot (now Kong) was another veteran of the mobile scene, not as a DJ but as a rapper—her stage name was Lani Luv, and she regularly performed alongside DJ crews in Daly City and San Francisco. In the early 2000s, Caganot was finishing an MA degree in art design and pitched the exhibit partially to fulfill her remaining requirements. Her extensive background in the mobile community gave her access to visual artifacts from the scene—audio and lighting equipment, photos, trophies, video footage, party flyers—and *Tales of the Turntable* constituted one of the only attempts to present the history of the mobile scene to the larger public, then *or* now.

I met Caganot when I wrote a short piece on her exhibit for the *San Francisco Bay Guardian* in the fall of 2001 (Wang 2001b). The following January, she invited me to the History Museum to moderate a panel discussion on the history of the mobile scene. That's where I met the DJs who formed my initial set of interviewees: Kormann Roque and Jay dela Cruz (Spintronix, Daly City), Francisco Pardorla (Images Inc. / AA Productions, Union City–Fremont), "Jazzy" Jim Archer (Skyway Sounds, San Jose), Burton "Burt" Kong (Sound Sequence, South San Francisco), Tra-

A Legion of Boom / 25

vis "Pone" Rimando (89' Skratch Gangstaz, Fairfield–Oakland), and John Francisco (Expressions Entertainment, San Francisco). Though there was no formal network or directory of Filipino American DJs, most of these DJs were still in touch with other people from the scene, and thus, through them, I began to use snowball sampling to build a list of other potential interviewees.

As with any study limited by time and resources, I made choices that highlighted certain crews and eras while minimizing others. For example, most—though not all—of my respondents came from the San Francisco or Daly City scenes, especially since these two cities were at the center of the overall Bay Area scene. Likewise, though the mobile era spanned from 1978 until roughly the mid-1990s, I leaned toward interviewing crews from the earlier part of that span, especially those who formed within the first five years. I felt these "pioneering" crews did much of the work to define the scene as a whole and thus could contribute to my understanding of how crews formed and functioned.

I did not presume—nor do I want to imply—that these older crews define any kind of "authentic" mobile culture. I take it for granted that the mobile scene was constantly changing throughout its history; that is why I also interviewed newer crews, expressly to see if styles and values changed as the mobile scene evolved. Besides mobile DJs, I also interviewed others who were part of the larger social scene. This included dancers, promoters, club and radio DJs, and ordinary revelers who frequented these parties. Given that part of my mission was to understand how DJing changed the larger community (beyond just the DJs) it was important to engage members of that broader community.

However, there were many more people and crews and subscenes that I was not able to address. At its height, the DJ scene covered over six counties and seven thousand square miles in the Bay Area alone, with potentially over one hundred crews who had come and gone over a fifteen-year period.[23] Even a "local" scene in an area such as San Jose likely involved dozens of crews, some of whom never performed outside Santa Clara County. Pursuing anything approaching a "definitive" history was beyond my capabilities, though I have tried to collect these other (hi)stories through other means, namely, the use of a dedicated website (http://legionsofboom.com) and via social networking sites, especially Facebook. What exists in this book is merely the first step in exploring a vastly rich and dense social world created by the mobile scene (and, as noted, the conclusion discusses some promising areas of future research).

I.4 / Vinyl sticker for the Legion of Boom, designed by Francisco Pardorla. Courtesy of Francisco Pardorla.

About the Title

This book's title was inspired by the Legion of Boom, an alliance formed in 1986 between five different DJ crews across the Bay Area: South San Francisco's Sound Sequence, Fremont's Images Incorporated, Union City's Creative Madness, and two Daly City crews: Midstar Productions and Styles Beyond Compare. It was Sound Sequence's Burton Kong who coined the name "Legion of Boom," playing off "Legion of Doom," the alliance of evil superheroes drawn from the DC Comics universe (Leva 2008). I elaborate later (chapter 4) on how alliances often addressed logistical needs—the sharing of equipment, for example—but they were also a way to join forces and form a mega-crew for special occasions, where the collective could stage a sonic and visual phalanx of massive speakers and lighting.

Alliances like the Legion of Boom embodied some of the best communal values the mobile scene engendered: working together across geography and individual concerns, lending support, seeking to entertain audiences with spectacular performances. Alliances also made for good marketing—"five crews for the price of one!"—but ultimately, it was not business concerns that held alliances together: DJs wanted to assemble the most elaborate sound system possible. As Images Inc.'s Francisco Pardorla explained, "down south, they had the sound, but no lights. SF crews are very flashy. They had all lights, but no sound. [The Legion] were right in the middle. We were the best of both worlds." As Pardorla explained this, it was obvious he took great pleasure in laying claim to such bragging rights, and this reminded me of how integral pleasure and play were within the mobile scene. After all, "having fun" was not a superficial or secondary concern but was very much at the forefront of what motivated these DJ crews. What made alliances so remarkable was that these were crews who were otherwise fiercely competitive with one another, for both business and status. Yet despite sometimes being rivals, these same crews forged alliances as a way to build constructive relationships, ones that rewarded crews for cooperating, not just competing.

In naming this book after the Legion of Boom, I not only nod to the name's cleverness and the visual image it evokes of a field full of subwoofers. It is also a homage to what the original Legion represented—the best of *all* worlds that united people in the pursuit of play, pleasure, and the desire to bring together a community within the reach of their speakers' range.

Chapter 1 / Cue It Up / Social Preconditions for the Mobile Scene

1.1 / Studio West jacket belonging to former DJ Paul John Weber. Studio West was a popular nightclub in the North Beach neighborhood of San Francisco. Photo courtesy of Paul John Weber.

If you want to sneak into a nightclub, first check the back door. That was the favored point-of-entry for Daly City's Anthony Carrion and his high school friends whenever they were trying to slip into their favorite San Francisco nightclub, Studio West. If the back door was locked though, they had to brave the front of the club. The thing was: Studio West was already fairly hospitable to younger patrons; after 2 a.m., once the alcohol taps were shut off, the discotheque allowed in everyone over eighteen. But Carrion and his buddies were still too young, even then. Some of them had fake ID to get them over the magic age number, others just hoped a friendly bouncer would look the other way and let them past the velvet rope. On the nights they made it inside, most of Carrion's friends would take off to dance or pursue romantic opportunities, but Carrion literally set his sights higher, seeking out the club's balcony. As he explained, "my friends were out chasing the girls and stuff. I was up there watching the DJ."

You could say Carrion inherited his interest in discotheques from his parents. Back in 1977, when *Saturday Night Fever* came out, the subsequent disco inferno swept up many, including Carrion's parents. "They liked to go out and party and basically they started throwing parties at our house," he recalled. "At least once a month, my mom and dad would throw a party at our house. . . . Any occasion that came up, he'd throw a party." Up to 150 friends, family, and coworkers would get the invite, and Carrion's father—by day an aircraft technician—would transform the large family room of their two-story house "into a little club, party room. . . . It was tile, black and white flooring. . . . He even put a little bar in there." Carrion's family supplied the music: "We were still playing those little 45s. My mom and dad were actually the ones buying the records. Sometimes I got to play it. I think that was my first time . . . playing records at a party but I didn't know how far it would go."

Carrion's journey up to the Studio West balcony did not only begin at the door (back, front, or otherwise). The club's very existence owed itself to a general boom in discotheque construction that swept through San Francisco in the late 1970s. Likewise, Anthony Carrion's travels to San Francisco did not just begin from his family's Daly City home. His parents had been in the United States only since 1969, beneficiaries of both his grandfather's U.S. military service and changes to immigration laws dating back to 1965. Between the thin edge of a twelve-inch single and the wide sweep of federal policies lay any number of forces, structures, and networks that composed the social milieu the mobile DJ scene eventually emerged from, what I describe as its social preconditions.

A precondition is not a *causal* force; it does not guarantee what actions may follow, but its existence creates the possibility. The mobile scene was never an inevitability simply because a certain set of social forces aligned, but its preconditions can explain its emergence in a particular time and place. The role of the individual—and happenstance—is still relevant: Carrion needed to sneak into Studio West. But these personal actions would have been immaterial if, for example, the discotheque craze had never come to the Bay Area.

In this chapter, I focus on what I see as three of the most significant preconditions of the mobile scene. First would be the aesthetic innovations within DJ culture and music production that helped produce and popularize the nonstop disco mixing styles that mobile crews adopted. Second are the immigration and settlement patterns of Filipino American families, not just to the Bay Area but specifically resettlement from urban centers to Bay Area suburbs. Third, I end with a discussion of a smaller scale yet no less significant precondition (and predictor) of the mobile scene: the garage party tradition.

All Night Long / Nonstop Disco Mixing

The movie *Saturday Night Fever* hardly created disco—many might argue that its success actually marked the beginning of the genre's end—but as Carrion's parents can attest, the film popularized a particular vision for the culture of disco. With its sensationalist portrayals of disco's fashion, lifestyles, and, of course, music, *Saturday Night Fever* and its best-selling soundtrack encouraged hundreds of entrepreneurs across the United States to start up nightclubs in hopes of capitalizing on the fad.[1]

San Francisco was no exception.[2] One of the city's pioneering discotheques was originally called Cabaret and then appropriately renamed City Disco. Though its founding circa 1975 was slightly ahead of the national curve, it would not take long for other competitors to enter the field. In 1977, the I-Beam opened in the Upper Haight, soon followed by the Trocadero Transfer in the South of Market Area (SOMA), Oil Can Harry's in the Tenderloin, and the Mineshaft on Market. One of the greatest concentrations of nightclubs sprouted in the same North Beach neighborhood that City Disco presided over. Within a ten-block radius of the neon-lit Broadway corridor, one could find not only Studio West but also Broadway Power and Light, the Palladium, and my personal favorite (name-wise): Dance Your Ass Off, Inc. (Diebold 1988; Keast 2000; Lawrence 2004).

This growth in nightclubs was such a key precondition because the discotheques served as key sites where people could witness innovations in DJing style and aesthetics happening throughout the 1970s and 1980s. They became, in essence, informal classrooms, where aspiring DJs could learn how to mix, what songs to play, the best techniques to build a floor. Cameron Paul, the DJ at Studio West whom Carrion and others would sneak in to see, explained: "From the moment I heard and saw Johnny 'Disco' Hedges spinning at Oil Can Harry's, I was entranced with what he was doing. It was absolutely hypnotic. I couldn't tell when one song ended and a new one began. There was a door to the DJ booth that he kept open all night long and I would stand there in awe" (Paul 2006b).[3] Paul's anecdote about watching Hedges is remarkably similar to what my respondents said about watching Paul and other DJs at Studio West. It was one of the more popular "mixed" (i.e., straight and gay) clubs in San Francisco, what Spintronix's Jay dela Cruz described as "the equivalent to Studio 54 in New York. If you were in the party scene in the Bay Area at that time, this was the place to be."[4] Studio West boasted any number of

DJs who became revered figures in the mobile scene: Mickey Carp, Alvin Bonifacio, Paul John Weber, and especially Cameron Paul.[5] Carrion described what it was like to see Paul commanding the dance floor: "When I went to the club, I heard the music mixing in, just one after the other, and the music was just blending. The crowd was into it and everything, I was like gosh, who's doing all this stuff? I went upstairs and I seen what [Paul] was doing . . . and it just caught me. . . . I thought it was just a fun thing to do, but it is kind of a power thing where you control the crowd and you control the tempo of the party, the way it goes." Midstar's Ray Viray also credited figures such as Paul and Bonifacio with being "my idols . . . I looked up to them. They had very clean mixes and it got me going more. I was underage at that time, I would wait for my friend to get tapes from him. I listened to it, started copying it, and that's when my creative mind started going." Non-Stop Boogie's Candido Anicete added, "Studio West's trademark was 'Studio West, redimension in disco tech' or something like that. Our [crew's motto] was 'new dimension in mobile disco tech.' So we were trying to emulate the wild side of disco and continuous nonstop music."

At the end of Anicete's quote, he uses the term "nonstop music." This alludes to a particular *style* of DJing that helped make disco—and later dance music forms—so popular. Disco may be more associated with polyester suits, lighted dance floors, and gold medallions, but disco, first and foremost, was a musical style. In the context of the discotheque itself, *how* DJs played records became as important as the records themselves.

As a musical practice, DJing is bound to various forms of technology: turntables to play records, a mixer to coordinate audio sources, the amplifier and speaker systems that transmit sound, et alia. Despite this, one of the biggest innovations in modern DJing was the application of a decidedly low-tech apparatus: a human thumb.

At some point in the late 1960s, a New York DJ named Francis Grasso discovered that if he used his thumb to keep a record still—while the turntable platter beneath it continued to spin—he could release the record at full speed, allowing him to drop a new song "on beat" into the existing rhythm. Previous to this, DJs would normally fade in and out of songs; most radio stations still feature this form of mixing.[6] With Grasso's new method—dubbed "slip-cueing"—he could slip in new songs on tempo, avoiding any jarring breaks in the rhythm that might throw off dancers. Slip-cueing became foundational in the development of what became known as "nonstop disco mixing" (Lawrence 2004: 35).

Walk into almost any American nightclub today playing hip-hop, R&B, or any genre filed under the broad electronic dance music umbrella. If the DJs are even halfway competent, the flow of songs you hear will never stop, never break, until last call is announced and the house lights come on. From opening to close, nightclub DJs seek to sustain a stream of music, attempting to segue between tracks so subtly that the casual listener will not be able to tell where one song ends and the next begins. This is the essence of nonstop mixing.

This style is so commonplace that it may not seem particularly significant, let alone innovative, but when nonstop mixing came into play in the 1970s, it had a tremendous impact on the dancing experience. Consider: on the parquet, a break in the music is essentially a break in momentum. An obvious segue between songs, especially one where tempos are thrown off or the volume lowered, even momentarily, can give dancers an excuse to leave the dance floor. Crafting a seamless, steady flow of songs helps maintain the crowd, but even more important, it *builds* a floor toward those aforementioned moments of climax and collective effervescence. Nonstop mixing is not absolutely necessary to make those moments happen—there are other ways of mixing—but for the last thirty to forty years, it has proven one of the most common and effective means for a DJ to build a floor.

However, nonstop mixing's proliferation depended on more than just changes in DJ technique; it also required shifts in music production and DJ technology. One of the most important of the early changes was what became known as the "disco break"—a long, steady passage within a song that tended to strip the track down to its percussive core, giving dancers a more focused rhythm to move with.[7] Especially as the twelve-inch single became the favored medium—it was longer than seven-inch singles and louder than LPs—the disco break could last for minutes, even more than half the song. Whether disco existed before the disco break or vice versa is a classic chicken-and-egg conundrum. Either way, those long disco breaks made nonstop mixing easier and thus helped DJs sustain and build the floor. As DJ Joey Negro puts it (quoted by historian Ulf Poschardt), "disco music was the first music that was engineered specifically for clubs—it was made with dance floors in mind" (Poschardt 1998: 122).

These innovations paralleled changes in DJ technology, especially the invention of DJ mixers specifically designed for club use such as the Bozak CMA-10-2DL, first introduced in 1971 (Lawrence 2004: 35). The modern club mixer not only allows DJs to move between multiple audio sources—two turntables, for example—but crucially, they also allow DJs to "cue" a record through their headphones, that is, privately preview an audio source before sending that signal through to the speakers. Though Grasso's innovations in nonstop mixing were often made in spite of technological limitations, by the mid-1970s the technology had caught up with the techniques, especially turntables with enough heft and stability to resist "jumping the needle" when a DJ slip-cued a record. Turntables also began to incorporate pitch-control, which is used to steadily and accurately slow down or speed up a record in order to match tempos (an essential component in nonstop mixing). For mobile DJs in particular, the "miniaturization" of this technology, especially in shrinking down heavy and cumbersome club mixers, was in full force by the mid-1970s, with audio firms in the United States and United Kingdom developing product lines specifically for mobile use. As early as 1976, music magazines regularly featured advertising and articles targeted at mobile DJs, including one *Billboard* story titled "Mobile Discos: From Nursing Homes to Country Clubs" (Pechansky 1974).[8]

The discotheque was ground zero for disseminating these new styles and techniques. In the 1970s, these styles of DJing barely mapped onto mass/mainstream media depictions of DJing itself. The current ubiquity of DJs in pop culture had not yet crested, let alone the ability to access hundreds of "how to DJ" videos online or on VHS or DVD. Learning how to DJ in the 1970s was literally a "peer-to-peer" activity. Your exposure to the craft and its techniques came by watching other DJs perform in real time.

This is why something like a balcony overlooking a DJ booth in Studio West could become so important to a generation of pioneering mobile DJs. These were some of the few spaces where they could study the act of DJing itself (until they, later, became the "teachers" for the generation of DJs who followed). As Paul Tumakay, founder of San Francisco's Universal Sounds/Kicks Company, explained, "I think the benchmark there was to take whatever you saw at Studio West and Palladium and bring it into a garage or high school gymnasium. That was our . . . goal, was to try to replicate that." Importantly, Tumakay highlights a key transfer of knowledge, not just in the figurative sense of mobile DJs learning from their club counterparts but in physically *moving* those styles from city discotheques to domestic, suburban spaces like garages and gyms.[9] The Filipino American mobile scene initially grounded itself in that symbolic transfer of DJ styles learned in the city and then brought "through the gateway" to the suburbs.[10]

Map 1.1 / Map of the San Francisco Bay Area. © Daniel Dalet, d-maps.com.

From City to Suburb / Filipino American Family (Re)Settlement

If you want to get a sense of *where* the Filipino American mobile scene eventually formed, begin with where Filipino American families settled (map 1.1). The biggest clusters of Filipino American families were in such cities as San Francisco, Daly City, Vallejo, Union City, Fremont, and San Jose. Logically, the fact that Filipino American DJs came out of places where Filipino Americans lived is intuitively obvious. However, family settlement patterns are crucial to understanding not only *where* the mobile scene developed but also *how*. Map 1.1 not only displays patterns of geographic dispersion but also is a cartography of *class*, pinpointing where families of upwardly mobile means ended up settling. Those neighborhoods—

almost exclusively suburban—where middle-class Filipino American families settled are the same neighborhoods where the DJ scene flourished. DJing may be a cultural activity with distinctly urban associations, but Filipino American mobile DJing was overwhelmingly a *suburban* phenomenon.

There is a subtle irony at work here. After all, DJing is seen as "cool" and "hip," yet the dominant caricature of suburban culture is one of stifling blandness. Just to double down on the irony in this particular context, one of the most famous songs ever written about suburban conformity was inspired by Daly City, unofficial capital of the mobile scene *and* the target of Malvina Reynolds's 1962 song "Little Boxes." Turned into chart hits by both Pete Seeger and The Womenfolk, "Little Boxes" refers to the rows of identically styled houses that line Daly City's hillsides. The song also introduced "ticky-tacky" into the lexicon of American idioms, and it caught on quickly ("Tacky into the Wind" 1964). A 1967 *Billboard* spotlight on the "musical revolutionaries" of San Francisco's psychedelic music scene laid out what would become an all-too-familiar straw man comparison between city and suburb when writer Philip Elwood described San Francisco as "a relatively rich and varied cosmopolitan center in the midst of the lackluster monotony presented by tens of thousands of suburban little-boxes made of 'ticky tacky'" (1967: SF-6). Perhaps Daly City of the 1960s was truly that static (however unlikely), but within a few scant years a steady demographic shift would change the complexion of not just Daly City but suburbs throughout the Bay Area.

The youth who made up the mobile scene predominantly came from the "third wave" of Filipino American immigration. The first wave included students and laborers who immigrated to the United States beginning after it annexed the Philippines and continuing until the 1934 Tydings-McDuffie Act.[11] The second wave began after World War II and included Filipinos who qualified for American citizenship due to military service. The third wave began with the 1965 Immigration Act, which, in response to everything from Cold War realpolitik considerations to momentum generated during the civil rights movement, finally loosened immigration quotas after decades of a near-moratorium (Bonus 2000: 44–45). This cohort transformed the Filipino American community in terms of sheer numbers but also in composition: especially in the first two decades following the act, many Filipino immigrants came from a well-educated, white-collar professional base (39). They possessed greater economic resources than previous immigrant waves of agricultural and factory laborers and military servicemen (52–53). However, it was also the case that many third-wave professionals were at risk of underemployment, forced to forgo their more advanced training in favor of less lucrative or prestigious white-collar work (52–53).

California port cities such as Los Angeles, San Francisco, and San Diego drew tens of thousands of third wavers (Bonus 2000: 47–50; Hing 1993: 94–95). As John Liu, Paul Ong, and Carolyn Rosenstein exhaustively document, these waves of immigration were always already heterogeneous, part of a "dual chain" of both (1) relatives of Filipino American citizens and permanent residents already residing in the United States pre-1965, and (2) high-skill professionals and their extended families, beneficiaries of legislative preferences given to such professionals, at least up through 1978 (Liu et al. 1991). Those large port cities were also the launching points for secondary, internal migration patterns, not just movements between states but local "internal" relocations within metropolitan areas (Gober 1999: 244–45). Daly City and Fremont may now have a reputation as key Filipino American hometowns, but they were rarely the first cities of residence for Filipino immigrants arriving in the 1960s and 1970s. Instead, many middle-class families first settled in dense, central city neighborhoods before moving out to suburban developments. This included most, if not almost all, of the families that eventually produced the mobile scene's participants.

Prior to 1965, the traditional Filipino community in San Francisco centered on various downtown neighborhoods. Best known was the ten-block Manilatown, located primarily along Kearny Street, north of Market and south of Broadway. Filled with single-residence occupancy hotels, Manilatown—at its height—was home to approximately ten thousand Filipino Americans, primarily single men (*manongs*) who had arrived in the United States as agricultural workers as early as the 1920s (Sobredo 1998: 277–78). However, despite this long-standing presence, San Francisco's aggressive redevelopment plans for the financial district (which flanked Manilatown to the east) all but erased the neighborhood during the course of the 1960s and 1970s, setting the stage for a dramatic August 1977 confrontation between police trying to serve evictions of elderly manongs residing at the International Hotel, an event that drew citywide protests and national media attention (Choy 1993; Habal 2007).[12]

Yet, even as the city displaced an older generation of Filipinos, other neighborhoods swelled with the arrival of thousands of third wavers, especially the Mission, the Fillmore, and most prominently SOMA, where by 1990 Filipinos constituted 30 percent of the local residents (Sobredo 1998: 285).[13] Their arrival expanded the amount of services and institutions catering specifically to Filipinos. Kim "KK Baby" Kantares, now a radio DJ at KPOO FM, grew up in the heart of SOMA, at Sixth and Minna, and recalled that in the 1970s, "the Filipino community was really growing. You were happy when you saw someone Filipino and everybody knew each other. You had a few Filipino organizations . . . one was Bayanihan, one was West Bay . . . and the local community rec[reation] center that was real popular in south of Market was Canyon Kip. . . . You had your few churches—St. Patrick's, then St. Joseph's—we had Filipino priests [like St. Patrick's] Father Bitanga, who's still there." These institutions helped provide direct services to newly arrived immigrant families, but beyond their material benefits, they also acted as community centers that assisted families in developing a sense of community within new surroundings.

St. Patrick's monsignor, the aforementioned Father Fred Bitanga, began to observe that this downtown community did not hold stable for long. He arrived in San Francisco in 1969 from the Philippines and witnessed that among other newly arrived immigrants, they would "live in cheap hotels here, in south of Market, just [for] cheaper rent, and they can save money, send it to the Philippines and save. In five years, I tell you, I lost many of them [when] Daly City was developed and most of them moved to Daly City, and I had to bless their houses. This is the diaspora of the Filipinos."[14] Father Bitanga's observations of his church flock seemingly held true for Filipinos across the Bay Area. Table 1.1 surveys population changes in selected Bay Area cities and counties from 1970 to 1990, spanning the time period in which the mobile crews and their families would have been settling across the Bay. The data suggest that while San Francisco's Filipino population grew over this time, it was dwarfed by the massive settlement of Filipino families happening elsewhere. As a city and county, San Francisco still boasted the highest number of Filipino residents compared to other cities, but in terms of per capita population *growth*, every other city and county in the Bay Area far outpaced San Francisco, even Marin.[15] In short, though many third-wave Filipino families continued to make San Francisco their home, the real growth was happening in the suburbs.

Nationally, between 1980 and 1990, the proportion of Filipino American households in the suburbs expanded by 58 percent (Alba and Denton

Table 1.1 / Bay Area Filipino Populations by City and County, 1970–1990

City/County	1970	1990	Increase
San Francisco	29,694	40,977	138%
Daly City	2,677	24,950	932%
San Jose	2,583	37,467	1,450%
Fremont	783	8,797	1,123%
Union City	246	9,850	4,004%
Vallejo	2,224	20,380	916%
San Mateo County	5,676	44,355	781%
Alameda County	10,597	53,760	507%
Santa Clara County	6,728	59,963	891%
Contra Costa County	2,763	25,288	915%
Solano County	3,363	28,958	861%

Source: Data drawn from http://www.bayareacensus.ca.gov.

2005: 253). As Richard Alba and Nancy Denton note, "in clear contrast to earlier European immigration groups, which generally first established ethnic enclaves and only after a generation or more migrated to suburbs, the new [post-1965] immigrants frequently settle either immediately upon arrival in the United States or soon after" (2005: 253).[16] However, while researchers have identified these statistical patterns of suburban settlement, they have less to say in regard to the underlying motivations behind them.[17] The assumption often seems to be that suburbs are the "natural" preference for upwardly mobile immigrants.

On the one hand there is a tempting logic to that presumption, given the idealized construction of suburbia broadcast around the world since at least the 1950s.[18] Especially with the saturation of U.S. television media in the Philippines up through the post-1965 era, it is not hard to imagine how "American life" and "suburban lifestyles" could become conflated ideals.[19] It is also the case that, at least in and around Manila, by the 1960s a suburban development explosion was already under way in neighborhoods such as Quezon City and Makati (Hedman and Sidel 2001: 124).[20]

However, cultural allure aside, there were other forces in the Bay Area compelling middle-class families to leave downtown neighborhoods. Beginning in the late 1960s, San Francisco was deep into its most ambitious—and tumultuous—redevelopment agenda since the 1907 earthquake. Under the banner of so-called urban renewal policies, the city razed thousands of low- to moderate-income housing units.²¹ This was especially acute in the downtown and SOMA areas, where the city's push to build high-rise commercial, retail, and tourism-centric facilities often meant the destruction of mixed-income housing.²² All these forces left the central city housing market irrevocably transformed, bifurcated between high-end, high-rise apartments and low-end, dilapidated tenements. In short, the exodus from downtown San Francisco cannot be seen through a narrative of Filipino American families "naturally" desiring to make that move. The "diaspora of the Filipinos" that Father Bitanga spoke of came partially in response to heavy economic pressures compelling families out of the downtown housing market.²³ The other half of the resettlement equation came with the expansion in housing opportunities elsewhere in the Bay Area.

The post–World War II boom in construction and redevelopment did not only affect the traditional "big cities" such as San Francisco and Oakland. The 1950s saw so many new subdivisions being constructed in previously unincorporated areas that they overwhelmed regional boards and government bodies (Scott 1985: 273; Wollenberg 1985: 258, 261). The passage of another federal legislative act in 1965—the Fair Housing Act—helped fuel this growth in at least two ways. First, by striking down some of the most pernicious forms of housing discrimination, the act created new opportunities for families of color—including Filipinos—to move beyond the ethnic enclaves of the inner city (Laguerre 2000: 85).²⁴ Second, post–Housing Act integration also spurred many white families to flee toward newer—and whiter—suburban developments, such as those in southern Alameda County or the ocean side of the San Mateo peninsula (Wollenberg 1985: 264).²⁵ Houses that fleeing white families left behind expanded the housing stock available to newer homeowners, including Filipino immigrants.

This is partially how Daly City went from the nearly all-white suburb of Reynolds's "Little Boxes" in the early 1960s to "the *adobo* capital of the U.S.A." two decades later (Vergara 2009: 24; see also Eljera 1996).²⁶ Between 1960 and 1980, the Filipino population surged from a mere 332 individuals in 1960 to 13,800 by 1980—a fortyfold increase. In explaining why Daly City attracted such a large Filipino population, Benito Vergara posits that "there are no simple explanations" but instead cites a convergence of specific factors, including Daly City's proximity to San Francisco and the presence of the Seton Medical Center, which recruited many workers directly from the Philippines (2009: 34). More important, though, as secondary migration brought more Filipino residents to the area, their very presence became a draw in and of itself for other Filipinos, including many of the mobile scene families.[27]

Apollo Novicio (aka DJ Apollo) first lived in the Mission district as a child, but his family later moved to Daly City when he was approximately ten years old. He suggested that his family's reasoning was "Hey, there's a lot of Filipinos in this part of town, we could feel at home here. . . . We're gonna make a life in U.S. and this is the part where all the Filipinos are going." Similarly, Ray Viray, a DJ with the mobile crews Unique Musique and Midstar Productions, recounted his own family's settlement route: "South of Market, that's where most of the Filipinos migrated to [from the Philippines]. We just followed the crowd, stayed there for a couple years. Then of course, everybody started moving to Daly City." Viray's use of the phrase "of course" is suggestive of the way many perceive Daly City as a default destination for Filipino families. That certainly may be true in quantifiable population numbers, but Daly City's reputation as a "Pinoy capital" was reason enough for other families to seek relocation there. Jay dela Cruz of Spintronix spent his early childhood in Jersey City, New Jersey, but even there he and his family knew of Daly City before they ever moved to the Bay. He said: "According to my parents, one of the main reasons they relocated out here is because of the large, long-established Filipino population. As long as I could remember, Daly City was always known as a 'Filipino town.'"[28]

Daly City is the most storied of Filipino American suburban communities, but it is hardly the only one. Many families stayed within San Francisco, moving from SOMA or the Fillmore out to the more suburban districts in the west ("The Avenues") and south (Excelsior and Visitacion Valley).[29] Similar patterns emerged throughout the Bay Area. With San Francisco as the origin point, Filipino families began moving to other cities located south of San Francisco, not only Daly City but also South San Francisco, Colma, and San Bruno. Others crossed the Bay toward the southeast to buy property in Union City and Fremont.[30] Still others went northeast to Vallejo, while others went an hour south to San Jose. In some cases, there would even be a *tertiary* resettlement to further outlying suburbs in the northeast part of the Bay Area, such as Pinole and Hercules.

While many of these neighborhoods were far from affluent, they still required stable, high(er)-wage incomes for moving to them. Table 1.2 shows changes in median family income for select Bay Area counties from 1969 to 1989. Not only were median family incomes lower (in absolute dollars) in San Francisco than heavily Filipino suburban cities but also San Fran-

Table 1.2 / Median Family Income by City, 1969–1989 (adjusted for inflation)

City	1969	1989
San Francisco	$10,503	$12,004
Vallejo	$8,237	$12,189
Daly City	$10,786	$13,466
San Jose	$10,043	$14,881
Fremont	$11,933	$16,400

Source: Data drawn from http://www.bayareacensus.ca.gov.

cisco experienced the slowest relative income growth during this period.[31] In short, as I noted earlier, the map of Filipino American resettlement in the Bay is as much a cartography of class as ethnicity. As later chapters discuss in greater detail, middle-class families were essential to the long-term growth and health of the mobile crews, as their financial resources helped nurture a fledging scene to a flourishing one.

I want to end this section by reemphasizing that it was not simply families and their financial capital moving between city and suburb; it was also cultural influences. Especially for Filipino youth, downtown San Francisco still constituted an important destination for recreation and entertainment. Filipino parents may have moved their families out to the burbs, but every weekend there was a reverse flow by their children, traveling back into the city to watch films, go dancing, listen to music. It was when these same youth began to brainstorm ways to bring the cultural elements of downtown clubs back through the gateway, to their suburban environs, that the mobile scene found its start. As future chapters explore, the mobile DJ crews created a social world where Filipino youth could work, play, and live all in the same blocks, bringing an energy and vitality to their local neighborhoods that was anything but "ticky-tacky." Nowhere could this creative burst be witnessed on a quotidian basis more than in that most spartan of domestic spaces: the garage.

Red Light Special / Garage Parties

The garage has its linguistic origins in French ("to store/shelter"), but its modern architectural manifestation is thoroughly American, especially in a region as notoriously car-centric as California (Jackson 1987: 25). Some affluent homes built in earlier eras included a carriage house that was physically separate from the main house, but the expansion of suburban housing after World War II usually involved building garages *into* the overall house structure. As Kenneth Jackson jokes (?), "in California, garages and driveways were often so prominent that the house could almost be described as accessory to the garage" (1987: 252).

Yet, even if the garage is now enclosed within the same structure as the rest of the house, it is still, by both design and purpose, a liminal space, "neither inside nor outside the home," as described by Christine Balance (2007: 141).[32] Unlike the rest of a house, a garage is not inherently designed for sleep or socializing or meals. It may provide household storage, but its primary purpose is to house automobiles. In other words, the garage is a transit hub through which families travel in and out of their domestic realm into public, civic space.

Part of the garage's liminality arises from its inherent flexibility; it is a space whose physical dimensions can be easily filled and emptied within a moment's notice, and as a result the suburban garage has often been tasked with all sorts of temporary functions that would not easily work in any other "room." The garage can be a space for a band to rehearse or an impromptu playroom or a workshop for tool tinkering. It is striking, for example, to think of how many tales of American entrepreneurship center on the "humble beginnings" of innovators working out of their garages, whether Polaroid's Edwin Land or Apple Computer's Steve Jobs and Steve Wozniak. Great ideas never seem to begin in the living room.

For the Bay Area's Filipino youth, one of the main creative uses for the garage was music and dancing, aka the garage party. The garage, once emptied of cars and other items, becomes an ideal party space—a blank, concrete canvas, if you will. In a two-car garage, you can easily accommodate audio equipment, a few lights, and most important, enough dance space for a few dozen revelers, especially in warmer months when people can congregate out of the garage and on the driveway.

In the pre–mobile DJing days of the 1970s, music for a garage party tended to be a communal affair. The host would provide the basic audio equipment—usually a simple family stereo system—and the attendees would help by bringing seven-inch singles, which were stacked into a queue next to the turntable. Sometimes one designated person would help pick and play the records; other times people took turns as the informal DJs. The music they played reflected similar dance music being played in city discotheques, with songs drawn from popular soul and funk artists, including James Brown; Rufus and Chaka Khan; Kool and the Gang; Cameo; Earth, Wind and Fire; and others.

It may be obvious to point out that garage parties were a particularly suburban phenomenon, since the garage itself was such a ubiquitous and specific feature of suburban homes, especially compared to denser, apartment-based housing in central city neighborhoods. San Jose's Yusuf Rashid noted: "You go to a party in San Francisco . . . it might be a little bungalow . . . but San Jose, you know you was gonna have a garage." Kantares added: "Back in the days, we didn't really have a lot of [garage] parties downtown. Mostly, we'd go out in the Mission, Daly City, the Avenues 'cause a lot of people who lived out there had bigger basements and garages and their parents were more well off. The Avenues was like heaven to us because that's two-car garages, that's going to fit a lot of people." In this respect, garage parties offer an interesting spin on the conventional caricature of suburban culture as being creatively bereft, what Karen Tongson relays as "an aesthetic vacuum, a place where art and creativity are domesticated and inevitably disappear altogether" (2011: 19). With garage parties, one could say that creativity and art are indeed being domesticated, insofar as they are being brought into a domestic space, but there is no creativity being erased in the process. Instead, the garage gave youth a space to repurpose with their own creative output: "think garage bands, garage parties, and a teenager's playroom," writes Balance.

She also notes: "Still part of the architecture of the home, garages allow parents the luxury of their children at proximity while relegating their noise production outside of the enclosed quarters of the domestic sphere" (Balance 2007: 141). That kind of division of property was common with garage parties, as Rashid recounted: "The parents would stage a party and in the living room and the kitchen . . . the elders would be hanging out there and they would have their card games and their mahjong, OK? And basically, the youngsters, they would be relegated to the garage. The whole attitude was, 'as long as you guys don't get violent we're just going to leave you alone.' It was weird because a lot of stuff was going on in the garage that . . . if the parents knew . . . they would have pulled the plug." This was a common anecdote among my respondents—the kitchen and living room belonged to the "elders," while the younger generation had the garage to themselves. That kind of claimed space allowed for social interactions not necessarily possible elsewhere, such as school or church, especially when it came to physical contact with potential romantic and sexual partners. A good garage party hardly needed fancy club lights, but the one essential component was a red lightbulb, whose romantic connotations (and soft shadows) facilitated momentary liaisons over the duration of a slow song. As Kantares joked, "that's the main reason we did it in garage and basements, so we could put the red light on and slow dance and get your grind on."

Garage parties became a central social activity for third-wave Filipino American youth. "You did not want to miss a garage party and that's why you went out every weekend. It was like everybody was there," said Leila Recania of the San Francisco crew the Go-Go's. Her crewmate Daphnie Anies added, "For me, it was a big impact on my whole life. From the time I was ten, I went with my brother to . . . it wasn't even a garage party, it was a living room party with lights out. I was the youngest one there. [I knew] it's always going to be my life."

Not only did the crews bring the entertainment value of the nightclubs closer to home but they were an important *youth* space that stood in contrast to discotheques catering to older, eighteen- or twenty-one-and-up crowds. Spintronix's Jay dela Cruz observed that during his teen years, "there weren't the clubs and the organized parties; it was all about the garage parties. These people needed an outlet to dance."[33] They utilized the outlets available to them rather than waiting for other institutions to fill those needs. In transforming these domestic spaces into their own entertainment zones, these DJs were claiming space for themselves, benefiting from a resource specific to the middle-class neighborhoods their families had moved to.

These kinds of adaptations of private spaces into social venues bring to mind the concept of "ephemeral forums" that urban historian Jorge Leal uses to discuss a different kind of suburban musical scene. In blue-collar, predominantly Latino neighborhoods in Southeast Los Angeles (Bell, South Gate, Downey, etc.), Leal argues, "due to the lack of music venues or public spaces in these deindustrialized cities, 'music activists' have created scores of 'ephemeral forums' to stage concerts even for one night. Locales such as empty storefronts, decaying movie theaters, decommissioned veterans' halls, rundown pizza parlors and even foreclosure homes have served as the sites where hundreds of young people create and nurture the South East L.A. music scene" (2011). Here we also have the transformation of existing private spaces into newly purposed, temporary public space, one where urban planning failures, municipal neglect, and local resistance is pushed back against by youth-driven creativity and a willingness to make do with whatever is at a band or community's disposal.[34]

Garage parties happened in a different kind of ephemeral forum. The cities where they took place were often spaces that actually had municipal venues, such as Hayward's Centennial Hall or San Francisco's California Hall, or at the very least public spaces (parks, memorials, etc.) that allowed for public congregation and performances. The conversion of a garage into a pseudoclub is not necessarily a guerrilla action (unless done without a homeowner's permission) in the same way as commandeering a liquor store parking lot.[35] As such, I prefer to think of garage parties as an example of a "liminal forum," on the blurred edge of private/public space. The fact that garages, as noted, are already liminal spaces within/outside a home only makes this comparison more apt.

Garage parties may seem small-scale, but they could draw youth from across great distances, requiring a fluency with multiple public transit systems. Dave "Dynamix" Refuerzo of 3-Style Attractions lived in San Jose, and in order to get to a party in San Francisco, he explained, "I used to always take the bus in San Jose to BART in Fremont and then MUNI in the City [San Francisco]."[36] This was no small investment in time, since a one-way trip from San Jose to San Francisco could have taken upward of two hours, and partygoers risked being stranded once BART shut down for the evening.

This kind of compulsion, to cross space and borders in search of a good garage party, speaks to a yearning of sorts, when different youth from across the Bay Area sought a rare form of social contact between one another. This point will become even more crucial in chapter 4 in explaining the importance of the DJ scene to the Filipino youth community. For now, it is enough to say that as *destinations*, the garage parties physically brought them together into shared spaces, undergoing shared experiences. Those acts of traveling set down roots to building an identity via cultural activity and participation. When the first mobile crews began to form, they would only widen and intensify the desire of youth to make these pilgrimages.

Chapter 2 / Team Building / Mobile Crew Formations

2.1 / Flyer for a 1979 dance, "Disco Extravaganza," in San Francisco. It was hosted by Sound Explosion, a crew formed at Balboa High School in San Francisco and recognized as the first Filipino American mobile crew in the Bay Area. Courtesy of Rafael Restauro.

Back in the mid-1970s, hiring a mobile disc jockey meant getting out the phonebook and flipping to the "D" section. If you were in the San Francisco area, you might end up with the Music Masters or Dr. Funk, two of the more popular phonebook DJs. They were competent at their job, possessing a decent sound system for school dances and having acceptable taste in the latest dance tunes, but as DJs, they mixed records in that old-fashioned fade-in, fade-out way. There was no nonstop mixing. There was not enough . . . flow.

For the Restauro clan at San Francisco's Balboa High, phonebook DJs were all they originally knew. The Restauros were led by brothers Rafael and Ricky, and their core clique also included nephew Edward (who was only a couple of years younger) and honorary family member Sam Beltran. They took music seriously, especially as leaders in the school's competitive ROTC drill team, considered one of the best in the city. Drill team is all about coordinated performances set to music, so perhaps it was only natural that they would take an interest in DJs but not the staid phonebook variety. They needed something different to spark their imagination; one night in 1978, they found that at a nightclub called The Firehouse.

The clique had crossed the bay to meet up with their friend Renel Bautista at the Firehouse, a new discotheque in the city of Danville. Within minutes of stepping inside, they could tell something novel was happening. The DJs at the Firehouse were different from their phonebook variety. Instead of fading songs in and out, these DJs segued seamlessly, with each song melding into the next.[1] This "nonstop" mixing was a revelation, a completely new way to experience music. Within days, the Restauros, Beltran, and Bautista made a decision: instead of bringing their friends out to the discotheque, they'd bring the experience of the discotheque back to their friends. Together, they formed the Bay Area's first Filipino American–led mobile DJ crew: Sound Explosion.

The members of Sound Explosion were already used to being ahead of the curve. The Restauro family, for example, had immigrated to the United States in the late 1950s, half a decade before the Immigration Act of 1965 finally undid over forty years of draconian immigration quotas. Ricky and Rafael's father had been a U.S. Army soldier for thirty years, and that had allowed him and other relatives to immigrate at a time when few other immigrants from Asia, let alone the Philippines, had the opportunity. In contrast to the Restauro children—all of whom were born in the United States—Sam Beltran followed a more conventional path. He was already twelve when his parents came to the United States in 1972—not coincidentally, the same year Ferdinand Marcos declared martial law in the Philippines.[2]

At Balboa, the Restauros and Beltran rose up the ranks of the school's social hierarchy thanks to their involvement in the ROTC drill team.[3] At Balboa, the ROTC rooms were where the "cool" Filipino American kids hung out, and to be on the drill team was practically like lettering in a varsity sport. Rafael Restauro eventually rose to become the drill team commander—Beltran was his XO (executive officer)—and their band of family and friends were prominent enough that the school principal would jokingly call them "the Mafia."

After their visit to the Firehouse in the summer of 1978, Bautista and Beltran had purchased turntables and were mastering the art of nonstop mixing. By the beginning of the school year that fall, Sound Explosion were ready to make their debut. Ricky Restauro, the crew's informal master of ceremonies and hype man, convinced Balboa's administration to allow the crew to DJ an upcoming fall dance. This became their coming out party. "It was the first school dance of the year . . . down in the cafeteria," Rafael recalled. "That's when we said, 'OK, let's break out Sound

Explosion.' We had a little paper sign that we plastered up on a little four-by-eight plywood and had this little shiny paper on top of it."

That first dance put Sound Explosion on the map. In their early months in 1978 and 1979, the crew did not have an organized marketing strategy, let alone access to anything akin to today's social media advertising tools. Instead they relied on word of mouth, with each gig serving as an opportunity to audition for future clients, a process Beltran described as "reverse invitations. It wasn't intended for us to market ourselves, but people would come up, 'do our party, do our party.'" It helped that Sound Explosion had little competition as mobile DJs versed in nonstop mixing. "We were mixing and [audiences] were tripping out on that. They just never heard that before," said Rafael.

Sound Explosion also brought an impressive visual flair. At that first Balboa dance, the crew spent most of their advance fee on a do-it-yourself fog machine—essentially, a fifty-gallon water tub into which they could drop dry ice. They also learned to assemble their own lighting rigs. Said Rafael, "We used to go to clubs back then and they would have all the lighting. So [we thought], 'let's bring our lighting here' rather than just the cafeteria lights being turned off and flashlights and all that. We had rope lighting, we had strobe lights," rented from theatrical supply stores.

There were no DJ specialty rental stores back then. If you could not rent the equipment you needed, you learned to build it. "Our stands for our lights and disco balls were rims of tires we put cement in [figure 2.2]. Screwed pipes in, all that stuff," said Rafael. Their most dramatic visual props were flash pots—simple but dangerous pyrotechnic devices made from hubcaps, tissue paper, and flash powder purchased at the local magic supplies store. Because flash powder ignites on contact, the tissue acted as a makeshift fuse, but it was far from an exact science. Rafael recalled one time when he lit the fuse but it seemed to take an inordinate amount of time: "I went over there and POOF, I burned all the hair off my arm."

Sound Explosion applied the same ingenuity to their promotions. After they saved up enough money from their gigs, they purchased a van to move their heavy equipment. On weekends when they did not have a gig, they loaded their speakers—professional-grade Klipsch La Scalas—in the back of the van and connected them to their stereo. "We used to have those Klipsch, in the van, bumping off a radio. No one had a system like we had back then in a car. We had a concert in the car, it was so damn loud," said Edward. With that mobile sound system, Rafael said, they

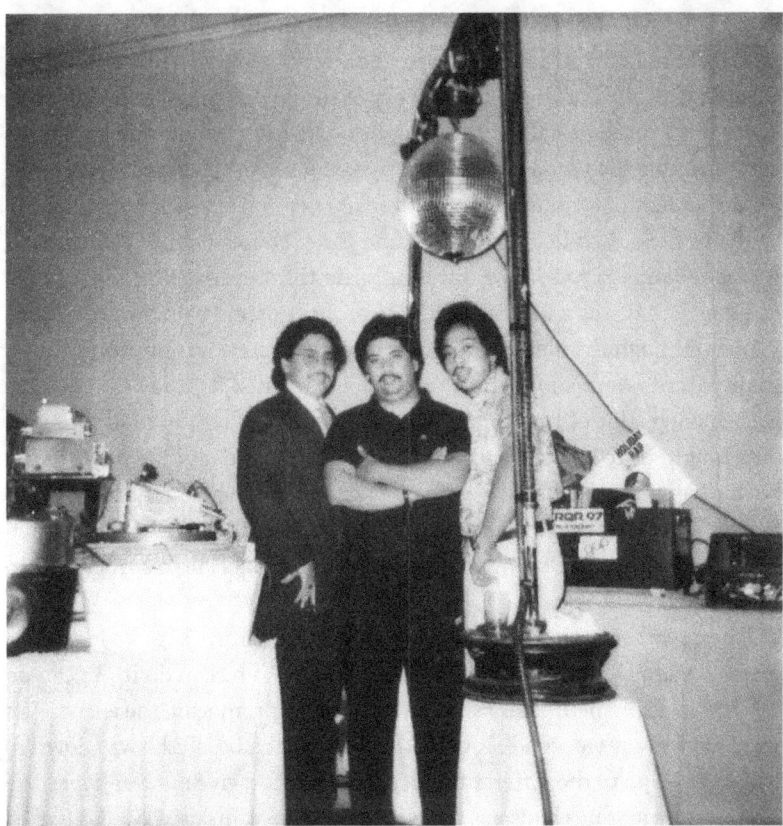

2.2 / Sound Explosion (San Francisco), c. 1979. Left to right: Rafael Restauro, Sam Beltran, Edward Restauro. Note that the light stand base they are standing next to is a repurposed car tire rim. Photo courtesy of Rafael Restauro.

would "run around with it and people would be drawn to [the music] and we'd give them flyers or whatever, let them know who we were."[4]

From a business standpoint Sound Explosion also broke new ground. Rafael registered the crew as an independent business, and by negotiating with school administrators, equipment rental stores, and venue managers, he helped to condition people to the then-unusual sight of a high school teenager handling contracts and other business agreements with adults.

Over their four-year reign, Sound Explosion were a remarkable success by any standard. As one of the few mobile crews operating in the late 1970s, they were hired throughout the Bay Area to spin at everything from garage parties to school dances to weddings. They gigged around

Team Building / 53

San Francisco and neighboring cities, as far away as the Solano County Fair, forty miles from San Francisco. "Some months, we were working five weekends in a row, every Friday, every Saturday, getting $350, up to $600 every day," recalled Rafael; this was a goodly sum not just by late 1970s standards but also for a crew of mostly sixteen- and seventeen-year-olds. Rafael added that money was not the only perk: "We used to make thousands of dollars and party at the same time. People would feed us, we'd go meet women, you know different girls from every different part [of the Bay]. . . . It was a lifestyle at the time and getting paid on top of it."

Even though the idea of starting a mobile DJ crew was unprecedented, their parents were supportive. As Rafael explained it, "they saw that we were having a lot of fun, clean fun, making money on top of it. Our parents taught us to be little entrepreneurs because, unfortunately, we didn't have silver spoons when we were born so we had to go out and get it." In fact, it was Rafael's mother who helped bankroll Sound Explosion's biggest gig, thrown on December 1, 1979, at California Hall in San Francisco (figure 2.1).

The idea came from watching existing DJs throw similar gigs. "Dr. Funk used to have a big following and we said, 'If he can do it, we can do it,'" Rafael explained. The crew spent six weeks promoting the event. "We used to go every weekend . . . to all the different clubs, all the way down to San Jose . . . go to the different high school dances, give out our flyers. We drew out about one thousand people at that dance," he said. Sound Explosion also included a dance competition as part of the event, buying their own trophies for the winners and inviting dance crews from across the Bay to participate. At the event itself, the crew also struck upon a simple moneymaking strategy. Rafael recalled, "We thought about . . . OK, we'll give them free popcorn and sell soda so we'll get them thirsty, then we get them soda." Edward added, "There was so much money being made there, we couldn't even handle it. It was just all our family handling it. We didn't really care about the money, it was all about having fun."

In the end, though, Sound Explosion's success generated its own discontents. In 1978, the crew had the scene practically to themselves. Within two years, their success had inspired the formation of four other mobile crews at Balboa alone, to say nothing of other nascent groups elsewhere in the Bay. These new crews might have been inspired by Sound Explosion, but they also became competitors, and Rafael complained of rampant underbidding by their new rivals. Sound Explosion's founding members were also getting older, and what had been a teenage pursuit now felt less important as they were advancing into adulthood. Rafael recalled: "We were getting older, we had all gotten out of high school, you know. Everybody was getting into the working field . . . then the younger guys were getting all the parties at a cheaper price and we couldn't really compete. Or, put it this way, we didn't want to. We didn't want to lower what we thought we were worth to what those guys were doing." Without much formality, Sound Explosion disbanded that year, and, surprisingly, when the members left, they left completely. They stopped DJing, their records went into storage, and they never looked back. When I spoke to Rafael, Edward, and Sam about their experiences with Sound Explosion, they had little idea of how the mobile DJ scene they helped birth had eventually grown into a movement that practically defined a generation.

The success of Sound Explosion created shock waves across San Francisco and Daly City; ground zero was the crew's own Balboa High. In 1979, Lowell High student Rene Anies met up with some friends at Balboa to attend a school dance where Sound Explosion was spinning. Anies recalled witnessing the crew's show for the first time: "They brought the club to the high school dance, in essence. And they just took it to another level. . . . I mean, dancing in those days, you grabbed a girl, go out and dance. But they told you what to do . . . they told you to say 'Yeah!' They told you to say 'Party over here!' And with that, everybody was just interactive, not just dancing, not just to their group, everybody became one. It just made the party that much better." After the dance, Anies turned to his friends at Balboa and said, "Hey, that's pretty cool, we should do that." Together, they went out and formed Electric Sounds.

Willie Sparks and Orlando Madrid were also Balboa students in that era. "I think Sound Explosion was the biggest inspiration for anybody," Sparks said. "I mean they had their lights set up, they were set up real well. . . . You got ideas off them and then you just kind of made it to where you could make it work, you know?" Madrid added, "Sound Explosion was the biggest crew back then that I knew of. They had all the big speakers and stuff, all the nice stuff. I was like, 'I want to be like them one day.'" In the late 1970s, the two became members of two new Balboa crews, respectively: Non-Stop Boogie and Sounds of Success. Yet another set of classmates kicked off Disco Tech Limited at the same school. By 1980, Balboa had seen five different mobile crews form—and they were not done yet.

In 1982, the first—and possibly only—Filipino American *female* mobile crew, the Go-Go's, formed at Balboa. Then, in 1984, a freshman by the name of Richard Quitevis enrolled at Balboa; he would later join the Live Style mobile crew and adopt a DJ name based on a video game character, Q-Bert. Within the mobile scene, no single school has quite as storied an alumni network as "Bal."

The web became even more interwoven. As Electric Sounds and Non-Stop Boogie began gigging around town, one of the people who caught them was Anthony Carrion, from across the Daly City border. Carrion, if you recall, was an acolyte of Studio West's resident DJ, Cameron Paul, but it was not until he saw these mobile crews that Carrion thought, "We could do that too, what they're doing. You know, even better. So we said, 'OK, let's put something together.' Got some money from my parents, got some equipment and went from there." That led to Unlimited Sounds.

Beginning with Sound Explosion, the Filipino American mobile scene began to grow slowly but exponentially, with each new crew inadvertently helping influence the formation of other crews. These were still the early days of the scene, but even back then, three important trends were already becoming evident.

First, as important as discotheque DJs were in spreading the gospel of nonstop disco mixing styles, the idea to form *mobile crews* came largely, if not almost exclusively, from watching *other mobile crews*. Thus, the budding popularity of mobile DJing depended heavily on peer-to-peer observation and interaction. Mobile DJing was not an activity one could witness via mass media; it was literally and figuratively interpersonal.

What made those encounters powerful was that the DJs whom people were watching were peers from the same neighborhoods, the same schools, and perhaps most important, the same ethnic background. I revisit this topic in more depth later, but for now, it is worth sharing Q-Bert's postulation that "it's the whole role model thing. To see a DJ that is a Filipino do something and have a good time [inspires people to think], 'Why can't I do it?' To be associated with other high-ranked DJs, it kind of set the standard for [thinking], 'If he can do it, I can do it too.'" That "I can do it too" realization—what I describe as the "lightbulb moment"—represented a formative, cognitive moment when new possibilities blossomed, inspiring youth to action.

Second, the peer-to-peer spread of mobile DJing can be thought of as the transmission of an idea within a network: the denser the network, the easier it was to quickly and broadly disseminate that idea.[5] This is partially what made those aforementioned Filipino American family settlement patterns so important. Neighborhoods where more families clustered led to denser networks of peer contact that abetted mobile crew formations. In contrast, those neighborhoods—even in large cities—where relatively fewer Filipino American families lived, such as Berkeley and Oakland, had sparser peer networks and, as a result, fewer mobile crews.[6] That may seem self-evident—Filipino mobile crews formed where Filipino families lived—but my point is to draw attention to the importance of social, family, and community networks in understanding how and where the scene took root.

Third, being inspired by an idea and actualizing that idea are two different phenomena. To form a crew required more than inspiration; you needed resources. There would have been expensive equipment and records to buy, storage spaces to secure, and transportation to arrange, and all that is before a crew might have even performed at their first gig. In most cases, those resources came from a crew's network of family members who could help with either direct capital (cash) or indirect assistance (referrals for gigs). As chapter 3 chronicles, Filipino American families, alongside community, church, and school groups, constituted an essential, soft "infrastructure" that supported the long-term health and growth of the scene; their role is as much part of the mobile scene story as the DJs themselves.

Chapter 1 explained the social preconditions that shaped the environment where the scene took root: nightclub disco mixing was an inspiration, garage parties provided a precedent, and Filipino American family settlement established where the scene would sprout. The next two chapters examine the social forces and processes at work in forming the scene itself, roughly covering 1978–1982. In particular, I focus on two distinct (but interconnected) sets of social forces. In the next chapter, I discuss those factors "external" to the crews, specifically the role of a community- and family-based infrastructure that helped transform a collection of crews into a fully realized scene. For the remainder of this chapter I will focus on forces "internal" to the scene that influenced how young men and women were likely to join and form crews . . . or not.

Psychic Income / Earning Symbolic Capital

Spintronix's Kormann Roque once described what he "earned" via DJing as "psychic income" (Portugal 2006). In other words, DJing came with modest incomes, but what mattered more to him—and many others—was *social* currency. Images Inc.'s Francisco Pardorla also observed: "A lot of these guys ... were flipping burgers twenty hours a week, and on the weekends, they would spin for people's parties for free just for the social aspect." I took "the social aspect" here to mean both the ability to socialize with friends, new and old, and the opportunity to burnish one's social status by being at the center of a party. In short, mobile DJing earned symbolic capital.

By "capital," I mean any resource that can be accrued, possessed, and/or spent, in both literal and figurative ways.[7] There is economic capital—money, for example—but while symbolic capital may not be as quantifiable, it can be no less valuable. Not only can symbolic capital be earned (and lost) but also it can be converted into other forms of capital. For example, Gil Olimpiada, of the San Francisco crew Ultimate Creations, recalled working out the performance fee with promoter Mark Bradford for one of Bradford's popular Imagine parties: "Each DJ group had to negotiate their own price for performing at his events. My brother Jose had to play hardball with him a few times as he would try to offer us a lowball offer. Bradford did mention to us about other DJ groups playing for free during contracts negotiations, but that didn't work with U.C.!" What Olimpiada alludes to is how Bradford could offer newer crews a lesser rate in exchange for exposure (symbolic capital offered in place of economic capital). However, crews who already enjoyed a strong reputation, such as Ultimate Creations, already had status, thus making it harder for Bradford to lowball their performance fee.

Throughout the scene, these various forms of capital fed into one another, with a crew's status (symbolic capital) justifying a higher pay rate (economic capital), which could enable them to purchase better equipment (cultural capital) that, in turn, could burnish their reputation (back to symbolic capital). Of these myriad forms, money was certainly important, but ultimately, it was social status that provided prospective DJs with their raison d'être.

Disk jockeys were the focal point of attention at parties—they "*made the party*" as the saying goes. As such, their reputations were analogous to other high-status social roles within a youth community. Electric Sounds' Rene Anies explained, "When you were known as a DJ, that was our little Hollywood. That was our way of being a star within the community." Spintronix's Jay dela Cruz chose an analogy closer to his background as a former athlete; when I asked him if well-known DJs enjoyed higher status, he replied, "Oh yeah, just like how the star quarterback would walk down the hallway."

In short, becoming a DJ held the promise of becoming an object of respect and admiration. Even the respondents who modestly tried to play down their celebrity status still admitted that they benefited from it. The following extended exchange was between Carrion and myself:

AC: Usually at school, I kind of just stayed low key until we started doing the school dances, then they did know who I was and what we did. That was when they did start hanging out and talking to me and stuff. You know, "that was a cool dance, blah blah." But I didn't really make a big deal out of it.

OW: But it did elevate your status?

AC: Yeah, definitely it did. One of the cool things when people start noticing who you are, is you go to a pizza place and you start getting free food. McDonald's: free food. Anywhere you go. We started getting free stuff. I was, like, cool.

There is a duality here in Carrion's responses. On the one hand he stated "I didn't really make a big deal" in regard to his social status, but at the same time, when it came to its perks, he also admitted he found it "cool." These are not contradictory impulses. Instead, they highlight that DJing conferred a special status that could be enjoyed even by those who did not actively solicit it.[8]

Notably, another measure of prestige was in the literal mobility a crew possessed in traveling out of town for gigs. Burt Kong of South San Francisco's Sound Sequence recalled that part of the allure of DJing came from how he was able to gain entry into social spaces beyond his hometown: "You're young, we were the best in our field—it's like being . . . the world champs at the time, you know? Anywhere you go . . . within the community, we were like, not movie stars or anything, but you know people would recognize us. We had friends all over and we could go, you know, to Vallejo, San Jose, anywhere we want. Get in to all the gigs for free, you know? It's [a] small world, but [you] have it."[9] Being part of Sound Sequence gave Kong and his partners entry into other spaces that they might not have enjoyed otherwise, expanding their social world beyond a local high school or neighborhood. As Kong described, the DJ scene may have constituted a "small world," but it was *their* world, one in which being a DJ carried status. The ability to travel within that world, to have people near and far respect your reputation, was both a sign of one's symbolic capital and a privilege to be "purchased" through that capital.

Social status also connected to an individual's sense of power and control. Part of the appeal of DJing is the feeling of control you have over a floor. For Roque, that meant "being able to mix the music, being able to control the music that everybody's listening to. Getting a reaction from the crowd at a party." Likewise, when Pardorla encountered his first mobile crew (City Lights), what stood out in his mind was "the control that they had over the crowd. In a way, sort of the 'celebrity-dom' that they had." Pardorla makes plain here the connection between symbolic capital ("celebrity-dom") and a DJ's power to "move the crowd."

However, more than just having an impact on an undifferentiated audience, many DJs wanted to leave a positive impression on a more select group of people. If you recall that most mobile crews were composed of straight-identified young men just coming into postpubescent sexual awareness, it should not be surprising that many of them would want to "spend" their symbolic capital by improving their social standing with young women in particular.

"Just for the Girls" / Erotic Capital and Gender Relations

Kormann Roque not only coined the term "psychic income"; in a separate interview, he explained that one of his other motivations in helping form Spintronix was that "we wanted to see what the girls looked like at the private schools."[10] The idea that young men would pursue activities that might heighten their sex appeal is certainly not a novel one or unique to the DJ scene. However, I highlight this dimension because sexual desire—and the idea of what Catherine Hakim terms "erotic capital"—was as central to the logic of crew formation as any other form of capital and partially addresses the layers of gender relations within the larger scene (Hakim 2010: 501).

After all, young men joined crews not just to enhance their own social stature with other male peers but also to raise their profiles among women in particular. Carrion explained:

> Some guys, they just got into it just for the girls. You're up on the stage and everybody's out there on the floor—you know you're the star up there. They want to hang out with you. When we used to do parties before, we basically had a party crew. We'd bring a party crew with us just to turn the party out, you know, make sure it was a good party. We'd have like fifteen to twenty people come with us, girls and guys, and a lot of times girls would want to come along with you. You'd meet

2.3 / Francisco Pardorla (Images Inc./AA Productions, Fremont) with the New York dance music group Sweet Sensation, 1987. Besides helping form the Fremont mobile crew Images Inc., Pardorla was also involved with AA Productions, one of the major party promoters during the mobile era, started by Arleen Alviar. Photo courtesy of Francisco Pardorla.

a lot of girls that way and you get to go to all these parties. Where[as], if you weren't a DJ, you would not be at all these parties, you know? There's no way.

Likewise, dela Cruz affirmed: "We wanted to meet girls, man, absolutely.... You're in the spotlight, you're the center of attention in front of three hundred people. The same could be said that's why they [women] wanted to go out with the star quarterback or the singer." What was telling is how dela Cruz quickly shifted from explaining why *men* wanted to become DJs (i.e., "to meet girls") to explaining why *women* would be drawn to DJs ("you're in the spotlight"). Both his and Carrion's comments suggest that symbolic and erotic capital were inextricably tied together.[11]

In contrast, for the few female mobile DJs, their concerns had little to do with "meeting guys."[12] Most of them got into DJing through boyfriends who were already in the scene, and therefore their primary concern at parties was to avoid being confused with "trophy girlfriends," says Daphnie Anies of the Go-Go's: "A lot of the groups that used to bring women with them, [these] girls just sat in the corner. We were active.

Team Building / 61

These girls would just sit in the corner and not dance all night because their boyfriends were DJing the party. They would just sit there. And they were just there, just to be there, watch their boyfriend, whatever. [When] we were there, we got into it. I would say that was the majority of the groups, all of them just had trophy girlfriends tagging along. We were just kind of different from that." Notably, even the nomenclature itself—a *trophy* girlfriend—intimately connected the symbolic (a trophy as a literal symbol of status) with the erotic (a sexual partner). Sunaina Maira suggested in her study of South Asian and South Asian American DJs: "A male deejay is also presumed to confer status on his girlfriend, who would then be known as 'DJ Karma's girl' or 'Lil' Jay's girl,' drawing subcultural capital from the achievement of her male partner" (Maira 2002: 61). (In this example, erotic capital is exchanged for symbolic capital.) Also, what bothered Anies was her perception of "trophy girlfriends" as *passive* players at a party. She thrice described how "they would just sit there," which seemed to be an affront to the whole point of being around DJs: you danced, you were active, you "got into it," as she said. For her, there was nothing wrong with being involved with a DJ—she herself ended up dating and marrying Electric Sounds' Rene Anies—but rather it was how that relationship changed the behavior of women, transforming active partygoers into passive corner decorations who "just sat there," much as a trophy actually would.

However, in the scene as a whole, women were generally quite active. The ranks of DJs themselves were overwhelmingly male, but women exerted a powerful presence *on the floor*. According to Allyson Tintiangco-Cubales, who grew up in the Union City–Fremont party scene, "behind the tables, it was very male, but at the actual party, no. It would be fifty-fifty in terms of how many [men and women] would be there, but I think a lot of times, there was a whole culture of women dogging each other during these parties, and it was dominated by women in terms of its culture." What Tintiangco-Cubales describes here are the ways competitive relations between women—manifesting in the form of insults and arguments (i.e., "dogging")—had the effect of turning the dance floor into a more female-dominated space, despite the presence of the DJs as the central entertainment.[13]

The dance floor is, at the very least, a highly charged sensual space, defined as much by the physicality of moving and pressing bodies together as the sounds and rhythms of the music itself. DJs do not just mediate social space; they also facilitate the sexual chemistry of that space. That too is a form of power to wield, especially as it—in the eyes of the DJs—enhanced their own erotic capital as that mediator. However, though men may have entered the mobile scene in hopes of forging heterosexual liaisons, I suggest that *homosocial* relationships were an equal, if not more powerful, draw.

Forging Brotherhoods / Homosociality within the Mobile Crews

Crews were homosocial formations; that is, they were largely same-sex social organizations. Mobile crew membership allowed young men an opportunity to interact and bond with other men, free of familial, school, or other outside pressures and expectations. This too was a draw, as the DJ crew served as an alternative to traditionally homosocial groups. For example, in a 2005 twentieth anniversary video assembled by Spintronix, different members described the importance of belonging to the crew: "We're more of a fraternity"; "The bonds and the relationships you have with these guys are going to stick with you for the rest of your lives"; "Spintronix is my brotherhood" (Portugal 2006). In a separate interview, Spintronix's dela Cruz stated: "The best thing was building this brotherhood of guys, who will become your best friends, your brothers, coming together, forming this crew, fighting for one cause. You learn many life lessons, you'll have relationships with these guys until the day you die. These guys are all brothers." Another common analogy compared crews to sports teams, especially with regard to how both organizations focus on common goals through competitive spirit. Images Inc.'s Pardorla suggested, "My cousin is a huge Raiders fan and so are many of my friends. I never understood this, how could someone feel so passionate about an organization where they have no control. Are these screams of support even heard by the players? To me it would be more logical to sport an SBC crew jacket even though I'm just the guy that hauls the equipment around. At least as a crew member I'll make a difference, a true member of the winning team." His sentiments were echoed by dela Cruz: "It's just like being on a championship sports team, working together for a common goal and celebrating all together. Collectively, as a crew, we spent many weeks, months, planning for just one night. Some young folks participated in Little League Baseball, Pop Warner Football, CYO Youth Basketball, in regards to team activities. Our outlet was the mobile DJing scene." Tellingly, it is the competitive *team* dynamic that serves as the key parallel between sports teams and mobile crews. Both use competitive

2.4 / Spintronix (Daly City), at a garage party at Kormann Roque's house, c. 1986. Garage parties were a key source of starter gigs for many crews. Left to right: Larry Alfonso, Mike Penas, Ron Mananquil, Ron Cada, Dino Rivera, Chris Miguel, Glenn Penas, Jonathan Mesa, Kormann Roque, Robert Cristobal. Photo courtesy of Ray Portugal.

goals as a way to build a collective, team-based identity. That shared goal is what turns groups into *crews*.

Mobile crews can also be situated within traditions of homosocial Filipino American organizations. In Bangele Alsaybar's study of Filipino American gangs and "party crews" in Los Angeles, he compares both organizations to the transplanted Filipino cultural institution of the *barkada*: "the indigenous peer grouping suffused by an egalitarian orientation emphasizing mutual caring, loyalty, and friendship that often tends to run deeper than blood relationships" (Alsaybar 1999: 120).[14] For Alsaybar, brotherhood was already a strong "organizing principle in Philippine culture, society and history" and "this indigenous propensity . . . was transplanted to America, undergoing modification in response to local conditions and expressing itself through the formation of fraternal organizations and various youth groups from gangs to car crews and party crews" (121).

While I do not believe mobile scene participants were consciously trying to replicate the model of the barkada (the term never entered any of our conversations), the parallels between them seem especially relevant in understanding the importance of homosocial organizations in the lives of different generations and communities of Filipino men. That also applied to another form of youth "group" that mobile crews were often compared to, or better said, confused with: street gangs.

When DJ crews first began to appear in the late 1970s, what people saw were groups of Filipino young men congregating together and wearing jackets and T-shirts with their crew names stitched or ironed onto them. Especially as DJ crews were a new phenomenon, many simply assumed crews were newly formed gangs, and this created problems for them with the police, school officials, and most dangerously, actual gangs. Rene Anies recounted: "There was one incident, we had our jackets, it said 'Electric Sounds,' and we were on Twenty-Fourth Street, and we got chased by a Mexican gang, 'cause they thought we were a gang. Because of the clothes we wore, because everybody wore the same jacket . . . there was a lot of confusion. . . . Even though we were DJs, they saw us as a gang."[15] Despite being mistaken for gangs, DJ crews led a separate existence from the gang scene. Some individual DJs were previously involved in youth gangs but broke ties when they joined DJ crews. Most of my respondents had no formal involvement in the gangs whatsoever, even if they knew gang members in their larger social networks. The two groups may have shared similar geographic turf, but for the most part they came from starkly different family and class backgrounds that would sustain a social separation between the two.[16]

Like gangs, sports teams, barkadas, fraternities, and the like, DJ crews offered members a sense of collective identity and purpose that enhanced their appeal. Sara Cohen investigated the rock band scene in Liverpool, but her observations could just as well be applied to the mobile crews when she writes: "The scene offers a social life, a sense of purpose, and dreams and aspirations outside any restrictions or responsibilities of work, family or home. It becomes an important source of individual and collective identity, and a means through which men can explore relationships with other men or relationships with women within the security of male groups" (Cohen 1997: 31). In short, homosocial formations offer a host of attractions: camaraderie, an intimate support network, a sense of safety within a collectivity, a team of people around you, working toward shared goals, and so on. However, these groups do not only draw men; I suggest they also help to *produce* men, or at least, produce a particular ideal of masculinity.

Music Masters / Producing Masculinity

When I first set out to study the mobile scene, I knew that I wanted to discuss gender relations in regard to why women were such a minority within crew ranks. However, in the course of collecting these oral histories, I realized that I needed to broaden my questions beyond "why were there not more women DJs?" and also ask "why would DJing attract so many men?"[17] This simple change in questioning became tremendously useful, as it helped me think through how DJing promotes a series of masculine ideals that can both attract men and potentially dissuade or marginalize women. In becoming DJs, then, part of what participants learned was how to adopt these values and, in this sense, become legible as men to others in the scene.

Much of what DJs value in the performance of their craft embodies and reifies popular ideals of hegemonic, Western manhood. Foremost among these is the emphasis on control and mastery. DJing celebrates the ability to exert control over music, to physically manipulate records and equipment to exacting specifications. Moreover, the crew structure, among other things, was designed to allow groups to have control over audio and lighting equipment rather than depending on the venue to provide them. Mobile crews also competed to control access to gigs at specific venues or in particular neighborhoods. Most of all, the DJ was presumed to be in control of himself, of his abilities, in order to be in control of the crowd. If the dance floor environment depended on the DJs to guide dancers' bodies through music and rhythms, DJs' mastery of their craft was crucial: if they chose the wrong song, or bumbled the mix, they risked losing the floor.

Moreover, DJing's competitive environment encourages constant expressions of bravado and machismo. Competitions are framed in military, conflict-based terms such as "battles" or "world wars." Turntables and records are often referred to as "weapons." If you defeat another DJ or crew soundly, you are said to have "destroyed" them. This kind of language is certainly not unique to the DJ scene—it is ubiquitous in playgrounds and sports venues everywhere—but the competitive environment of DJing especially lends itself to these expressions and celebrations of machismo. As Arthur Flannigan-Saint-Aubin argues, "contest/opposition appears to be the masculine modality par excellence and the obvious route to self-identity: I come to know myself only by knowing that something else is not me and is to some extent opposed to or set against me" (1994:

244). Nancy MacDonald makes a similar point: "Masculinity is not a free-standing asset. It depends on comparison and thus, competition and challenge for its significance and profile" (2001: 105). In the graffiti scenes that MacDonald explored, competition between writers and crews was part of the fabric of their practice, thus constantly reproducing an idealized form of masculinity—emphasizing risk and danger, that is, "resilience, bravery and fortitude"—that, to her, helped explained why graffiti crews, much like the mobile DJ crews, were overwhelmingly male (105).[18]

For DJs, "mastery" and "control" go hand in hand (quite literally, in using their hands). Unlike other feats of masculine display in athletics or even in other music genres, such as rock, DJing emphasizes displays of mastery that minimize the visual display. Some DJs may be very physical in their performances—constantly bobbing their heads, pushing buttons, twisting knobs, touching vinyl, and so on—but their movements are often subtle, meant to look meticulous, deliberate, and finely controlled. If the ideal posture of a rock guitarist is captured in overt spectacle—the phallic posturing of a guitar between a player's legs or a head-thrashing, arm-swinging drum solo, for example—it is telling that one of the most famous anthems to DJing is the 1989 Gang Starr song "DJ Premier in Deep Concentration." DJs are meant to stay in cool, collected control so that everyone around them can abandon themselves to the music.[19]

In a sense, DJ mastery is a performance of nonperformance. The language with which one can laud a DJ includes describing their mixing as "effortless." That praise means a DJ can accomplish a difficult task—mixing seamlessly—while simultaneously hiding the obvious signs of that labor. This is not a universal value: some DJs, for example, are quite visibly performative in a conventional "rock star" sense—hopping up and down, using exaggerated, violent motions to work a mixer, throwing vinyl records into a crowd after being done with them—but these displays generally only happen in environments where the audience is visually fixated on the DJ, such as on a concert stage. In a nightclub setting, the DJ is ideally meant to be heard, not seen. The ideal is not to distract the audience through one's bodily presence since that would interrupt the "flow" of the music and dancing. With apologies to Adam Smith, the DJ also demonstrates the power of the invisible hand.

DJ mastery extends also to the "tools of the trade," especially hyperknowledge about records. While not all record collectors are DJs, most DJs have to collect records by the nature of their profession. As a result, DJs are often in possession of arcane knowledge about music that those outside their community—and even within it—are not privy to. When I was actively DJing in the Bay Area, I would often run into Derrick "D" Damian, formerly of Just 2 Hype, and he would always have some newly acquired obscurity to show me, often preceded with the question (or perhaps it was a challenge?): "You got this?" or "You know about this?"

Especially when many DJs are competing for attention, knowing or "discovering" a previously unknown song accrues symbolic capital: DJs enjoy bragging about how they "broke" a particular record in the scene. Fusion's Ken Anolin shared: "We were expected to break something new. . . . I thought that was one of the coolest things around. 'Hey, I've got something that you don't have.'" In turn, displays of insider knowledge are studied and copied by their peers to help build their collections. For that reason, DJs are known to keep certain records in their collections secret as a way of maintaining exclusivity. For example, pioneering hip-hop DJs like Kool Herc and Afrika Bambaataa were notorious for taking the labels off their records in order to prevent other DJs from learning what songs they played (Katz 2012: 46). Anolin mentioned that DJs in the mobile community would do the same, "ripping labels off." Will Straw argues that symbolically, this kind of secrecy also served to reinforce insider versus outsider status and thus was part of the way social hierarchies were maintained (Straw 1997: 9).

Record collections become a metric of both cultural and symbolic capital, where the number of records one owns, and the exclusivity of those titles, are ways through which DJs can measure up to one another; some DJs even joke that they are "comparing stacks," which seems to have a phallocentric allusion, intentionally or not. To that point, Straw argues that record collecting is a key bonding force in homosocial circles: "Record collections, like sports statistics, provide the raw materials around which the rituals of homosocial interaction take shape. Just as ongoing conversation between men shapes the composition and extension of each man's collection, so each man finds, in the similarity of his points of reference to those of his peers, confirmation of a shared universe of critical judgment" (Straw 1997: 5). As collectors, though, DJs maintain an unstable relationship with conventional masculinity. While maintaining an exclusive collection is a form of mastery, Straw argues that it also puts DJs at risk of being classified as "nerds," if their collecting comes to be seen as a retreat from social interactions into private insularity: "For the nerd, knowledge (or, more precisely, the distraction which is its by-product) stands as the easily diagnosed cause of performative social failure" (8).

For Straw, the DJ is able to avoid being classified as a "nerd" by fashioning himself as a "hipster," a distinction that, while compelling in its own right, is not as useful for my purposes (Straw 1997: 9). The difference is that Straw is focused on discussing DJs as solitary figures; he does not consider the dynamic at play with *crews* of DJs. Unlike a lone figure, a crew fostered a team identity analogous to athletics and, by extension, aggressive, competitive attitudes. The fact that crews were also confused with youth gangs also boosted their image as dangerous and powerful men. Therefore, I would suggest that while record mastery was clearly an important quality of DJing in the mobile scene, it was not as necessary a move to counter a concern over being perceived as a nerd; grouping themselves into crews, with visible, exclusively male memberships already did much of the work to bring crew members into closer alignment with conventional masculinity.

Admittedly, I leave underaddressed the role race plays in the construction of these masculine identities. I discuss the role of ethnic and racial identity in greater detail elsewhere, but for now it is important to note that throughout the history of Filipino men in America, anxieties around both their race and gender have often been combined and conflated. One only needs to remember that in the nineteenth and twentieth centuries, antimiscegenation legislation and residential segregation were designed in large part to corral Asian immigrant men, perceived as racialized and sexualized threats, into enclaves from white society (see España-Maram 2006 or Espiritu 1997).

However, for the Filipino men I interviewed, it was difficult to ascertain how their experiences as a racialized community factored into how they negotiated masculine identities. For *some*, being Filipino was fraught with uncertainties around where they fit into their immediate social settings, especially when marginalized by a dominant black–white paradigm in their local schools or neighborhoods. It would also seem reasonable to suggest that, given how much deeply entrenched normative definitions of masculinity are bound up in that binary, Filipino men who fall outside of it experience social distance from dominant masculinity as well. Therefore, becoming DJs, benefiting from symbolic capital, and belonging to that community—especially a homosocial community of fellow men—could be seen as ways these Filipino youth recouped a sense not only of racial but also of masculine identity.

However, many young Filipinos, especially those in predominantly Filipino social spaces, grew up as a part of a visible central population. Surrounded by a community of other Filipinos, their masculine identities would likely have been more complete and well-developed, especially given the cultural persistence of machismo within the Filipino community. Therefore, entering into a DJ crew might have been less a way of recouping masculinity and more a way of enhancing it, especially for those teens who were already popular within their social circles as a result of being athletes, campus leaders, and so on, both within and outside a Filipino social context; remember Balboa High School's ROTC-centered social hierarchy of Filipino-ness, for example.[20] There certainly is more work to be done in probing how masculinity and gender identities play out within this community, but the challenge lies in understanding what makes Filipino American youth unique, given their particular positions in regard to their unique racial experiences and class privileges.[21] Especially given the complex intersection of heterosexual desire, homosocial networks, and the production of masculinity, a more thorough and focused study of gender within this scene might help contribute additional insights into the processes that generate social identities and relations among racialized youth. In that regard, I end this chapter with a discussion of where Filipina girls and women fit into the scene. If homosociality and the circulation of masculine identities created an inclusive environment for its male participants within the crews, they also influenced an environment that was exclusive of women, not from the scene as a whole but specifically from behind the DJ booth.

Locked Down and Out / Whither the Filipina Mobile DJ?

They came from Templeton, the outer Mission, South City; friends since childhood and Balboa High classmates by the early 1980s. When Sound Explosion were first blowing up, they were still in junior high—several at Denman Middle, right across the street from Balboa. Amy Gramlich (née Celis) used to cajole her older sister into taking her to the early mobile parties: "I knew Sound Explosion because I used to hang out with my sister in the older crowd. She hated me coming along but she had to bring me." By the time they all got to high school, the Balboa students would congregate in the basement. "There was a whole floor where the hip Filipinos would stay," Daphnie Anies (née Gambol) explained. "That was where the ROTC was."[22]

Since the days of Sound Explosion, the ROTC floor had become the informal stomping ground for all the school's mobile crews, and several

2.5 / Scrapbook page for the Go-Go's (San Francisco–Daly City). The Go-Go's were the only all-female DJ crew to assemble and perform at several events during the course of the mobile scene. Left to right: Leila Apostol, Liza Dizon, Daphnie Gambol, Amy Celis, Theresa Barellano, Stella Jolley, Rebecca Dumlao. Courtesy of Daphnie Gambol Anies.

of the women already had close ties to different existing crews: Anies's older brother Mike was a member of Electric Sounds, and she herself fell in with Disco Tech Limited. Gramlich dated Noel Villenueva of Disco Tech Limited, while Liza Vargas (née Dizon) was involved with Orlando Madrid of another Balboa crew: Sounds of Success. When Sounds of Success folded themselves into Disco Tech Limited, it brought them all together in a single crew.

Given that Gramlich and Vargas were dating other DJs, they knew how others might treat them as "trophy girlfriends," and they were quick to assert their own agency in pursuing the craft. Anies stressed that "Amy got into [DJing] on her own," independent of her boyfriend happening to be a DJ. When they were all in Disco Tech Limited together, they made sure they were not just part of the background and instead carried equipment and records, helped energize the party atmosphere by always being front and center on the dance floor, and in the cases of Gramlich and Vargas, stepped off the parquet and behind the DJ boards.

Gramlich's early reputation was as an ace dancer: "I was a tomboy. I just picked up . . . first locking, then strutting. It was just for fun." Rebecca Ruaro (née Dumlao) added, "At parties, [people] would lock or strut and we would push her out there." She began to pick up DJing by practicing at Madrid's house. Leila Recania (née Apostol) recalled, "When we'd go to [Madrid's] house, that's all it was—just music playing all the time. He used to tell her to learn, and she would just be on [the equipment]." Meanwhile, Madrid was also training Vargas, and eventually, the two women began to spin guest sets at Sounds of Success and Disco Tech Limited gigs. "Liza and I were both good on the turntables," said Gramlich; "we knew we could hang with the other crews."

Other friends came into the mix as the idea to form a crew took shape: Recania, who lived in South City, was part of the core, as was Ruaro, another Balboa classmate.[23] In the beginning, the women would joke, "Yeah, we'll be the first lady DJs. We'll come, wearing the same clothes, we're going to have this little dance. Amy and Liza will be the main lady DJs. . . . And then it just started happening," Recania recalled. Anies was the crew's MC (master of ceremonies)—one of the first in what would become a notable line of Pinay MCs in mobile crews—responsible for hyping up the crowd through her rapping and for helping to introduce the crew. "We thought if we formed a DJ group, just the girls, we'd get more exposure that way and more gigs," said Gramlich, adding, "we picked the Go-Go's because they were a popular girl band—we looked at the group as our role models. We weren't into the rock thing but when the Go-Go's were hot, we figured we'd name ourselves the Go-Go's too." It was the summer of 1982.

The Go-Go's began doing hall parties, including at the Masonic, but one of their early gigs was a battle at Assyrian Church of the East in San Francisco, involving themselves and three (male) crews: Non-Stop Boogie, Ultimate Creations, and Studio Sounds (see figure 3.1). Anies recounted:

> The first battle, we battled guys and they wanted to battle us. We were like, "OK!" We were kind of being picked on just because we were the girls. [Rumors would be] "Oh, they think they're all that but they got help from all their little guys, let's see what they can really do." ... Amy was better than a lot of the guys out there and I think that was really pissing them off. When you see a girl up there who was doing so much better than you, I think that was a reason they challenged us the very first time.

Anies felt that Gramlich's skills as a DJ threatened the masculine pride of male DJs who previously had dealt with women only on the dance floor and not as competitors behind the boards. Battles typically invite more established crews to join; inviting the Go-Go's, as a fledging crew, was unusual (though not unprecedented). When they placed second in the battle, their competence could not be easily dismissed. However, that did not stop others from challenging them, including other women.

According to the Go-Go's, following their initial visibility, a nemesis arose in the form of another female DJ crew, Young 'N' Tough (YNT), out of San Francisco's Wilson High.[24] The Go-Go's insisted that Young 'N' Tough only came into existence to challenge them: "I think [they formed out of] jealousy because they came out of nowhere. They really came out of nowhere," said Anies. Furthermore, Ruaro recounted that after the St. Joseph's Hall battle, "YNT, they spread a rumor that we were using a tape."[25] Accusing another crew of "using a tape" was akin to calling them cheaters, attacking the very integrity of the crew itself.

In order to settle this emerging conflict, the two crews held a DJ battle in the fall of 1982 in San Francisco. The Go-Go's walked away victorious, but this did little to quell the divisiveness coming from others. "After the YNT gig, everybody was just picking on us," said Anies. Again, most new crews did not attract such intensive scrutiny or criticism simply by virtue of being new—few people would know of you well enough to lobby a criticism. But the Go-Go's situation, precisely because they were the first female crew, was different: the level of scrutiny of these young women was far greater than a novice male crew would normally have experienced. Ruaro felt that to many audiences, "we were just girls and all show. They really needed to know that [we] could DJ."

The negativity eventually took its toll: "We still all hung out, we just didn't . . . pursue [more gigs]. We just didn't want to deal with everybody talking about us," said Anies. These young women continued to stay active in the mobile scene. Gramlich continued to spin with Disco Tech Limited and, years later, convinced Electric Sounds DJ Rene Anies to return to the craft after he had given it up. However, as a crew, the Go-Go's were over. It was the winter of 1982 by the time of their disbandment; the mobile scene never saw another all-Pinay DJ crew come through again.

Pinay DJs certainly existed in the mobile scene. Beside the Go-Go's, there were Sound Sequence's Daisy Ycmat, Cosmix Sounds' Suzie "Suzie Q" Racho, Just 2 Hype's Kristine Javier, and a handful of others, but in most of these cases, these women's tenure with their respective crews was short-lived. These women were exceptional, in multiple meanings of the word.

The male-ness of DJing is often taken for granted. It is telling that in the preface of their DJ history *Last Night a DJ Saved My Life*, Bill Brewster and Frank Broughton offer this qualifier: "We've called the DJ 'he' throughout. One, for grammatical reasons and two, because 98 percent of DJs have a penis" (1999: x). They do not seek to *explain* that disparity, however.[26] That casual, almost dismissive qualifier speaks to the ways masculinity has historically been normalized in discussions around gender and DJing, in both popular and academic publications.[27] This has shifted in more recent years, thanks to scholarship by the likes of Katz (2012) and Tiongson (2013), where the gender disparity receives far more than a token glance. Nonetheless, the traditional dearth of discussion of gender and DJing reflects, in my mind, a general privilege of masculinity where gender domination becomes normalized and naturalized. There is, of course, nothing "natural" at play here—homosocial formations do not form out of thin air; they are social constructions made up of actions (or inactions) that are both discrete *and* discreet.[28]

My wordplay here is deliberate insofar as the paucity of female DJs in the mobile scene was a product of any number of distinct forces (discrete) but rarely in obvious or explicit ways (discreet). My male and female respondents alike insisted that no one in the scene tried to actively discourage, let alone prohibit, Pinay DJs from participating. The Go-Go's' Ruaro insisted, "If the women really wanted to, the men would have given them the opportunity. That's part of their show. It only makes them look good too. I didn't think a lot of the women out there had the desire to do it as much as [Go-Go's DJ] Amy [Gramlich] did." However, as Ruaro inadvertently hints at, the forces curtailing female involvement did not have to be explicit prohibitions; they were often discouragements so buried into the logic and culture of the mobile scene that overt exclusion was not necessary to achieve the same effect.

For starters, an activity like DJing requires participants to stay out nights in opposite-sex environments. This created problems for teenage Pinays living in homes where daughters were expected to stay home and forgo social interactions. Allyson Tintiangco-Cubales grew up in the Fremont–Union City scene and fell in with the local crew, Nite Lime. However, "I couldn't follow them because my mom was really strict," she said, adding, "Even as a bad child, I could only really defy her to a certain point." She went to their gigs when they performed locally, but if Nite Lime crossed the Bay for a gig, that was literally a bridge too far for her to follow. In Dina Maramba's research on Filipino college students, one Pinay subject compared these kinds of situations to being on "lock down" (Maramba 2008: 343; see also Wolf 1997: 466).

Even the women in the Go-Go's had to pursue their activities surreptitiously, despite *running their own crew*. Gramlich shared: "My dad would give us a curfew and said 'If you're not home by eleven [p.m.], I'll lock the doors.' So we would sneak over to [a friend's] house." Daphnie Anies similarly had to resort to subterfuge to escape her parents' oversight: "If [my father set a curfew of] twelve o'clock and I wasn't home by twelve o'clock, I'd get in really big trouble. We snuck out too. My mom knew who I hung out with but she didn't know what we were doing specifically. She just knew we were going to parties." These and other Pinay respondents were intensely aware of the double standard applied to them in comparison to their male siblings and relatives, who rarely had such restrictions put on their movements.

The same may also have applied to familial support for purchasing equipment. Most of the female DJs I spoke to learned how to spin on someone else's equipment, not their own. This would have made learning the craft more difficult and was a barrier that male DJs were less likely to contend with. As chapter 3 details, family support for DJ crews was absolutely essential in helping the mobile scene form; the absence of financial support—let alone parental prohibitions—would have been a tremendously difficult resource hurdle for prospective Pinay DJs to surmount.

In addition, I have stressed the importance of the way DJ knowledge is transmitted peer-to-peer. One learns how to DJ, how to run a crew, largely by training with peers and mentors.[29] That form of knowledge transmission privileges "insider" relationships while creating a subtle barrier to "outsiders" trying to acquire those skills. This is especially true in a field such as DJing, which requires both technical knowledge (operating audio and lighting equipment) and cultural knowledge (records). As Straw describes it, "if the worlds of club disc jockeys . . . seem characterized by shared knowledge which excludes the would-be entrant, this functions not only to preserve the homosocial character of such worlds, but to block females from the social and economic advancement which they may offer" (Straw 1997: 10). In her work on gender politics in New York's hip-hop scene, Tricia Rose observed similar forces at work in how women often lacked access to the tools of musical production: "Women in general are not encouraged in and often actively discouraged from learning about and using mechanical equipment. This takes place informally in socialization and formally in gender-segregated vocational tracking in public school curriculum. Given rap music's early reliance on stereo equipment, participating in rap music production requires mechanical and technical skills that women are much less likely to have developed" (1994: 57). In addition, as the sharing of DJ knowledge is often dependent on role model–mentorship relationships, the relative absence of elder female DJs meant that aspiring female DJs would have had almost no mentors to work with. Notably, most of the female mobile DJs I ever spoke with or heard about were mentored by male DJs—sometimes, though not always, their boyfriends—rather than other women. Q-Bert, who previously discussed the importance of role models for producing his generation of (male) DJs, opined that the inverse could also explain the absence of more women behind the turntables: "I think females looked at [DJing] as a guy thing. I think there were just no role models for them. There were no females to just stand out and [say] 'Fuck this, I'm going to do this.'"

This said, in thinking about the mobile scene as a whole, there is an important difference between being "marginal" and being "absent." Cohen makes this distinction in her work, observing that within the Liverpool rock scene relationships between men in the scene are strongly influenced by their relationships with women. For some men, involvement in the scene might offer close and intense social interaction and male companionship free from the pressures of relating to women; for others music promises status, identity, success and the possibility of attracting women; for many, music represents an escape or retreat from women and a way out of domestic obligations, and many come from backgrounds where the division of labor between men and women is marked and single-sex leisure activity commonplace. Women are thus very much present in the scene despite their absence. (Cohen 1997: 21)

One key difference with the mobile scene is that, unlike in Cohen's field site, where women were "present yet absent," Filipinas were far more visible members—and key contributors—to the overall scene *beyond* the crews themselves: as clients, as promoters, as masters of ceremonies, and most basically—but vitally—as dancers and partygoers. It is a DJ truism—actually true or not—that you DJ to keep your female patrons happy; where they go, so goes the party. If we think of music scenes as Jennifer Lena describes them—"nested rings of groups characterized by varying levels of commitment to the community" (2012: 33)—then women were major players in most of the mobile scene's nested rings . . . albeit not at the core occupied by the DJs themselves. As discussed, that asymmetry was a product of patriarchy and other forces that maintained a predominantly male, homosocial DJ corps. If, in Cohen's study, women were "present yet absent," Pinays in the mobile scene might be described as "everywhere but the center."

Chapter 3 / Unlimited Creations /
The Mobile Scene Takes Off

3.1 / Flyer for a 1982 DJ battle, "Competition of DJs," held in San Francisco, hosted by the Jr. Optimist Club of Balboa High School. The Go-Go's won this battle. Courtesy of Daphnie Gambol Anies.

Mobile DJing may have offered "psychic income," but it also paid in "Denny's money." For many Daly City–South City DJs, the Denny's diner on Westborough became the designated after-gig spot: "Whether they were enemies or not, you would see them," said Spintronix's Dino Rivera. If there was profit left over by the end of the evening, the crew leader would treat everyone to a late-night meal.

"Denny's money" might not sound that glamorous, but for cliques of teenagers, even a little spending cash was a luxury. At the very least, it meant your crew was making money. New crews especially, eager to make a name, might underbid or simply offer to do a gig for free just to get their name out there. Even if they were getting paid, profits were either used to pay off debts—equipment rentals, parental loans—or invest in equipment upgrades and new record purchases. To be able to roll through Denny's and treat the crew to a meal meant, in a sense, you were "making it," and on the busiest party nights, the Denny's would be thick with different crews, new and veteran, an auspicious sign for the overall health of the mobile scene.

The early to mid-1980s saw an exponential growth in new crews. My database-in-progress lists at least twenty-five forming between 1982 and 1985 alone (almost certainly an underestimate).[1] However, as I mentioned in chapter 2, these crews did not spring forth, fully formed, purely out of youthful interest and energy. Forming a crew was an expensive ambition on the front end, and building a long-term career—which in the scene meant lasting for more than a year—required crews to become self-sufficient. That meant a constant infusion of economic capital, but as this chapter details, what ultimately mattered more was *social* capital: networks of friends, community groups, and especially family members who helped funnel paying gigs to different crews. In other words, the viability of the mobile scene needed more than just the crews themselves; it needed others to support them, and for a decade-plus, that support came mostly from members within the Bay Area's Filipino American community. The story of the mobile scene is as much theirs as the DJs'.

Doing Something for Themselves / The Symbolic Worth of DJ Work

Given that most people pursued DJing for social (rather than financial) reasons, there was a certain amount of incredulity that DJs experienced on their first paid gigs. Images Inc.'s Francisco Pardorla recalled:

> We just meant to help someone out, but at the end of the night, the parents came up and gave us $40. And I'm thinking, "$40!! Just for helping out? This is a good deal!" . . . We realized that there was money to be made doing this. Honestly, I thought $40 was good money to do something to just go to someone's house. You were gonna go anyways. You have a choice to either be a guest and stand up against the wall like everyone else or be in charge and get paid for it. We used to have a saying, "We come to eat your food and drink your beer, and you pay us."

The key awareness that Pardorla acquired was that his leisure activities could also serve as an employment opportunity. As he pointed out, he could go to a party, "be in charge," and be fed, and yet he was the person being paid at the end of the evening. That realization was made all the more powerful by the fact that, given his youth, he had few other options available to him, especially employment avenues that would afford him the same kind of agency and control. He continued: "When I was a senior in high school, what were guys doing? Flipping burgers? Minimum wage back then was $3.25. Even if you worked a twenty-hour work week, which was the most you could work when school's on, they didn't make a fraction of what we made." Compared to low-skill, low-wage employment, DJing could be a more attractive alternative. Being in a crew meant answering only to yourselves, setting your own work parameters, and most enticing: transforming what would otherwise have been play into a profession.[2] Historian Robin Kelley observes that in the wake of post-deindustrialization, American youth have pursued innovative ways to make a living by collapsing the distance between "work" and "play." In writing about these emergent forms of cultural work, Kelley argues: "These arenas have provided young people with a wider range of options for survival, space for creative expression, and at least a modicum of control over their own labor. In other words, neither an entrepreneurial spirit nor a work ethic is lacking in many of these inner city youths. Indeed, the terms *work* and *play* themselves presume a binarism that simply does not do justice to the meaning of labor, for they obscure the degree to which young people attempt to turn a realm of consumption (leisure time / play time) into a site of production" (Kelley 1997: 75).[3] Indeed, mobile DJing is very much a form of "play time" turned into a productive site: for income, for creative expression, for a sense of personal or social empowerment.

That said, though, the actual income was modest for most crews. Money made from gigs was, first and foremost, used to cover immediate costs—venue rentals, equipment rentals, gas, and so on—and leftover profit was best invested into the crew's long-term needs, especially upgrades to their audio and lighting systems or new records. What remained was what made it into people's pockets—either that or Denny's money—but in many cases, it was so little as to put the "trickle" in "trickle down."

Each crew worked out different formulas for their monetary distribution; this is how Orlando Madrid, who was a member of both Sound of Success and Non-Stop Boogie, broke down the balance sheet for a typical gig:

> It was more about making money for your pocket. Doing parties for $100, $150, $200 if you're lucky.[4] We'd buy new records, a new needle if you needed it. Stuff like that, the essentials. It was hard to make money off it. It's a trip, people don't realize that. You'll charge them $400 and they'll say, "What about $300?" They say, "You're only playing for two hours." But the event is five hours. It takes an hour to get there, an hour to set up, then you got to stay the whole duration of the event. You're there the whole time and they don't see that.

Despite the outside perception that DJs are paid a high rate for relatively little time, Madrid pointed out that much of the work they had to accomplish was beyond just manning the turntables. Especially given the amount of equipment that needed to be assembled—either rented or bought—and then factoring the size of the crew into the profit equation, I knew of no DJs who made anything approaching a full-time living off of mobile work alone.[5] Toward the late part of the mobile era, DJs who branched into clubs and radio could substantially increase their earnings, but that tended to benefit individuals, not crews.

Nonetheless, the money earned was less important than the symbolic worth of DJ work. Engaging in an activity seen as "professional" had its own particular rewards, bringing with it an aura of economic self-reliance that shaped the perception of it as a constructive activity. That kind of symbolic capital was particularly important for the families of DJs. They were more likely to see DJ work as promoting "positive" values, especially in contrast to popular parental fears often attached to other youth activities, that is, crime, gang membership, violence, and drugs. Sound Explosion's Rafael Restauro mentioned: "I'd be the one to go out to talk to the principals and faculty advisors or go out to the different employee credit unions. I'd be a young kid, talking to adults who'd been around and it's business. We're talking business here. They'd look at us like 'These guys are doing something for themselves. They're not doing drugs, that kind of stuff, they're making money.'" His comments reflected the perception that mobile crews taught youth how to become more responsible, professional, and mature. Unlike negative associations linking youth with crime or deviance, DJing was a teenage activity that community elders legitimized and endorsed (at least for men). The dichotomy between "good youth" and "bad youth" is especially meaningful in the mobile scene, since the DJ crews were sometimes seen as alternative organizations to the youth gangs of that era. Whereas elders may have seen gangs as indolent, violent, and troublemaking, crews carried a reputation as hardworking and keepers of the peace. Just 2 Hype's Derrick Damian put it plainly: "First and foremost, my dad was happy I didn't get into drugs, thugs, or colors and all that stuff. DJing was just an outlet for us, a recreational thing that got us off the streets." Others echoed this same framing, including the store manager of Pacifica's Manor Music, Sarah Glew: "I used to tell their mothers when they came in . . . they were afraid that [DJing] was going to lead to crime and bad habits and drinking and smoking—you have to understand these kids were quite young. The grandmother and mother would come in with their credit cards and would be expected to pony up several thousand dollars for equipment and I would have to reassure them that it would build good work ethic, and good habits because I had seen this based on other Filipino kids I had known." Again, the symbolic capital of DJ work embodying "good ethics and habits" helped to solidify support by older Filipino American family members for the endeavors of the younger generation.

This intergenerational dynamic raises several ideas worth pondering (though I draw no firm conclusions). First, given that many third-wave, post-1965 Filipino immigrants were well-educated and socially mobile, it is worth considering how the symbolic capital of DJ work would have particular resonance in a community in which the narrative of immigrant social mobility is presumably present. Rafael Restauro stated, "Our parents taught us to be little entrepreneurs because, unfortunately, we didn't have silver spoons when we were born so we had to go out and get it." Many Filipino American youth would likely have witnessed relatives or community members pursuing new lines of work (not the least of reasons for which being that immigration had displaced them from their former occupations) as a way to create opportunities where none might have existed before—a skill DJs would end up replicating within a nascent mobile scene. Similarly, they may also have been better prepared to accept and deal with uncertainty, a useful trait in trying to navigate through obstacles such as logistical challenges or bureaucratic tangles. And most of all, many of them would have grown up in an environment colored by a particular immigrant ambition for social mobility, reflected in the suburban migration patterns I discussed in chapter 1. At the very least, pursuing mobile DJing required a minimum amount of ambition, as well as the fortitude to explore what amounted to a cultural terra incognito, especially in the scene's early years. Growing up in immigrant families may very well have prepared these youth to take on these kinds of challenges and uncertainties.[6]

These questions around immigrant cultural influence are mostly conjectural on my part and certainly could be one area of future research. What was more concrete were the ways in which aspiring mobile DJs benefited from the *material* resources that middle-class families could literally afford. Sound system equipment is expensive, as historian Norman Stolzoff observed in regard to Jamaican mobile DJ culture: "Even though the sound systems were a cheap source of musical entertainment, they were not easily obtained by the average working person. As a result, most of the early sound system owners were men who straddled the lower-class / middle-class social divide. For the most part, these men were members of the petite bourgeoisie: government clerks, merchants and owners of small downtown shops" (2000: 43). The early proto-reggae DJs of Stolzoff's research share similarities with the Filipino American mobile crews, especially in their reliance on family resources to help get started. For example, when Orlando Madrid first began DJing, he was using inexpensive but poorly made speakers. Needing money to upgrade his equipment, he turned to his parents: "When I was getting deeper into DJing, I asked my dad, 'Pops, I'm tired of blowing out the house speakers, can we get some real speakers?' So we go down to the Guitar Center and buy a pair of Yamahas . . . and an amplifier. Happiest guy on earth that day. I owe my parents a lot for that because I could have been doing a lot of other crazy crap but I guess they saw that keeping me into this hobby that I was in would keep me out of trouble." Gary Millare from Ultimate Creations had a similar experience: "My mom said, 'You guys are doing a lot of parties. I'll loan you a thousand bucks, just buy some decent equipment.' It was kind of a controversy because everybody would think, 'Oh, they buy him everything.' We paid her back in two months, each time, OK? We asked a few times, 'We need to put it on [your credit] card and we'll pay you back.'" For many, parental support came in the form of a loan to be repaid via future gig money. However, other DJs were gifted money or equipment outright, and as Millare's comments suggest, these differences—loans versus gifts—fueled subtle but significant class tensions within the scene.

Spintronix's Dino Rivera noted, "If your parents were either rich or the kid was spoiled, they would ask their parents [to buy all their equipment]. A lot of guys I knew weren't well off, so they would have to save and buy little by little." In other interviews, DJs would scoff at "certain crews"—notably, never named but often alluded to—who reportedly were given money rather than having it loaned.[7] I sensed that this difference between who received loans versus gifts helped establish a certain kind of authenticity within the scene. Financial struggle and hardship were markers that a crew had "paid its dues."[8] To receive money or equipment as a gift was to bypass that dues-paying process.

The fact that the vast majority of mobile DJs came from middle-class backgrounds suggests that the dividing line here was less about quantifiable differences in family net worth and had more to do with the *process* through which family support arrived. Receiving a loan and paying it back fell in line with a "bootstraps" theory of hard work and self-reliance—again, not an unusual value system in an immigrant community—whereas bypassing that process via a gift made a crew appear to be more dilettante-like and therefore less "authentic."

However, while DJs may have frowned upon family members gifting money to a new crew, accepting help from relatives to land gigs was an entirely different story. Here, too, the aura of constructive work surrounding DJing encouraged parents and other family members to help fledging crews get off the ground. When I asked Ray Viray from Daly City's Midstar Productions if his parents were supportive of his activities, he replied, "At first, no. They would say, 'What are you doing?' But when they saw us as a group and how we presented ourselves, they were pretty impressed. They started telling their friends, 'Hey, my son is a DJ.' They were a big help." What Viray highlights is how larger Filipino American family and community networks formed a soft "infrastructure" of social capital that helped support the mobile scene's long-term growth and success.

Word of Mouth / The Social Capital of Filipino American Family and Community Networks

One of the most successful mobile DJs I know is New York's Moe "Choimatic" Choi. A thirtysomething Korean American who began his DJ career in the 1990s, Choi went from spinning hip-hop in basement clubs to earning five-figure commissions working with clients that include the financial company Bloomberg and such fashion houses as Kate Spade and Yves Saint Laurent. As for many mobile DJs, though, weddings are his bread and butter, and he averages over twenty a year, needing a management team to help him sort through the dozens of well-heeled couples bidding for his services on the most desired wedding dates of the year (usually in June or July).

Surprisingly, Choi barely markets himself. Overwhelmingly, his clients find him through word-of-mouth referrals: guests who attended weddings he DJed or friends and family members of past clients. Because many of these couples come from what we might conventionally describe as "high society" or the "moneyed class," his reputation with past clients is essential to him gaining entrée into this particular social world.[9] In other words, Choi possesses both symbolic capital (he has a stellar reputation) and social capital (he is known by the "right" people). This pays off (literally) in unexpected ways: in the summer of 2013, he landed a lucrative gig to DJ a Bloomberg-sponsored party on the roof of New

3.2 / Flyer for a 1983 graduation party in Newark, California, featuring Images Inc. (Fremont). Courtesy of Francisco Pardorla.

York's Metropolitan Museum; it helped that one of his former wedding clients was the granddaughter of the late sculptor Louise Bourgeois. That Met gig, in turn, led to the Guggenheim Museum, the Museum of Modern Art, and the Whitney Museum all inviting him to DJ similar events. There is no "museum DJ circuit," no "go-to" list of DJs that these cultural institutions keep on hand. Choi's pathway into these museum gigs may have been serendipitous, but it was not random. Like many mobile DJs before him, he has benefited from the power of social capital.

In the mobile scene, these "who you know" networks were absolutely essential to their long-term prospects. If symbolic capital was the beacon and economic capital was the electricity that powered it, social capital was the transmission lines that delivered the power. For most mobile crews, social capital began with their families.

Spintronix's Jay dela Cruz recalled: "Cotillions, the family parties, that's where you usually start off. I know when I first started DJing, I played for my mom. As soon as you started that, everything started falling into place." DJing for his family was a way to get the crew's proverbial "foot in the door." Even though these gigs were normally small and not

Unlimited Creations / 87

necessarily well-paying, they were a way for Spintronix to build a reputation, which in turn allowed the crew to pursue higher paying gigs, which in turn burnished their reputation. And so the cycle came back around.

Garage parties once again proved to be important, as they were some of the easiest gigs for a new crew to land. Regardless of whether they paid well or not, they provided that crucial foundation for crews to get their start. Electric Sounds' Rene Anies described it this way: "Our mainstay in the beginning was garage parties. Being from a Filipino background, as far as our group, we always had weekly garage parties in the City [San Francisco]. So we started hitting 'em up, [offering] 'Hey, we'll do it for free, we'll do it for twenty-five bucks here, fifty bucks here, just to get in and show it.' And our focus was how much could we make the garage live, like in a club, we got lights, we even put fog machines in the garages." Immediate family members were one source of these kinds of basic gigs, but just as relevant were *extended* family networks. Madrid recalled: "[One friend] had an older sister so she set up parties for us to do. I had an older cousin, she used to hook me up with her friends for their garage parties." Likewise, dela Cruz explained, "Someone always knew somebody who wanted to throw a party. We were all connected. . . . That's how everyone first starts, whether it's a cousin's birthday party or someone's company party . . . in the living room of your aunt's house." Carrion added, "Basically, anytime anybody mentioned that they needed a DJ, [our relatives] would always recommend us. We never did any advertising, basically all of our business was from word of mouth." What all three men describe is how their crews benefited from social networks created by close relations between extended family members. This did not only apply to so-called blood relations; some of my respondents would joke that everyone in the scene was their "cousin," even though, technically, there was no direct (or at least, close) bloodline between them.

This is also one area where the role of women—as clients—was quite significant in the scene; for many house and garage parties, the hosts/sponsors were often women; Rivera estimated that "most, if not 90 percent, of the parties were always thrown by girls for events like birthday parties, sorority sisterhood parties, et cetera." Even if that 90 percent figure is an overestimate, it once again highlights the presence and importance of women within the "nested rings" of the scene, even if they were a tiny minority within the crews themselves.

Beyond these family and friend networks, DJ crews could also rely on broader community support, especially in the form of Filipino youth and student groups at high schools, colleges, churches, and community centers who helped sponsor larger "hall parties." Many of the high schools with large Filipino student enrollment had Filipino or Asian student clubs that would sponsor dances and invite DJs to perform—Balboa High's Octogon [sic] Club, for example. Local church youth groups were also vital. John Castro, coscreenwriter of the Filipino American feature film *The Debut* (2000), recalled that even as far back as the 1970s, "every Filipino neighborhood had a church and the church would have a Filipino organization and they would throw parties. Like, my family church was St. Victor's, which is in the heart of the Berryessa District [San Jose] where all the Filipinos are. They would throw a dance and they would have a band and at the same time, maybe get the younger kids to DJ it also."[10] In the 1980s, especially in Daly City, the Young Adult Group at St. Augustine's Church became a major sponsor of DJ events. Unlimited Sounds' "DJ Apollo" Novicio remembered that "every weekend, they would host a different mobile DJ group right here in Daly City. That was a big platform. Churches were starting to throw fundraisers so they would throw dances. Holy Angels, St. Andrew's, we used to do them too."

Castro noted other Filipino social organizations that sponsored dances, such as provincial groups: "You'd have your organizations, the ones outside of church, like the ones that are broken down by provinces. Filipinos are very proud of what province they came from, especially the ones that immigrate here, and so they would develop their associations for their province, and throw parties and dances." This community and family client base created an ideal situation for the growing DJ scene. As knowledge of the crews expanded, more and more party hosts wanted to hire DJs as their entertainment. Dela Cruz opined that "with Filipino Americans, they like to party, they like to dance. The fiestas, the debuts. There's always a need, as long as there's debuts, there's always a need for DJs."[11]

Whether parties took place in a garage, school gym, or social or church hall, the important dynamic was that they existed *in abundance*, tied to a preponderance of Filipino family and community events and celebrations. During the 2002 San Mateo County History Museum panel discussion, Sound Sequence's Burt Kong quipped: "I'm Chinese American but I grew up in Daly City so I'm pretty much honorary Filipino. Just from the culture itself, since I'm an outsider, maybe I can see it differently. They have a lot more parties than Chinese folks, I can tell you that. They have debuts, they have christenings, you name it." In a separate interview I did with Melanie Caganot, erstwhile rapper and mobile scene veteran (as well as Kong's spouse), she echoed similar points about the relevance and abundance of family parties to the economic lifeblood of the mobile scene: "A lot of DJs stayed alive because they probably had a lot of gigs within their family. There's weddings, there's christenings. We actually had a DJ group in the family. You have to understand—Filipinos are all about [parties] for any reason. A lot of DJs—that's how they started off, DJing for their family. Eventually, there were just so many gigs, people had garage parties all the time." Likewise, journalist Jinni Bartolome, whose son Richard was a member of Unique Musique, commented in an email: "Pilipino parents were supportive of so many DJs because they would come out for a plethora of events such as installation of officers, beauty pageants, queen contests, and birthdays, baptisms, weddings, etc." As San Francisco's Patrick dela Cruz, of Beyond the Limit, put it, "being in the Filipino community, there's parties all the time. There's a party for when you're born. There's a party for when you're being christened. There's a party for when you turn eighteen. There's parties for everything." Perhaps most important, as the Go-Go's Daphnie Anies suggested, "there was never a party where there was no music. I could not see us just sitting there talking. We never really sat a football game together. That's to me, the traditional thing in most communities, especially suburbs, was going to football games. That was not what the Filipinos were into."

I once joked to a respondent that the gist of these comments could be summed up as the "Filipinos party more" thesis. Social capital in the mobile scene was made up of two interrelated components: a high frequency of events and parties that needed and desired DJs as entertainment *and* a close relationship between Filipino families and other community members that directed those gigs toward the crews.

In other words, whether Filipino Americans quantifiably "party more" or not is less relevant than the ability of this family and community network to pool and distribute economic capital (in the form of paying gigs) to all the various crews. As I mentioned in the introduction, mobile crews existed in other ethnic communities in the Bay Area, but I suggest that the Filipino family- and community-based support system was a clear advantage to the long-term growth and sustenance of the Filipino scene specifically.[12]

I describe these networks as forming a kind of "soft infrastructure," meaning that they functioned as a critical support system around the crews. The same concept exists throughout research on other cultural scenes, though under different names and descriptions. Howard Becker famously described them as "art worlds," that is, "a network of cooperating people, all of whose work is essential to the final outcome" (1982: 25). Ken Spring describes it as "an underlying complex of social networks" (2004: 49). As noted in chapter 2, I am quite partial to Jennifer Lena's metaphor of "nested rings of groups characterized by varying levels of commitment to the community" (2012: 33).

What these ideas all share is the understanding that cultural activity does not burst fully formed from the heads of individual auteurs. The myth of the genius musician, painter, sculptor, and so on is seductive in pop culture, but even the most gifted violinist still requires someone who can turn animal intestines into catgut for the bow. In Spring's (2004) study of the rise and fall of a techno scene in a small Michigan town, it was not just DJs and promoters who were vital to the scene; so were security staff, local city officials, even fire marshals.[13] In the mobile DJ scene, the nested rings would have started with the crews at center, followed by their families, then school and church youth groups, then community organizations and school officials, then independent promoters, then general audience members, and on the outermost rings would be record stores, equipment sales and rental stores, manufacturers, and so on.

As should be clear, the partners who make up any particular cultural infrastructure change depending on context; there is no "one size fits all" logic.[14] What matters is the understanding that artistic/cultural endeavors happen through these kinds of collaborative processes, where supporting players may not be obvious but their role is still essential. Moreover, social networks are not passive representations or reflections of a community; the very notion of a "community" exists only insofar as these social ties are constantly activated to maintain and build relationships that, in turn, produce a collective identity.

Sociologist Robert Putnam describes this phenomenon as an example of "bonding social capital," that is, a kind of "sociological superglue," useful for "undergirding specific reciprocity and mobilizing solidarity" (2001: 22). In particular, Putnam specifically highlights "dense networks in ethnic enclaves" as a key source of "social and psychological support" as well as a useful way to generate and distribute "start-up financing" for members of that community (22). As I have suggested, strong interpersonal ties and relationships within the larger Filipino American community made it easier for people to lend support to the DJ crews by providing or funneling financial resources to them. In doing so, not only did the

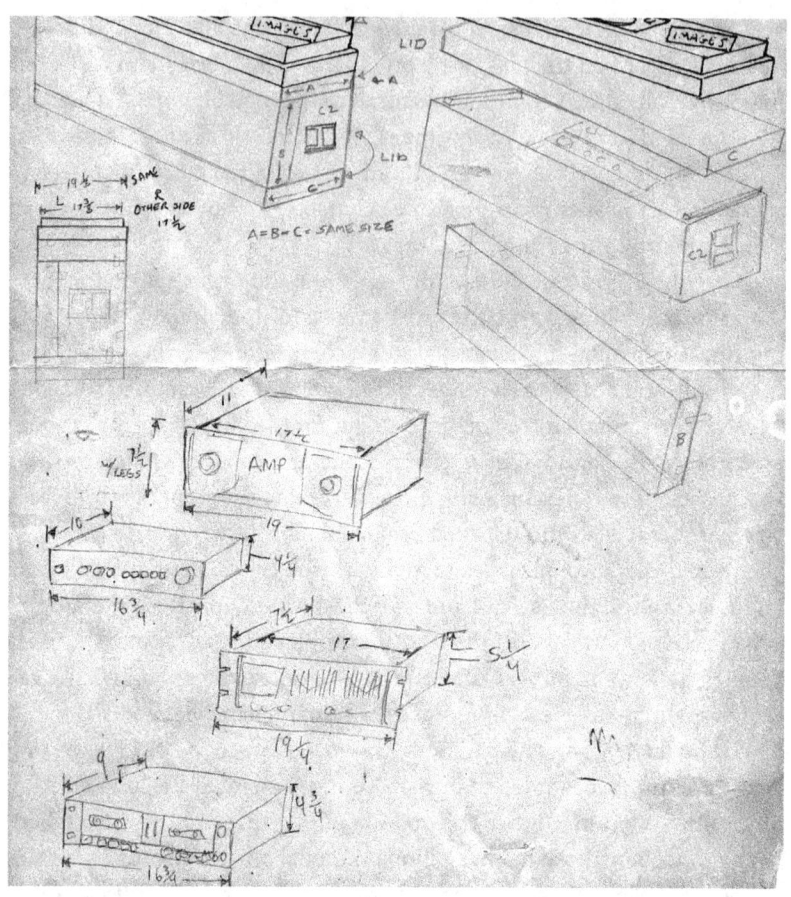

3.3 / Schematic for a turntable "coffin" (i.e., case) from Images Inc. (Fremont). Courtesy of Francisco Pardorla.

activation of these networks act as a form of bonding social capital but also, I suggest, their existence and use helped make a "Filipino American mobile scene" an identifiable, legible entity itself.

In his research on the value of social capital within London and Manchester's respective punk scenes, Nick Crossley argues: "Whatever artistic influences and social strains are expressed in punk, *it only took off as a recognizable cultural movement in virtue of the pattern of connections and interactions* linking its key actors. . . . UK punk was the product of interactions within a concrete social network. *To understand the movement we need to understand the network*" (2008: 90; emphasis mine). I see the Filipino American mobile scene as having operated similarly; its emergence as an identifiable "scene" was highly dependent on that "pattern of connections and interactions" between mobile crews themselves, families, and community organizations.[15] Mobile crews certainly can exist independent of that support system; that is a daily reality for thousands of mobile DJs already. However, the existence of mobile crews themselves was not what made the Filipino mobile scene "a scene." For that scene to coalesce, it needed a broader art world, those nested rings. In that sense, I suggest that part of how we can understand DJing as a "Filipino practice" has less to do with cultural and ethnic traditions and far more to do with mobile DJing being so deeply embedded in the Filipino family, friend, church, and community networks whose support made the scene's existence possible. To put it a different way, the defining "Filipino quality" of the mobile scene was not simply that Filipino Americans made up the crews; it was that the entire social world within which the crews formed the scene was also so integrally tied in to other nodes of the greater Filipino American community.

All this said, I also suggest that this relationship ran in both directions: as much as the crews depended on the Filipino community to give their scene life, the mobile scene in turn also helped to define what it meant to be a member of that community. In other words, it was participation in the mobile scene—as DJs and audience members alike—that provided young people of this era with a common set of experiences that bonded them in their identity as Filipinos. Crews were able to do so with a particular form of social power they wielded, to literally bring people together from across the Bay Area via their events and parties. Nowhere was that form of bonding social capital more evident than during the showcase era.

Chapter 4 / Imaginings / Building Community in the Showcase Era

4.1 / Flyer for a 1987 showcase, "Don't Stop the Madness," aka "DJ Expo 87," aka "Imagine 7," held in San Mateo, hosted by Imagine. This was the largest recorded event in the history of the Filipino American mobile scene. Courtesy of Ricky Viray.

One of the largest events in the history of the Bay Area mobile scene was Imagine 7 (formerly dubbed "Don't Stop the Madness"), held April 25, 1987, at the San Mateo Fairgrounds (figure 4.1). Since debuting in 1984, the Imagine party series had become one of the region's most popular. Founder-promoter Mark Bradford spent heavily on posters and flyers to advertise his events, so much so that even the first Imagine show in 1984—held in the swank Green Room at the San Francisco War Memorial building—sold out to capacity.

Imagine 7 was on a new scale, however. Imagine 6, held the previous November, had only one headlining act—DJ Genie G and his crew, Ultimate Creations—with six other crews billed. Imagine 7 had *twenty-four* crews listed with equal billing and a couple dozen more listed in the acknowledgments. In order to manage that massive congregation, the Imagine staff produced a highly detailed schedule, part of which I excerpt here to illustrate the level of precise organization that went into events of this scope:

    8:00 AM   HALL OPENS
    3:00 PM   SET-UPS COMPLETE
    . . .   SOUND TESTS

6:35 PM	BOX OFFICE OPENS
7:00 PM	Audio Visions / Style Beyond Compare / Divine Style
7:55 PM	Beyond the Limit / ATOC / Genie G / Royal Sounds …
11:35 PM	Starlight / Sound Invasion / Mystical Legacy / New Dimensions
12:45 AM	IMAGINE! Medley
1:00 AM	HALL CLEARED
	HALL CLEANED
	PARKING LOT CLEARED
2:00 AM	HALL IS CLOSED

The overall size of the event was not the only thing that made Imagine 7 different from its predecessors. As Images Inc.'s Francisco Pardorla recalled, "it was the first [Imagine] outside of San Francisco," and in choosing the San Mateo Fairgrounds Bradford showed both practical and strategic acumen. For one, the size of the fairgrounds was an attractively affordable option to accommodate the number of crews and their expected audiences. However, San Mateo also made sense geographically. Short of building a new island in the middle of the Bay, the city was as central a location one could ask for, roughly equidistant from San Francisco and San Jose while still accessible via bridge from the East Bay cities. One quick glance at the Imagine 7 flyer would show how Bradford made good use of the location—the twenty-four crews he invited reflected the greater diversity of local scenes beyond just the San Francisco–Daly City nucleus. "He tried to hit everyone from each county and each city," said Gary "Genie G" Millare, and that included Oakland's Ladda Sounds, Daly City's Midstar, South San Francisco's Sound Sequence, San Jose's Unlimited Play, San Francisco's Beyond the Limit, Fremont's Images Inc., and others. In inviting such a broad spread of crews, Imagine's planners were shrewdly counting on each region's crews helping get the word out to encourage local fans to come to the event.

Given the size and scope of the event, Bradford booked one of the largest halls at the fairgrounds. Millare described it as "a big space, almost like an airplane hangar." It was so spacious that Pardorla was struck by the fact that "we could drive our trucks in," a necessary feature given the amount of heavy equipment that had to be assembled within the space. However, staging was going to be an issue; the hall was massive, but it still was not going to be big enough to allow two dozen separate crews to build their own stages. Instead, Bradford grouped the crews into six "teams" and divvied up the hangar space between them. It is not clear whether crews were even consulted as to what teams they would be grouped with. Pardorla does not recall ever being asked, and his Images Inc. ended up in a motley bunch that also included the small Hayward crew Universal Beats, San Jose's Unlimited Play, and High Energy from farther-flung Fairfield. Pardorla had not even met members of High Energy until the day of the event. Though each grouping was expected to share the same setup, in Pardorla's case there was little advanced planning: "We all just brought everything and figured it out from there."

For this kind of mega-event, crews spared no favors or expense in constructing the best sound systems they could assemble. Patrick dela Cruz was one of the main DJs for San Francisco's Beyond the Limit, a crew mentored by Ultimate Creations. Beyond the Limit were not as well established, so Bradford had slotted them to perform earlier in the evening, but that did not deter the crew's ambitions. "I had a set of what I wanted to do. I wanted to open up with some sound effects and special effects, stuff like that," said dela Cruz. "We all had matching Adidas jumpsuits. And we would run in and do our thing. I really wanted a big, booming sound system. And, you know, us, by ourselves, we didn't have that." Instead, Beyond the Limit turned to an ally, Alden Chen, of the Chinese American crew Altered Images, and were able to borrow a massive, low-end set of speakers from him: "crazy PAS1818 bass cabs [cabinets]," dela Cruz recalled.

Beyond the Limit's collaborations extended beyond just speakers. The crew were to share a stage with their mentors, Ultimate Creations, and the latter's road van carried all the equipment for both crews. When they arrived at the hangar at around 2 p.m., Cruz recalled,

> we grabbed as many banquet tables as we could. Six-foot, eight-foot banquet tables, and we stacked them. The secret was to clamp them down with C-clamps. That was [Jose] Olimpiada's thing. You had just this milk crate full of C-clamps to keep all these banquet tables together and it also [formed] a sort of barrier between the audience and us. [Using] this black tarp that we use for gigs, we made a fortress with banquet tables and a stage. We put [Chen's bass cabinets] right in front, just to blast everybody who would be standing in front of the fortress. That was our idea.

At the bottom of the schedule were clear instructions on how the segues between each performance should go: "**NO TIME LAG BETWEEN STAGES: EACH GROUP READY TO PERFORM IMMEDIATELY UPON COM-

PLETION OF PREVIOUS GROUP." Only slightly less aggressive print beneath read: "Switching among DJ's on any given stage to be accomplished smoothly and without any interruption in the music whatsoever." Millare explained the impact of that: "One DJ ends, boom, another one [begins]. People would rush, literally run, to the other stage setup. That was actually pretty interesting for the time. You didn't really see stuff like that."

Beyond the Limit, especially as a younger crew, wanted to make as big an entrance as possible. They had decided that Cruz's intro music would be from the movie *Rambo*, and someone in the crew had found machine gun water guns, and that gave them this idea: "I would start the music, and the other guys in the crew would run in there in their Adidas jumpsuits, right?" said Cruz. "Everyone would just laugh and see us running through with these big guns and then they would shoot everybody with water. We would just be out there and just throw stuff. We didn't care." Some in the audience cared, though, as Cruz remembered: "The water pistol thing got a lot of girls mad at us. Hairspray and water do not mix."

As much as any other event during the history of the mobile scene, Imagine 7 captured the essence of what a "showcase" was: a spectacular, multicrew event that, in drawing crews from across different cities, also drew together fans from those same neighborhoods, literally bringing together hundreds, if not thousands, of people. Within the Filipino American scene in particular, the Imagine showcases, alongside those by other production outfits like AA Productions and Expressions, became a key means through which like-minded youth would traverse the geographic distances between them and form social bonds that might not otherwise have easily formed. In that respect, the spectacles that came with showcases weren't the only thing that attendees "didn't really see" elsewhere; there were also entire groups of youth from far-flung parts of the Bay Area. The showcases created a social scene, to be sure, but they also helped plant the seeds for a community to grow.

Look at All These Rumors / Competition and Cooperation

A showcase could be defined as any gig where at least two or more crews participated. From a business point of view, the logic behind a showcase was simple: by inviting different crews to participate, you were also inviting their fan bases, boosting attendance. Beyond fattening door receipts, however, showcases also allowed participating crews to distinguish themselves next to their peers, whether on the basis of their sound system, presentation, or mixing skills, and so on. In that sense, all showcases were inherently competitions, and not surprisingly, the earliest forms that showcases took on were as "battles," that is, intercrew competitions in which one crew would be announced a winner.

Battles began to appear by the early 1980s, especially once enough crews had formed in the same schools or neighborhoods. In San Francisco, for example, Ultimate Creations appeared to have been involved in at least two different 1982 battles, one hosted by Balboa High's Octogon [sic] Club, the other hosted at St. Joseph's Church (with the Go-Go's competing). However, though school and church youth groups were key sponsors of these events, the biggest development came with the emergence of party promoters.

The term "promoter" stems from their function in helping to market and publicize (i.e., promote) an event, but generally speaking, a promoter is also the event planner and producer. In the mobile scene, party promoters existed independent of the DJ crews, even though many had close ties to certain crews. Up through the mid- to late 1980s, the biggest name in showcases was Imagine, and the biggest promoter was its creator: Imagine's Mark Bradford.

It would be hard to invent a more colorful—or controversial—character in the story of the mobile scene. Though he died in 1992—victim of a still-unsolved murder—he was well remembered by my respondents for both positive and negative reasons. Bradford was, in many ways, an outsider compared to most other scene participants: he was white, a generation older (thirtysomething), and independently well-to-do as a real estate agent. He was also gay, an important detail given how people recall their interactions with him.

Bradford threw the first Imagine party in the spring of 1984 with a DJ/dance battle titled "Let the Music Play." He booked it in the swank Green Room at the San Francisco War Memorial building, and though this was his first showcase in the Filipino mobile scene—it is unclear whether he had promotions experience previously or elsewhere—he was a shrewd and aggressive marketer, blanketing the city with flyers for the event.

Three Daly City crews from the same Serramonte subdivision participated in the DJ battle: Unique Musique, Eternal Sound Productions, and Futuristic Sounds. Unique Musique's Henry "G" Geronimo recalled: "The scene was crazy . . . one could barely walk through the hallways and dance floor. It was packed! I recall Mark being really worried about the vandalism that may occur to the building, since it was such a fancy place for a bunch of kids." As with many battles, debate raged as to who actually won—Futuristic Sounds was initially given the award at the event, but in later months Bradford stated that Unique Musique had won, sowing confusion.

This kind of controversy was frequent, reflecting how battles and showcases served a crucial purpose as arbitrators of status in a DJ community filled with scores of competing crews. Crushtown Chill Crew's Dell Farinas explained: "You had four to five groups there. And it was pretty much who could provide the best 'wow!' The opening part, the intro, who could make you [say] 'wow!' with the best light show, music. It was a combination of stuff. As opposed to just a big party . . . when [a showcase] had four to five groups in one big room, you had the crowd moving from DJ to DJ to DJ. So it was interesting. You could watch which people rocked out to which DJ the best." If family and community groups doled out economic capital, showcases became a primary arbitrator of symbolic capital. For more veteran crews, a showcase or battle could burnish their reputation, but they were equally beneficial for new crews seeking to make their names. Unlimited Sounds' Anthony Carrion explained: "I think it was real important to get the newer DJs out there. That was, if you wanted to get known quick, you would do these showcases and people would know you right away. Rather than just doing gigs here and there, it would take a long time before you established how good you were and what you had. If you did the showcases, you got known very fast." The gains of participating in a showcase or battle could cut the other way as well. Carrion continued, "Battles were more stressful because you did not want to lose, you did not want to be the worst out of four or five DJs. You had to be the best. Especially for us, we wanted to be there at the top. We didn't want to be last."

The Imagine parties, in particular, grew to have tremendous influence within the scene. As Melanie Caganot put it, "Imagine was the first, at a professional level. The showcases were just grand. [Bradford] produced ten thousand flyers per gig, which is not cheap. This guy was totally saturating everything. He was the first to put them in big halls, to have several DJs under one roof. He had trophies, he had the whole program. There's just this big ceremony about the whole thing." Imagine's clout grew to such an extent that crews found their reputations improved simply by getting their names on an Imagine event flyer. Unique Musique's Ray Viray explained: "[Bradford's] flyers alone are good enough. If your name is there, to some people you are untouchable. You want to make his list."

Imaginings / 101

Caganot added, "Imagine was important in the sense that everybody knew [about it]—if you did an Imagine gig, you would have tremendous exposure. And if you won an Imagine [battle], forget it, you'd have gigs left and right."

Showcases fed off a competitive dynamic already endemic among the crews, who regularly vied with one another for gigs. As Carrion mentioned, the high-profile events pushed crews to represent themselves in the best light possible, since DJs were putting their symbolic capital—and by extension, potential livelihoods—on the line. How crews responded to that pressure, both destructively and productively, reveals the ways these DJs negotiated community *within* their own ranks.

On the most extreme end, there were isolated instances of violence between crews. Daly City's Paul Canson of Second To None recalled that at a party in Daly City a South Bay crew allegedly attacked a DJ from Daly City's Styles Beyond Compare with a baseball bat. "Who knows what the beef was over?" Canson asked, but he added that "people hated each other. When it came down to it, it was all good clean fun, but shit gets personal." Competition could also lead to sabotage. Fusion's Ken Anolin remembered that at one gig, "I was in the middle of spinning, one of the group members came up . . . and showed me the sliced end of an extension cord, which shocked and pissed off all of us. Luckily it wasn't a cord that affected our sound system, which would have been disastrous!"

These cases were severe yet arguably less damaging than the more common form of attacking a rival crew: by undercutting their reputation. As I mentioned earlier, the Go-Go's said that a rival crew (Young 'N' Tough) had accused them of substituting a prerecorded tape mix for a live performance. Such a charge was taken seriously; not only was it a suggestion that a crew was cheating but furthermore it implicitly suggested that the cheating crew lacked the skills or confidence to pull off their mix in a "live" setting. Even without proof, the accusation of "using a tape" could be enough to sway people's perception and opinions. Spintronix's Jay dela Cruz recalled, "My very first Spintronix gig I attended was a battle, and I think it was our very first party collectively. It was us against Fresh Beats Incorporated, who were African American, and Dreamscape, who were Chinese. This was in April, May of 1985, after school. We lost because Chris [Miguel] and Dino [Rivera] were on four turntables and they accused us of playing a tape. We had trussing, we had lights—nobody else had that—but we lost." Ironically, because many crews did tape their sets and distribute them to others in the scene, it created opportunities for other crews to, in essence, "plagiarize" mixes.

Rewind a moment: a mix is composed of song selection, song sequencing, and the segues between them. In the mobile scene, a "good mix" would be one where every one of those attributes is executed not just flawlessly but ingeniously, where the DJ is credited with "discovering" the particularly memorable combination of those qualities. Therefore, mixes could be recognized and *attributed*, similar to the way songwriters and composers can be known for a particular melody or riff. In other words, they could become known as "signature" mixes.

This would have obvious relevance in a scene where cultural and symbolic capital were held in such high regard, and especially given the intense competition between DJs. To have your authorship of a mix recognized was a high compliment, reflecting not just on your skill but also your *taste*, that elusive marker of cultural capital that DJs may hope to cultivate but that can only be conferred onto them by colleagues and audiences.[1]

As signature mixes emerged, this also meant that situations could arise where DJs and crews could accuse others of "stealing" a mix. For example, John Francisco remembers a situation at one battle where a DJ mixed a sequence of records identical to a mix Spintronix had once recorded on a set tape:

> I remember judging a battle in Union City and this one kid swore up and down that his set was his very own. I think he took the first part of every Spintronix tape that I had ever heard and made it into his set. And so he was sitting there having an argument with the promoter saying, "Why did I lose?" [The response was] "Well one of the judges [Francisco] feels that you're a biter."[2] And he's all "No I'm not, that's not the case. This is all me, my original set." I said, "We can go back to my house and I can pull out all my Spintronix tapes and show you where you got it from." I guess he figured that since they were in the South Bay [whereas Spintronix was from Daly City], we wouldn't know.

In essence, the mobile scene had its own form of creative copyright, and the members of that scene were responsible for communally enforcing it.

The popularity of the Imagine parties created a unique set of tensions, especially given Bradford's status as an informal "kingmaker" who could boost a crew's profile simply by putting their name on an Imagine flyer.

However, complicating this was the fact that he was also older, white, gay, and, most controversially, someone who displayed and communicated sexualized interest in younger Filipino boys. For my respondents, his sexuality was not the primary issue; it was that he would use his influence in the scene to pressure or solicit the teenagers in the crews—most of them underage—for sexual favors.

Arleen Alviar, a promoter whom Bradford mentored, worked closely with him, and she alleged that he was "basically molesting, preying on these youngsters," adding that he "offered boys, 'If you do a little "something something," whatever, then I can get you those speakers.' And they would comply. A few times some of the boys have admitted to me—I won't mention who they are but they wouldn't deny it—they kind of admitted to me that they would give Mark a little 'something something' and they got like a car or like they got like a suit."[3] Alviar's allegations were echoed by other respondents who claimed Bradford had approached them as well, offering financial favors in exchange for sexual ones.[4]

At the same time, many crews dealt with Bradford on a professional level, regardless of whatever rumors may have swirled around him. Unique Musique's Henry Geronimo stated, "[Bradford's] sexuality didn't matter to me. A lot of people hated him, didn't like him, because he was gay or because they were afraid they were going to be touched by him, you know things like that. I didn't care anything about that. All I knew is the guy knew what he was doing and I wanted to deal with people that professional and he was professional. Although there were rumors about what he did or who he hung out with, but things like that never fazed me." Bradford's reputation helped fuel a rumor mill that could stir dissension within the crews. Ken Anolin experienced this after his crew, Fusion, lost the Imagine 2 battle but came back to win Imagine 3. He recalled that their victory at Imagine 3 was called into question and disgruntled people suggested that Fusion had won on more than just talent: "The rumor had it that there was some relationship between me and Bradford and that he's going [to allow us to win Imagine] 3." To simply suggest that a crew achieved success through any kind of favoritism—rather than merit—was a serious insult; to layer the accusation that they prostituted themselves to acquire that favoritism would have only compounded things far more.

These are examples of the scene at its most destructively competitive, but lest I paint too dark a picture, it must also be said that showcases and battles also encouraged a great deal of cooperation and camaraderie.

Mobile groups may have been rivals for reputation and business, but they still came from the same schools and neighborhoods. Even if DJs battled one another, they could do so while maintaining a sense of friendship and support.

One of the most common examples was mentorship. Older crews often outreached to younger ones, bringing them under their proverbial wings. Sometimes that meant bringing them to gigs or offering surplus business to them. For example, students at both San Francisco's Balboa High and Daly City's Westmoor High formed Live Style Productions in the mid-1980s. At the time, Spintronix was a dominant crew out of Westmoor, and they mentored Live Style, inviting their DJs to Spintronix gigs and allowing them to spin at those events. Especially for the crews who were most in demand, that mentorship could help younger crews land gigs that the more experienced crews handed off. Q-Bert belonged to Live Style and recalled, "We did a lot of shows with Spintronix, and whatever shows they couldn't do, they would hand it down to us." Through that relationship, a crew like Live Style could gain an advantageous foothold within the competitive mobile field.

As noted earlier, Ultimate Creations mentored Beyond the Limit. The latter's Patrick dela Cruz recalled that Ultimate Creations would often hand over gigs involving younger crowds. "We were younger, and we were doing the younger parties, they were doing the older parties," said dela Cruz. "It kind of worked out that way." In fact, Stockton promoter Brian "MC Fly" Samson had sought to book Ultimate Creations for a battle in Stockton, but the Ultimate Creations DJs were not familiar with Samson's operation at the time and ended up referring the promoter to Beyond the Limit instead. "That was our first battle we won. That's the first and only battle we won actually," dela Cruz said.

If mentoring younger crews was one form of intercrew cooperation, the other major form was through the creation of informal and formal *alliances*. An alliance was a partnership between two or more DJ groups to loan equipment or provide assistance to one another. They came into being mostly out of the rise in showcases and battles—times when a participating or headlining crew needed to have as grand and impressive a setup as possible. If their own equipment was insufficient—lacking enough speakers or amplifiers or lighting, for example—crews would turn to crews in their alliance to borrow hardware from them. Melanie Caganot explained that with battles, "people would go all out because it was a competition. They'd bring one hundred feet of truss and all their lights and borrow stuff from other groups. At this point, people would ally—borrowing speakers, or lights because they wanted to beat this other group." Skyway Sounds' Jim Archer concurred: "If I had a big battle, I'm going to Burt [Kong from Sound Sequence, asking], 'Hey dog, let me get twenty feet of truss, two helicopters, and smoke.' At the end of the day, it was alliances . . . there was a network that they would pull off of."

Most of these alliances were informal, created on case-by-case bases. However, a few alliances were officially billed by name. Carrion recounted how three Daly City crews—Unlimited Sounds, Midstar, and Unique Musique—briefly formed and performed together in an alliance named the Juice Crew.[5] In the South Bay, there was an alliance called Empire. Even as late as 1991, in the twilight of the mobile era, new alliances were being formed. On the back of the "Stompin' Into Tha 90s" flyer from 1991, an announcement declares a performance by "Daly City's newest alliance, The Power (Featuring Spintronix and The Beat)."

As mentioned in the introduction, this book takes its name from one of the biggest alliances, the Legion of Boom, formed in 1986. Named by Burt Kong of South City's Sound Sequence, the Legion eventually included Fremont's Images, Union City's Creative Madness, and both Midstar and Styles Beyond Compare of Daly City. In the summer of 1987, the Legion made highly visible appearances by headlining both AA Productions' Summer Showcase III and the Imagine 8 All-Star Summer DJ Battle.

From Kong and Pardorla's perspective, the Legion was a way for groups not just to share equipment but also to find new ways to perform. As the Legion, they boasted a sound system that was bigger than practically any rival's, and Kong added:

> It was another way also to market ourselves. . . . If you were an independent promoter, you could just book us all . . . at a good price, you know what I mean? It's cheaper for all of us too. Every member and every crew would just divvy [up the] equipment. . . . We'd have a couple of meetings before each gig to figure out what we're going to bring and stuff like that. And it's fun . . . we used to have around sixteen quakes [i.e., large club speakers] and that's a lot of eighteen-inch woofers.

That potential—to build the ideal sound system—was as much an incentive behind the alliances as any business concern. When I asked Pardorla which alliance was superior, he beamed and insisted, "Legion of Boom of course! We were the loudest, and we always used to say, down South, they had the sound, but no lights. S.F. crews are very flashy. They had all lights, but no sound. We were right in the middle. We were the best of both worlds."

Not all alliances were as formal as the Legion of Boom, but even casual alliances still reflected a spirit of cooperation. For example, during the late 1980s and early 1990s, the Westlake scene in Daly City was built by two local crews—Second To None and Style Beyond Compare—who cosponsored showcases together. Second To None provided the lighting, and Style Beyond Compare brought their audio equipment. These alliances, both informal and formal, represented some of the best communal values and qualities that the mobile scene engendered: the desire to work together across geography and individual concerns to not only lend support but also offer the audience larger and more spectacular performances. As Kong noted, there were financial incentives, but for him and Pardorla, being able to create the most elaborate sound system seemed even more pleasurable than whatever extra business they might have earned with the Legion of Boom.

These motivating factors highlight the role of play and pleasure within the scene. Having "fun" was not a superficial or secondary concern but was very much at the forefront of what motivated these DJ crews. While intense competition could detract from their enjoyment by creating tensions, not only did alliances encourage enjoyable, positive relationships between crews but also the ultimate goal was to create more spectacular performances to entertain audiences. In that way, the alliances not only were a boon to the crews who took part but also helped enhance the mobile DJ experience for all involved. It was an unexpected, but constructive, outcome from the rise of the showcases.[6]

Imagine may have been the most prominent of the showcase series, but it was hardly the only one. One of Bradford's protégés was Arleen Alviar (now Marcelo), a Pinay from Union City.[7] She started AA Productions in 1985, ostensibly to host her own high school graduation party, but it turned out to be such a major success that it encouraged her to continue to promote other events. Alviar initially learned the trade from Bradford, but she eventually took AA Productions in directions that distinguished its parties from Imagine's. For example, Bradford worked mostly within the Filipino (and, to a lesser extent, Chinese) mobile scenes in San Francisco and Daly City, but Alviar wanted to market AA Productions events to a greater ethnic mix, one that took advantage of Union City's geo-

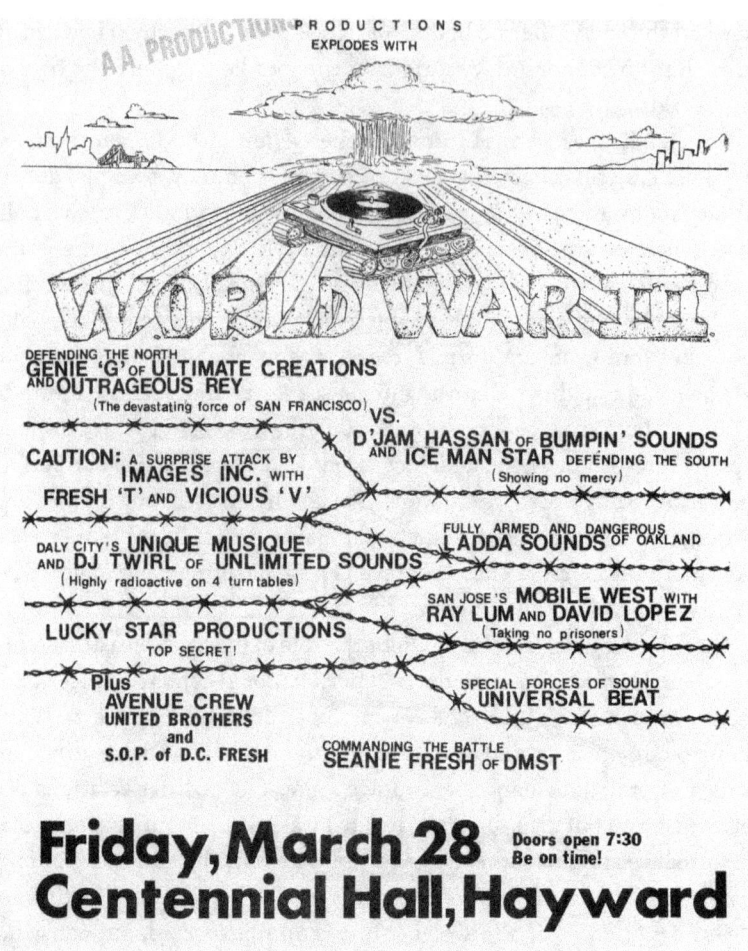

4.2 / Flyer for a 1986 showcase, "World War III," in Hayward, hosted by AA Productions. The Imagine series of showcases tended to lean more toward San Francisco–Daly City crews, while AA Productions tapped talent in the East Bay and South Bay. Courtesy of Francisco Pardorla.

graphic centrality between the heavily African American Oakland to the north, Latino-dominated San Jose to the south, and the many Filipino youth who lived around the tricity cluster of Union City, Fremont, and Hayward.

Images Inc.'s Francisco Pardorla joined AA Productions early on and described how they purposely recruited crews from across the Bay as a way to increase the popularity of their events: "It was unprecedented at the time to bring these guys from the South and these guys from the

North and put them together. So we started putting the battles like that, we were pitting North versus South. Just like a fight promoter, it's all promotions. In real life, these guys had no grudges against each other, but it brings the people in." Alviar herself offered some interesting claims as to why mixed parties were, in her opinion, better: "[I had] Samoan, Mexican, and blacks but majority Filipinos still.... I was purposely targeting other groups. You know, because Filipinos and Asians to me are pretty dead... they're boring. They just kind of hang out, they hold up the walls. You want to get like some blacks and Mexicans and stuff because they'll dance." Allowing that Alviar is generalizing quite broadly, the salient point here is that she actively sought to diversify her parties in ways that Imagine did not.[8] At the very least, it reflected some of the regional differences in how the scene developed. Demographically, the San Francisco–Daly City subscene benefited from a high density of Filipino crews living in a relatively isolated space at the tip of the San Mateo peninsula. As the popularity of the early Imagine parties suggested, one could promote almost exclusively to a Filipino American clientele and be successful. In the East Bay, populations of youth were diffused over a greater geographic area, and to maximize participants it made sense to appeal to a broader range of audiences as opposed to a predominantly Filipino one. Showcases existed to maximize audience, and as these parties evolved and shifted to venues all around the Bay Area, they began to bring together youth from across the region in a way that profoundly impacted a generation of Filipino American youth.

Combining as One / Parties as Pilgrimage

These days, Dr. Allyson Tintiangco-Cubales teaches Asian American and Filipino American studies classes at both San Francisco State University and Balboa High School. Back in the 1980s, though, her family lived on the border between Union City and Fremont, and though she attended American High in Fremont, she used to tell people she was from Union City: "Growing up, I would say I was from U.C. It was cooler, people would associate hip-hop with U.C."

At American, Tintiangco-Cubales befriended members of the Nite Lime crew, but growing up in a traditional, patriarchal household made it difficult for her to follow the crew to their out-of-town gigs. "Crossing the [Bay] Bridge was a big deal for us ... [it] meant that we were leaving the suburban and entering the urban ... where all the action was. For me, my parents were super protective so anytime I would leave Fremont–Union City . . . it was like sneaking out and going to the big city. We would go that far because we would hear from other folks that there were famous DJs there." As she suggested, even if making that trip across the bridge was fraught with risk (of being caught) and symbolic meaning (suburban to urban), what drew her was the desire to see other crews and DJs in the scene.

Her anecdote brought to mind many testimonials focused on the act of traveling. Yusuf Rashid grew up in the 1970s garage party era, and when he was a teenager, he and his friends would go great lengths, literally, in their quest to attend different parties. "We would take the bus, we'd take BART, [or] you tried to hustle a ride," he said, adding: "We definitely wasn't going to hit up our parents. Our parents wasn't going to be seen dropping you off at a party. We'd get to the party one way or another."

Coming from the other direction was Electric Sounds' Rene Anies, who reflected on his mobile years via travel as well: "Because we were DJing, we were going to [places] that we didn't know, that we would never have thought of venturing into." In all these examples, the desire to "get to the party one way or another" compelled the effort to travel, sometimes at great distance, expense, or both. Especially in the showcase era, given the spectacle of the parties, many hundreds if not thousands of youth, every weekend, found themselves "venturing into" new neighborhoods.

As a result of those travels, I suggest, the mobile scene helped produce a site- and time-specific identity for a generation of Filipino American youth. In other words, as much as the mobile crews came "out of" the larger Filipino American community, by creating a cultural activity that bridged different pockets of youth from across the Bay Area, the mobile scene also helped produce a sense of community in its wake.

To elaborate: the Bay Area's geography, in the words of urban historian Joseph Rodriguez, "mandated a dispersed pattern of settlement," and this was especially true for Filipino American communities (1999: 10). As a result, most people need at least forty minutes to travel between any two points between the four major hubs: (1) San Francisco–Daly City, (2) Vallejo, (3) Union City–Fremont, and (4) San Jose (to say nothing of the farther-flung Stockton and Sacramento). Especially for teenagers, traversing that distance was not made easy; many were too young to have a driver's license or lacked access to a personal car. Public transit options were inefficient and time-consuming. Yet, despite those challenges, youth crisscrossed the Bay Area, in search of the perfect party. Travel was not an incidental part of the mobile scene; it is quite essential to making the scene a "scene."

The building of social connections and relationships via shared travel has several important precedents, including one of the most famous mobile DJ scenes: the British Northern Soul movement. Beginning in the late 1960s, northern English cities such as Wigan, Manchester, and Blackpool became focal points for a series of parties where DJs would play obscure R&B singles from the United States.[9] Northern Soul constituted what could be thought of as "the first rave culture," which is to say it was a mobile DJ scene involving "working class kids [coming] together in larger numbers, across great distances, to obscure places, to take drugs and dance to music that no one else cared about" (Brewster and Broughton 1999: 77). Like the Bay Area mobile scene, Northern Soul parties often circulated through a variety of changing venue locations, given the turnover in club spaces. This made travel absolutely essential to the scene but, more specifically, to the experience of *belonging* in the scene. Investing in Northern Soul meant more than simply being at the party, it also meant finding a way to *get to* the party. As a result, Joanne Hollows and Katie Milestone argued, "the sense of 'community' within northern soul is not one based on locality or neighborhood but instead is 'produced' through travel and an attachment to the spaces that are usually considered mundane but that acquire an 'aura' as sacred places because they are central to the scene" (1998: 94). This idea of community being produced *via* travel is key; rather than seeing identity as something preformed and then taken on the proverbial road, what Milestone and Hollows suggest is that identity was formed through the act of traveling itself. Music fans who work their way to parties, shows, and festivals inevitably bond with one another through that shared act, whether in the literal act of traveling together (as in carpooling, in caravans, etc.) or in the knowledge that they have this shared experience with one another. In that process, Paul Hodkinson, writing about goth music fans, suggests that "traveling often resulted in the development of translocal friendship networks. Once established, such friendships created an extra incentive to make future trips" (2004: 136).[10]

For fans of the Filipino mobile scene, the frequent parties and showcases provided such an incentive to create and build on friendships begun at these events. Dame Cruz was a student at Presentation, a private girls school, and grew up between the Sunset district and Daly City.[11] She recalled the ways major mobile scene events provided her and her friends from other schools and neighborhoods an opportunity to see one another. "It was kind of like six degrees [of separation]," she said, comparing mobile parties to a social network in which each person is fewer than six degrees separated from anyone else. She added, "It was like . . . networking with friends I haven't seen in a while. . . . I don't think there would have been another venue where everybody just hung out." This speaks to the unique function of mobile scene parties, providing a liminal forum in which people from different parts of the Bay could socialize.

The process of bonding via travel can be so powerful that many are moved to invoke religious analogies. Mark Olson, writing about traveling fans in local rock scenes of the 1990s, described them as "diasporic pilgrims on their way there in hopes of finding their salvation from everyday life" (1998: 283). Not only does this metaphor connote the deep, fervent attachments that fans can have to music, but also the analogy of a "pilgrimage" emphasizes how the act of going to a show is not simply a means to an end; the journey itself is productive of identity and community.

Olson provided an elaboration, comparing "place-based scenes" to "meccas" (once again invoking religious connotations). He wrote that these scenes produce a shared identity, "predicated not upon *already* being there, upon an arrival, but in terms of a common desire to be there, a shared investment in a particular place: a movement" (1998: 283). He writes elsewhere: "In discussing the spatial singularity of scenes and their functions in contemporary culture, I hope to return to the issues [of] . . . 'being there,' movement, authenticity, and belonging—for these terms are integral to understanding scenes *not only as places produced but as productive places*" (275; emphasis mine). In other words, as much as our notion of "place" is shaped by activities that occur in a place, Olson also stressed how a sense of place is a productive force unto itself, creating what he described as "flows and trajectories" that make other things possible. In short, he argued that the gathering places of a "scene" are not "empty containers" or "mere scenery in front of which take place the politics and pleasures of music production and consumption." They create identity rather than just reflecting or representing it (271).

The "productive" qualities, in this sense, of the Filipino American mobile DJ scene were a major theme in my interviews. When I was interviewing Ultimate Creations' Gil Olimpiada, he had this to say about Bradford and the Imagine parties: "He put an organization together to actually have the Filipino community come together, combine as one." As

Olimpiada implies, one of the most important legacies of the showcases was the way they drew together so many people from across the Bay Area. If mobile crews spread out to travel to different cities and counties, showcases worked in reverse, bringing audiences from all over to congregate in a single venue. In that process, young Filipinos could meet, interact, and form a sense of what "community" meant for them and their generation.

Jeremy "Uprise" Monsayac, a scratch generation DJ from San Francisco, offered this take in an email: "You knew you were part of something special back then. Everybody knew everybody. It was definitely a shared experience. The party scene in the eighties helped give Filipinos an identity. As an ethnic group that had no real 'identity' in the same manner as the Chinese or Koreans, for example, the party scene helped give us something to claim as our own." There is much to unpack here, especially the idea that, prior to the mobile scene, Monsayac did not feel that he possessed a "real identity" as a Filipino in contrast to other Asian ethnic groups—shades of social invisibility. However, for Monsayac, mobile DJing was a cultural activity that allowed him to forge a common identity with other Filipinos of that era through their shared participation.

I do not want to overextrapolate from these testimonials to suggest that this was a universal experience for all respondents. As I have noted, for most of my respondents there was no transparent, self-conscious relationship between the mobile scene and their identities as Filipino Americans. However, I believe that as a social force, part of what showcases tapped into were the curiosities of young people to meet other likeminded young people—ethnic heritage being one aspect of that. This is obviously a hazy area to plumb, since "like-minded" could also mean people within their extended social circles—acquaintances from other high schools, friends of friends—but given the particular social network of the mobile scene, that would still mean coming into contact with hundreds, if not thousands, of other Filipino Americans throughout the course of the 1980s. In other words, whether by intention or accident, the mobile scene created an environment—especially via showcases—that not only encouraged social interaction between different Filipino American youth but also provided a cultural activity that could bond them through the shared experience of traveling and attending mobile events.

Cruz attempted to explain how the mobile parties helped to define a series of experiences that both anchored her memories of the era and linked her with others from the same time and place:

You had to understand, growing up in that area, what an Imagine was. I don't know if they have the same thing in LA or any other place, but it's . . . a unique culture thing in my circle, or at least my generation. For example, my husband, when we got married, he said, "Did you ever go to Imagine?" "Oh I did, I was at the Fairgrounds, I was at the one at the Irish Cultural Center." We joke because we share that same connection. Or if I happen to bump into an old school person on Facebook or one of my old friends, it's like we all have that shared memory, where we all liked the same mixes, we liked the same DJs, we all went to the same places.

This brings back Frith's postulation of how "[social groups] only get to know themselves as groups . . . through cultural activity" (1996a: 111). In that sense, I would advance that the mobile DJ scene was one (if not *the*) key cultural activity from which participation generated an awareness of a communal identity—predominantly among Filipino American youth—that may not have manifested otherwise, especially in the absence of a Filipino American mass media presence.

To return to the idea of pilgrimages, it may seem overly dramatic to describe a trip up the Nimitz Freeway from Fremont and then across the Bay Bridge in religious terms, but Filipino youth indisputably were drawn to mobile events through a powerful, shared desire to "be there," no matter what it required. Paul Tumakay (Kicks Company) recalled: "When mobile DJing started catching on . . . that's when you had people who preferred to go to garage parties than clubs. And it was kind of unique because people would not only go to garage parties by means of cars and private transportation, but they took the bus, and you don't see that happening nowadays, people taking the bus. There would [also] be stories [about] a small, compact car, and fifteen people in there trying to get to the garage parties." As Rashid said, "we'd get to the party one way or another."

On one level, the attraction of these DJ events was very simple: they provided entertainment in the form of music and dancing. As social gatherings, they facilitated the mixing and mingling of different people, offering the potential of finding new friends and potential lovers. As Rodriguez noted about the Bay Area, "the urbanized region encourages anonymity and individualism. We feel like outsiders since we so frequently venture beyond our neighborhoods and communities" (1999: 111). Yet here was a cultural force encouraging the exactly opposite: pilgrimages beyond local neighborhoods in the quest for social contact and community bonding.

However, it was not just social encounters these youth sought, but encounters with youth like them, that is, other Filipinos. The mobile DJ scene was both the creator of, and creation of, shared desires by Filipino youth to forge contact with one another. Promoters benefited from a circular logic: by promising that youth from across the Bay would be at their event, they were able to draw youth from across the Bay. Stockton promoter Brian Samson suggested that his parties were attended by a diverse set of audiences because of "the fact that you can follow that particular DJ crew to that party or event and you can, all of the sudden, hang out with people from Daly City and South City or San Francisco and South City or Hayward and San Francisco." Likewise, Rene Anies suggested,

> These DJ groups formed, we were doing parties for each other and got to see how other people [lived] . . . taste their food, down to the food, everybody cooked one dish differently, ten different ways to cook one dish. As something as little, as trivial as that, really, in essence, that's what it was. We were tasting each other's [lifestyles], how we celebrated our lifestyles. [My crewmates] used to make fun of me because we all did things differently and they said my language sounded backwards. But that was the thing, we learned about that and part of that was going to their family's parties and talking to their elders. In that sense, it did teach us a lot. People would never have thought of that, but it did.

Importantly, when Anies refers to "other people" he is not talking about non-Filipinos; he is referring to Filipinos of different cultural and linguistic regions. Anies's family was originally from Illocos Sur and spoke Illocano, but other members of his crew included those from Tagalog- and Cebuano-speaking parts of the Philippines. As Anies indicated, these differences in language also accompanied differences in culture and customs (not the least of which was culinary, apparently).

It is crucial to remember that Filipino America is a deeply diverse community, possessed of "a wild heterogeneity."[12] Anies's comments speak to that kind of internal diversity within the mobile scene as well as how participation within a crew was one way he was able to bond across those differences. The DJ scene was something Monsayac saw "as our own," in reference to an organic form of Filipino American cultural practice. If the mobile DJing was a path via which Filipino youth could lay claim to a sense of cultural ownership and identity, one can see how the mobile scene did not "emerge" out of the Filipino community so much as it was a lived practice through which that community actually came into being, or better said, came to understand itself, as a community. Along these lines, Tumakay offered this observation:

> In my opinion, one of the major positive things that the Filipino DJ really helped to bring about is getting familiar with the different community groups out there in a more social scene. Hanging out at Serra Bowl, you'd have to know someone or be part of a clique or gang. But . . . when you're at the dance party . . . you have to behave in a certain way, so I think that's what helped . . . to sort of start binding all these different, disparate Filipino groups in different areas of the Bay. . . . We weren't mature enough to [be aware of this], we were just like "this is cool." But when it comes to people enjoying themselves and trying to bond, the DJ groups really started that.[13]

Tumakay recognized that part of what was happening at these events was the crossing of borders—not just literal geographic borders but social divisions as well. The decision to make the journey to attend a showcase (or even a garage party) was premised, at some level, in a desire to make contact, to travel across space in order to meet other youth like themselves. There is a belief among sociologists and urban planners that "mobility makes community formation and maintenance difficult. It supports an individualistic, striving lifestyle," as put by Rodriguez (1999: 136). I agree that this may very well be true in a general sense that mobility creates social instabilities through the breaking of local ties, but in the case of the mobile scene, we also see ways mobility can enhance and maintain community.

What also stands out is that these youth, themselves, were products of a transnational migrancy and mobility that dispersed families across wide geographic regions, thus potentially tearing common bonds asunder. Yet what the DJ mobile scene may have helped to do was create the social glue to piece together a new kind of community, one that was unique to the participants' generational experiences. And they did this through their own form of mobility, by traveling with their crews and encouraging people to follow. While the ultimate destinations may have been parties and showcases, Filipino youth built community within this by going into motion, moving toward their destinations in unison with many others, seeking a sense of belonging. In searching for that "home," they found it on the move.

4.3 / Sound Effex (Union City), c. 1989. Members of Sound Effex were part of the stable of DJs that partnered with Expressions, a party promotions team founded by John Francisco in the late 1980s. Left to right: Fred Omaque, Jerome Palacious. Photo courtesy of John Francisco.

Rites of Passage / DJing as a "Filipino Thing"

As I was reminded throughout my interviews, few of my respondents thought of the mobile scene as what might colloquially be described as "a Filipino thing," that is, a self-aware or intentional expression of ethnic or racial identity. However, that does not mean that participants lacked a sense of ethnic identity. Rather, as with any community, a diversity of opinions and perspectives existed as to what or how such an identity factored into their daily lives, individually or collectively.[14]

For some, like Images Inc.'s Francisco Pardorla, seeing a DJ who was Filipino was integral to his own lightbulb moment when he first saw San Francisco's City Lights crew perform at Alameda City College: "See, the City Lights guys are the first Filipino guys I saw. That's when you think that you can do it. . . . If he could do it, then I could do it. And that's what

Imaginings / 117

it was for me. When I saw that these guys could do it, I didn't have to be Venus Flytrap, I didn't have to be Cameron Paul." That last comment was especially important; Pardorla knew of other DJs, both real (Cameron Paul) and fictional (Venus Flytrap from the 1970s TV show *WKRP in Cincinnati*), but neither were of Filipino descent.[15] It took witnessing Filipino Americans like himself—the City Lights crew—to make him feel that he "could do it too." Simply being aware of DJ culture was not sufficient to tip Pardorla into imagining himself as one; his lightbulb moment was inherently tied in to the recognition of his own self in other Filipinos. Ironically, all this happened despite Pardorla's own conflicted identity as a Filipino American. He explained:

> I saw myself as American. I think the fact that I didn't speak Tagalog segregated me from the other Filipinos. And that's how it was in our high school, that's how we separated. All the guys that spoke English hung out together. All the ones that spoke Tagalog, we labeled them as "FOBs" [fresh off the boat]. In actuality, these "FOBs" were born here in the U.S., but because their parents spoke Tagalog around the house . . . whereas me, I was born in the P.I. [Philippine Islands], but my parents spoke English. My grandfather was an English teacher. I saw myself as American, not that I wasn't proud of my Pilipino heritage, but I'll admit it, I was embarrassed by the FOBs. They were embarrassing because here we were trying to be cool, but I didn't want Joe Blow white guy to think that I was associated with the guy who could barely speak English, when in actuality he could speak English, but just chooses to speak Tagalog.

These kinds of internal tensions and separations are certainly not unique to Filipino Americans.[16] They suggest how identity, especially in the teenage years, is fraught with fractures, frictions, and contradictions. To the extent that identity is a form of alliance ("I identify myself with others who share that identity"), for someone like Pardorla, it was not just enough to identify as Filipino; it mattered which "kind" of Filipino you aligned with—or feared being aligned with.[17]

Then, there were those, such as Sound Explosion's Rafael Restauro, who at times simply rejected being labeled as Filipino at all (especially by other Filipinos): "I hated the stereotypical Filipino asking another Filipino, 'Are you Filipino?' No, I'm a Californian. No matter what, I'm a Californian even if I'm Filipino American. I don't know, for me, I just didn't like that. I'm just a San Franciscan, no colors about it." In Restauro's case, though he does not deny his ethnic heritage, it was not the foremost part of his identity; he preferred an identification based on geography rather than ethnicity.

Still another contrast came via the Spintronix founders, several of whom spoke about Filipino identity as something they grew into. For Jay dela Cruz, college-age experiences transformed his perception: "Honestly, I became very conscious of my Filipino background as I got older, into my college years because I was going to SF State and there was the PACE [Pilipino American Collegiate Endeavor] club and I was aware of that and their issues. As I got older, I began to learn more about what's going on in the Philippines. I did get to visit the P.I. once when I was nineteen. But growing up in my teen years, no, I wasn't aware of it." For others in the crew, their identifications were more cross-racial. Kormann Roque said, "Looking back now, I think most of my high school time, I felt like I wanted to be more black than I was Asian. Not that I'm not proud to be Asian but my icons were AfAm—Run DMC, you know? Whodini. UTFO." Rivera, on the other hand, identified more strongly with the Latino community initially: "When I moved to Daly City in middle school, I was Filipino. Then [was] my Latino era. At the time, they were called *cholos*, that's when Latino gangs came out, so I thought I was one of them. And then, came . . . high school, where I didn't know what I was anymore, and after high school, I thought I was black for five years. Then I realized I was Filipino." The common thread among these three Spintronix DJs was a relationship between age and identity; all three suggested that as teenagers (i.e., when they first entered the mobile scene) they all lacked a clear, self-aware identity as Filipinos or Filipino Americans. This may be an outcome of youthfulness, where a language of racial and ethnic identity is still in formation. It may also reflect the general absence of Filipinos from conventional American racial narratives—the "social invisibility" factor—which would help explain how people like Roque and Rivera identified more strongly with other racial groups (black and Latino, respectively) that had a more dominant presence in the American social landscape.

In contrast to this diversity of opinions around Filipino identity, there was far more uniformity when it came to whether respondents perceived mobile DJing as a Filipino American activity: the initial answer was almost universally "no" or "we didn't see it like that." However, in the course of those interviews, with the benefit of hindsight, some respondents began to develop an analysis of how ethnic identity may have played out in the scene. For example, Restauro offered this thought on what he saw as Sound Explosion's legacy: "I think, when [peers] saw us, these young, Filipino Americans, [they thought] 'Look at those guys, they're Flips. They're making money, they're having fun, they're partying, let's try to do that.' I think that's how it became a *Filipino thing*. But we weren't looking at it that way. We were doing it as family and friends having fun. But as these young kids were looking up at us, they just started doing their thing" (emphasis mine). For Restauro, DJing was not a "Filipino thing" at the time when Sound Explosion first formed. But as he observed, when his Filipino peers saw the success and fun that Sound Explosion were enjoying, it may have influenced them to think of DJing as a particularly Filipino American activity, if for no other reason than the fact that Sound Explosion happened to be made up of Filipinos. Like any good self-fulfilling prophecy, as more Filipino teens flocked to form their own mobile crews, it only served to validate the idea that DJing was "a Filipino thing," until the connection between ethnicity and activity became "naturalized," that is, the point where participants could simply take it for granted. DJ Apollo put it like this: "A lot of the old school [crews] were Filipino and we wanted to follow in their footsteps and it sort of became a tradition. It was like, 'Damn, there's hella Filipino groups. That must be the thing that everyone's doing.' And everyone just wanted to fit in and do what everyone else was doing. . . . Everybody just wanted to be like each other, and that just created more and more of it." On the one hand Apollo noted that for his generation of Filipino youth, joining a mobile crew was seen not just as a natural part of being young and Filipino but as practically an *expected* part, that is, "everybody just wanted to be like each other." That belief became self-reinforcing as more people joined, thus making it seem even more obvious that DJing "must be the thing that everyone's doing."

Travis Rimando made a similar point when discussing his participation in a younger generation of DJs who got their start in the late 1980s: "DJing is just so built into the social structure. You always have someone in the family who DJs or friends that DJ. It's almost like a rite of passage to be one." He again calls attention to the social networks and peer-to-peer interactions at play within the scene—"you always have someone in the family who DJs"—but even more telling is his suggestion that DJing was "built into the social structure," that is, that DJing was an integral, systemic part of the Filipino American community. Most provocative, though, is his remark about DJing as a "rite of passage," highlighting the productive quality of DJing, one in which ethnic identity is something to be achieved via DJing. Notably, Antonio Tiongson, writing about the same younger generation of Filipino American turntablists that Romando belonged to, argues a similar point: "DJing has come to serve as a rite of passage among Filipino youth and [has been] interwoven into their everyday lives" (2013: 52).

To put it simply, being Filipino is not what defined you as a DJ so much as *being a DJ is what defined you as a Filipino*, or, to follow Rimando and Tiongson's analogy, becoming a DJ was the ritual through which one *became* Filipino. This did not happen through any process (formal or otherwise) that participants were aware of at the time; as I have stressed, these were observations made with the benefit of hindsight and a more sophisticated, adult language of race and identity. Nonetheless, it suggests how "being a DJ" and "being Filipino" was a "natural" fit even when respondents could not articulate how or why. Even Refuerzo, who possessed a very strong self-identity as Filipino, had trouble connecting that identity with his career in the mobiles: "I was just fascinated by [DJing]. I don't know, it just grabbed me, I don't know. It was just the thing—it was the 'in thing' then. But I mean, everybody always wanted a ticket. Every neighborhood had their own DJ group. I just wanted to do it. . . . We wanted to be the younger kids to do it. So we started making our own speakers and hooking up home stereo stuff. I don't know, I guess it was in our blood or something because all the Filipino guys were like DJs. It's weird." Note how Refuerzo kept repeating "I don't know" even while he was espousing a theory of why DJing was so popular among his friends and classmates. I received the same reaction from many respondents—they had rarely contemplated the relationship between DJing and ethnicity, but in struggling to probe that link, many restated some variation on Refuerzo's point: DJing was the "in thing" that defined their cultural world, so much so that one could describe that compulsion as something "in our blood." There is an uncomfortable irony in that statement: throughout U.S. history, Filipino youth, especially men, have long been persecuted for viciously racist stereotypes—vice, greed, lust, violence—that white supremacists also presumed were "in the blood" (see Takaki 1989, chapter 9). However, what Refuerzo's statements suggest is how deeply ingrained DJing was in his identity; he thought of it as literally *natural*, an embodied part of what it meant to be Filipino, at least for the mobile DJ generation.

I should stress: there does seem to be a generational trend at play here. In Tiongson's research on Bay Area Filipino American scratch DJs (the generation that came after the mobile DJs), his respondents display much higher levels of ethnic self-consciousness *as it applies to DJing* (2013, chapter 4). Clearly, some kind of shift occurred within this broadly constituted community of Filipino American youth as DJing transitioned from the mobile to the scratchers. (I take up that transition in DJ practice in more detail in chapter 5). These generational differences were not a central part of my research, given that mobile and scratch DJs represented distinct eras, but I offer three explanations for consideration.

First, the politics of Filipino American identity have changed since the 1990s, especially through the expansion of Asian American and Filipino American studies in college curriculums, exposing more young people to histories and narratives that have inspired greater pride in ethnic identification. These are included in what Susanah Mendoza has described as the "'Born-Again Filipino' movement," which she identifies as directly confronting the "prior assimilationist orientation [that] had earned for the community the unflattering title, 'the invisible minority'" (2002: 12; see also Root 1997: 192–94).

Second, the rise of interest in hip-hop—an intensely identity-oriented cultural practice—plays a crucial role in explaining this rise in Filipino self-identification as well. Ethnographer Anthony Harrison described this as an "emergent Filipino hip hop script" (2009: 133). Finally, the mainstream, mass media visibility of Filipino American scratch DJs, such as Invisibl Skratch Piklz and members of Los Angeles's Beat Junkies, has helped bring attention to the very existence of Filipinos as an ethnic group, countering social invisibility and making it easier for younger DJs to identity as Filipino. As Tiongson puts it, "DJing has provided [Filipino youth] with a cultural space they can claim as their domain, contributing to a sense of group pride and belonging" (2013: 56). I would simply add that scratch DJs may have been a capstone on this process, but it first began with the mobiles.[18]

Postscript / A Shoe in the Chandelier

AA Productions' crowning event was supposed to be 1989's "Summer Girls Showcase," held at the San Jose Civic Auditorium. According to Pardorla, this was their largest event ever—attracting over 3,600 people to a sold-out event. However, despite its outward success, the showcase proved to be a devastating financial disaster, as the AA only recouped half their upfront costs. Alviar explained: "I spent like . . . $64,000 and only $32,000 came back. . . . I spent more than I was charging, you know, I . . . wanted everyone to be having fun so . . . I gave everybody limos and stuff. I was trying to do like how Imagine rolled—[Bradford] had to put everybody in the Hilton, you know? So I lost $30,000. It was hard." Alviar's mother, who had helped manage her finances throughout, helped cover part of the loss and told her, "That's it."[19]

Imagine did not survive much longer either. According to Alviar, who helped Bradford with his accounting, the events never made money; they were primarily a vanity project, with Bradford's real estate business absorbing the cost. For Bradford 1987 was a banner year, with no fewer than four Imagine events. However, within just a few years, Imagine had lost much of its clout, at least within the Bay Area. Bradford, for one, was less present, as he began traveling down to Southern California to throw parties there. He still held some stature with Bay Area DJs, however. Paul "Pauly Tek" Canson of Second To None explained that for younger DJs, "the new generation, meeting Mark Bradford, was like, 'I heard a lot about you, you're fucking weird but I have a lot of respect for you still because you were making moves back then.'"

Respected or not, Imagine in the early 1990s was not on the same footing as it had been just a few years prior. Not only had the name "Imagine" been forgotten among younger partygoers but also Bradford had to contend with a far more competitive field of promoters than he was used to. Out of Union City, John Francisco had turned over the remnants of his old Foreplay crew into the new promotions outfit Expressions Entertainment, sponsoring showcases and battles in Hayward, Newark, and other East and South Bay cities. Billed as "Daly City's Unity 2 Crew," Styles Beyond Compare and Second To None also promoted their own showcases in locations such as Daly City's Westlake district, Foster City, and San Francisco. As late as 1992, large showcases—the DJs Extravaganza series—were also sponsored out of Santa Clara University in the South Bay.

In his heyday, Bradford had the power to muscle out competing promoters; that era was long over now. Bradford held his last major Imagine party—Imagine 20—on November 27, 1991, at the Cathedral Hill Hotel in San Francisco.[20] Canson's dance crew, the Raggawinos, performed at the event, and he recalled its less than graceful end: "[My friend] Alvin was in a circle and he was doing those gyros, flung his shoe off, straight up in the air.[21] It hit one of the huge chandeliers and pieces started to crash down. They shut the party down right there. That was that."

Less than a year later, on September 5, 1992, San Francisco police would discover Bradford shot to death, his body and car set afire. His murder remains unsolved (Bartolome 1992: 1).[22]

Chapter 5 / Take Me Out with the Fader /
The Decline of the Mobile Scene

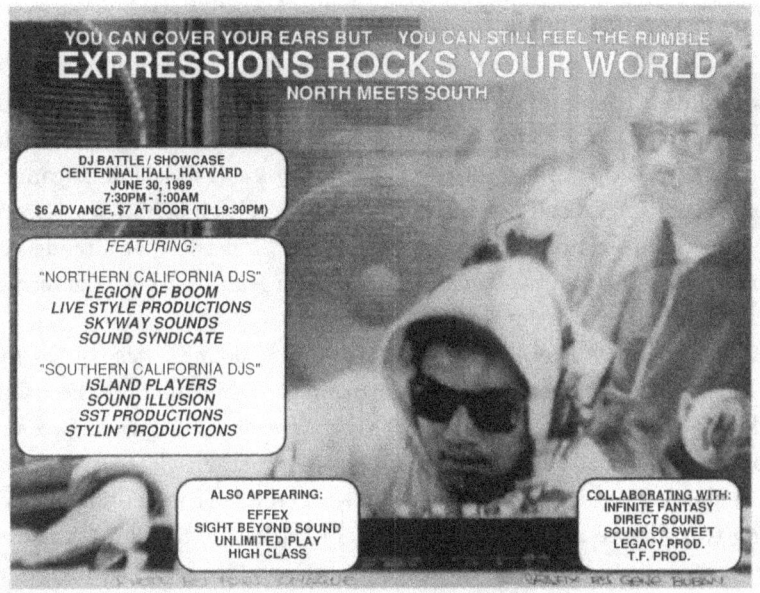

5.1 / Flyer for a 1989 showcase, "Expressions Rocks Your World," in Hayward. Though billed as a battle between DJs from Northern and Southern California, it is best remembered as being a key battle between "Jazzy" Jim Archer (representing older mix DJs) and Richard "Q-Bert" Quitevis (representing emergent scratch DJs). Courtesy of John Francisco.

On June 30, 1989, John Francisco's Expressions Entertainment sponsored its most ambitious showcase to date (figure 5.1). Held at Hayward's Centennial Hall, the showcase included several local and national stars, including DJ Johnny Juice of the rap group Public Enemy, then-up-and-coming rapper and radio personality MC Sway, and the mobile community's own MC Lani Luv (aka *Tales of the Turntable*'s Melanie Caganot). However, the real stars of the show—and the conceit behind the "North Meets South" concept—was the eight-team DJ battle that intended to put four crews from the Bay Area against four from Southern California. It did not quite turn out that way, though.

"Jazzy" Jim Archer, from San Jose's Skyway Sounds, was part of the Northern California contingent and explained, "I think that Northern California DJs started getting such a buzz that none of the LA guys showed up, or they showed up but didn't perform, it was something like that." Instead, the showcase ended up pitting the Bay Area crews in competition, including two alliance teams—Legion of Boom and Sound Syndicate—as well as Skyway Sounds and San Francisco–Daly City's Live Style Productions.

In the finals, the event still got its geographic showdown: San Francisco's Richard "Q-Bert" Quitevis (Live Style) versus the South Bay's Jazzy Jim. From Jim's perspective, this was more than crew versus crew; it was also a generational battle of sorts: "At that point, I was getting a decent name for myself and Q-Bert was just coming on. People were wondering about me, 'Is Jazzy done, has he had his time, is Q-Bert the next guy who is going to take over?' This is something people wanted to see." Jim mentally dissected what the potential matchups would look like in the battle, especially in relation to each of their styles: "I know that Q-Bert is going to get a ten on scratching, but I know I can probably . . . get a seven or an eight. I do not think Q-Bert is going to do much mixing so he's probably going to get a three, but I am going to get a ten."

Jim's predictions turned out to be quite precise. He went first, putting on a show of quick-mixing skills as he seamlessly whittled his way through two stacks of records on either side of him. Q-Bert's routine also featured some quick-mixing, but as Jim assumed, it was his scratch routines that really caught people's attention. Promoter John Francisco described his impressions of listening to Q-Bert: "I was walking from one side of the hall to the other. I stopped dead in my tracks. I was like 'Jesus Christ, who the hell is this guy?' I mean, he was doing things to that record that I never heard in my life. I mean I heard people scratching before, but not like that. He was like a damn madman up there."[1] At the end of the battle, the judges were left in a quandary. As Francisco explained, "it actually threw off a lot of judges, they couldn't figure out exactly how to judge them. You had two different styles on two different parts of the spectrum, how do you deal with that?" Debate ensued, but the judges eventually awarded the contest to Jim, a decision that attendees still debate today. No one questioned the skill of either DJ, but the difficulty in establishing a consensus on which DJ style was "better" reflected an emerging split within the larger mobile DJ community.

In hindsight, it is tempting to frame that 1989 battle as marking a symbolic crossroads in the history of the scene, one that also predicted changes happening among DJs globally. Scratching and mixing were not necessarily opposing styles—scratching can be a useful skill in enhancing a mix transition, for example—but the adherents of each skill set were beginning to form into different communities. On that summer day in 1989, Q-Bert might have lost the battle, but within only a few years, many could claim that scratch DJing would eventually win the war.

The death of Mark Bradford and decline of Imagine and AA Productions did not spell the end of the showcase era, but the scene was changing rapidly by the early 1990s. One of the most stark examples came with the way showcases began to focus heavily on single DJs rather than just crews. For example, on the flyer for a "DJs Extravaganza" showcase from 1992, two different categories appeared: battling DJs (i.e., individuals) and showcasing DJs (i.e., crews). This was a new kind of delineation, a nod to the emergence of the scratch DJ, and a harbinger of a fundamental transformation happening within the mobile scene. The scene's valorization of the communal unit (i.e., the crew) was steadily being displaced by a cult of personality surrounding individual, iconic DJ figures. This shift both reflected—and hastened—changing values within the scene.

As I have stressed throughout, mobile DJ crews offered many kinds of benefits and attractions for members: friendship and camaraderie, a modest source of income, social status. However, what may get lost is the most basic function of a mobile *crew*: labor. Crews provided the physical labor needed to tote crates of records and move and assemble heavy audio and lighting equipment. Remove the need for that assistance, and the logic of a crew organization begins to fall apart. When that happens among many crews, the scene itself withers.

Within this context, scratch DJing may have contributed to declining interest in mobile crews, but it was far from the only—or even main— reason the scene began to fade by the early to mid-1990s. As this chapter details, it was a confluence of factors, both internal and external to the scene, that gradually chipped away at its import within the cultural lives of the Bay Area's Filipino American youth. Some of those forces worked to elevate the successes of individual DJs but inadvertently weakened the need of a support crew. Other forces siphoned off youth into other cultural activities. And specific to the crews themselves, insufficient recruitment of younger members meant that those who "aged out" were not replaced in the ranks. The scene might have survived any single one of these forces, but in concert they helped catalyze the scene's decline. Yet even as the heyday of the mobiles began to pass, the generation of DJs they helped to develop began to make their own power felt. That emergent cadre of turntablists would go on to reach heights of global recognition that their forebears could scarcely have imagined.

An Itch to Scratch / The Rise of Scratch DJing in the Mobile Crews

The invention of "the scratch" dates back to 1977, when a teenage DJ named Theodore Livingston idly cued a record back and forth and became intrigued by the sound it made under the stylus.[2] Livingston, better known as Grandwizard Theodore, began to introduce his scratching technique into public gigs, and it caught on quickly with nascent hip-hop DJs in the New York area. By the early 1980s, scratching had become a central style among hip-hop DJs; one of the most lauded of "old school" hip-hop records, from 1981, is essentially a scratch and mix routine put on vinyl, Grandmaster Flash's "The Adventures of Grandmaster Flash on the Wheels of Steel" (1981).

Scratching enjoyed a massive boost in visibility in 1983 with the success of Herbie Hancock's "Rockit" (1983). Not only did Grandmaster D.S.T. provide scratching on the song, but the jazz-rock single came with an eye-catching video that put D.S.T. on display alongside a chorus line of disembodied, robotic legs kicking in rhythm. "Rockit" was so successful that it supposedly helped break through the infamous "no black music" policy at the then-fledgling MTV (Brewster and Broughton 1999: 260). Grandmaster D.S.T. accompanied Hancock on a series of prominent live performances of "Rockit," including on *Saturday Night Live* and the Grammys, and these appearances, along with the video, likely did far more to spread scratching than any audio recording. Spintronix's Kormann Roque could have spoken for an entire generation when he explained how he first learned about scratching: "For me, it was watching Grandmaster D.S.T. doing the 'Rockit' thing. Man, when I heard that I was like 'Damn.'"[3]

The appeal of scratching has partially to do with how it sounds. A scratch is, on one level, a conscious act of dissonance, creating a rupture from the expected, linear flow of a record. However, when scratching is done in tempo with a record, it adds a layer of sound and syncopation that enhances rather than distracts. In accomplishing this, scratching profoundly transforms the very function of the turntable and the person behind it. As musicologist Mark Katz notes in his book on DJ culture, *Groove Music*, "traditionally, it's not the person playing the turntable who is making the music—the music has already been made, and is simply *reproduced* by the turntable. . . . [Grandwizard] Theodore went even further; when he pushed [a record] back and forth underneath the stylus, he was transforming it into something entirely different. It is because of this real-time manipulation that the turntable can be a musical instrument" (2012: 61–62). If the turntable could be turned into a musical instrument, it followed that the DJ could become a musician. In the 1990s, Chris "Babu" Oroc, a Filipino American DJ from Southern California, came up with the neologism "turntablist" (turntable + instrumentalist) as another way to describe scratch DJs (Katz 2012: 127). The term stuck;

by the late 1990s, an International Turntablist Federation even arose to compete with the more venerable Disco Mix Competition (better known as "the DMC"). Turntablist became a useful way to describe the scratch DJ as both musician and performer. As I have suggested throughout, the act of mix DJing is always a performance, based around both song selection and mixing skills. However, scratch DJing pushed the performative element even further.

In the beginning, scratching added a layer of creative expression "on top" of the mix; for example, instead of tempo-matching two songs, one could instead "scratch in" the next song as a transition. However, as scratching evolved—especially through the participation of Bay Area Filipino American DJs—mixing receded into the background, leaving scratching as the primary musical expression. A scratch performance was no longer the sideshow; it became the main event.

For this reason, mobile crews often met the growing popularity of scratching with some ambivalence. This was a generational tension to some extent, with younger members enthusiastically learning the style while more veteran members remained wary. After all, nonstop mixing is meant to sustain and contain the energy of the dance floor, guiding the dancer-listeners into a state of "surrender" where they "lose themselves" in the moment. Scratch DJs operate on a divergent—some might say oppositional—set of ideals and needs. Scratching, as an act of rupture, calls attention to itself; an ideal scratch performance seeks a receptive, observant audience rather than one that is "lost in the music." To put it another way, if DJs are like drummers, the best mixers sustain a danceable backbeat, but the scratch DJ is all about the drum solo.

One of my most vivid, early memories of watching a scratch DJ was in 1994, when Daly City's DJ Shortkut (Jonathan Cruz) competed in the West Coast regional DMC contest. A Filipino American from Daly City's Templeton High School and originally a member of the Just 2 Hype mobile crew, Shortkut was a rising star in the turntablism scene in 1994, the heir apparent of older mentors like Q-Bert and Mixmaster Mike. At the competition, Shortkut unveiled a routine that he would later become famous for: the "Impeach the President" juggle.

A juggle (aka beat-juggle) is a scratch technique, dating back to at least 1987, where the DJ uses copies of the same song, one on each turntable.[4] By moving back and forth between each record, constantly rewinding or pushing them forward, the DJ can deconstruct and reconstruct the song to emphasize specific musical or vocal moments or completely reshuffle them. Juggling requires a deft hand, quick eye, and hyperattentive mind, since the DJ has to move between both turntables while also manipulating the DJ mixer, all within fractions of a second. It is a difficult skill set to master and as such became a staple in scratch competitions.

Shortkut's routine used two copies of the Honeydrippers' 1972 single "Impeach the President," a song that opens with a distinctive drum break, well sampled by hip-hop groups.[5] His song choice here was quite deliberate; scratch routines often rely on using songs that are part of the hip-hop or pop music canon but then transforming them, thus blending familiarity with surprise. In Shortkut's case, he took that famous drum break and then beat-juggled it to create an entirely new drum pattern, something that left the crowd (myself included) in awe.

My point is that Shortkut's routine was created specifically to draw and hone in our attention as a crowd. He needed us to (1) recognize the song being played as "Impeach the President," and (2) recognize how he was transforming it. In theory, a DJ could try to pull off a juggle in the middle of a mixing set, but if the crowd is "lost in the music," then a well-executed juggle might go unnoticed, therefore negating the reason a DJ would attempt to pull off such a difficult trick to begin with. As I am stressing, scratching is meant to call attention to itself, and as such, its integration into a mix-centric mobile scene was always going to face resistance.

Images Inc.'s Francisco Pardorla recalled: "When scratching first came out, it was annoying. It would kill a vibe." Unlimited Sounds' Anthony Carrion remembered when "DJ Apollo" Novicio, one of the crew's younger members, started scratching in the middle of a wedding and Carrion had to reprimand him: "Apollo was actually the first one to show me some tricks and stuff. He ended up at a gig, it was a wedding and he was trying to show me, and I was like, 'No, not now, this is a wedding.' He was transforming and scratching. [I told him,] 'Don't do it now, you know, we're right in the middle of a wedding.'" Non-Stop Boogie's Orlando Madrid recounted similar incidents: "We'll be at a wedding and a teenager will come up and ask, 'Can you scratch?' We're at a wedding . . . hello?" Like Carrion, Madrid imparted that scratching during a dance (especially at a wedding) was particularly inappropriate; as Pardorla said, scratching could threaten to "kill a vibe," the antithesis of what most DJs seek to build and protect throughout an evening.

As a result, many crews relegated scratching to the side. As Pardorla explained it, "everyone gets their fifteen minutes of fame. That's what scratching was. . . . There were these promoters that would have a dance, and for the majority of the night, there were DJs playing records, then it would stop so that these guys [scratch DJs] could show off." Pardorla's suggestion that scratching was partially about fame-seeking reveals an interesting tension within the mobile crews. To be fair, as I have suggested throughout, part of the appeal of DJing to these young men was the potential of accruing social capital; fame-seeking existed long before "Rockit" came out. However, what scratching introduced was a different route to fame, a point I will return to later in the chapter.

Once scratching began to catch on with a younger generation of mobile DJs, a generation gap was almost inevitable, as crews had to contend with two different kinds of DJs in their midst. While giving scratch DJs their "fifteen minutes to show off" could serve as a stopgap compromise, as scratching grew in popularity, that schism would eventually widen, especially once turntablists discovered they could headline their own stages instead.

The transition toward that break was slow and hardly linear. For the most part, mobile crews accepted scratch DJs in their ranks; some, such as Unlimited Sounds, had what amounted to a "designated scratcher"—a scratch specialist specifically given stage time during battles and showcases. Inadvertently, the use of designated scratchers, especially in high-visibility events, allowed those DJs to identify and seek out one another, regardless of which crews they belonged to. Marginal within their own organizations, these nascent turntablists had a vested interest in finding like-minded souls elsewhere.

This is how the nucleus of Apollo, Mixmaster Mike, and Q-Bert came together in the late 1980s.[6] They would later go on to form one of the most lauded and famed turntablist crews in the world—the Invisibl Skratch Piklz—but back then, they were all high school students, scattered about the Bay. Apollo Novicio was a student at Westmoor High in Daly City and was already a renowned participant in the b-boy dance scene centered at Daly City's War Memorial.[7] He then turned to DJing when he joined the prestigious Unlimited Sounds crew and became DJ Apollo. Richard Quitevis grew up in the nearby Excelsior district in San Francisco and was a student at Balboa High—birthplace of Sound Explosion, Non-Stop Boogie, Electric Sounds, the Go-Go's, and other pioneering Filipino mobile crews.[8] There, he joined Live Style Productions, becoming DJ Q-Bert. Michael Schwartz spent much of his teen years living between Daly City and Vallejo; he eventually joined the mobile crew High Tech Soundz in Sacramento, where his handle was Mixmaster Mike.

As I stress here, like almost all the prominent Bay Area scratch DJs from the 1990s, these three men first started with mobile crews in the 1980s.[9]

The three were childhood friends, with Apollo being the common link; he and Q-Bert's high schools were less than five miles apart, and they used to battle one another in school cafeterias during lunchtime. Apollo and Mike were close friends as well; Mike lived with Apollo's family for a spell. In the late 1980s and early 1990s, the three—calling themselves FM2O (Furious Minds 2 Observe)—began to lay down the foundation of what would become their groundbreaking innovation in scratch DJing, one dependent on a *collective* dynamic rather than just individual skill.[10]

Tandem mixing, with two DJs and four turntables, had already been a part of the mobile scene, especially for major showcase battles, but FM2O's innovation was in giving each DJ a specialized, sonic role within the larger ensemble. For example, one DJ would act as the rhythm section, scratching a percussive beat. Another DJ would add in melodic elements, scratching up a horn line for example. The last DJ could find some vocals to play with, adding in another sonic layer, and the three would coordinate their routines with one another. In essence, FM2O discovered how to organize DJs into a band.

This kind of coordinated group effort was virtually unknown in the rest of the scratch DJ world, but that would change dramatically by 1992, when the three, now called the Rocksteady DJs, took the U.S. and then world DMC titles.[11] Two things stand out here. First of all, prior to this, the DMC championships had been overwhelmingly dominated by African American DJs from the East Coast as well as British and German DJs. Bay Area—let alone Filipino American—DJs had almost no presence in these competitions until Q-Bert won the U.S. national championship in 1991.

Remember: much of this was happening in a relative mass media vacuum. As I have stressed throughout, the Bay Area mobile—and early scratch—DJ scenes came together through direct peer-to-peer interactions. DJs like Apollo and Q-Bert may have been turned on to scratching via "Rockit" or other televised hip-hop performances, but their *collaboration* was primarily made possible because of the mobile crew networks. And because their innovations had no easy path to mass self-distribution (i.e., nothing remotely similar to YouTube, Facebook, or Twitter), this media isolation also gave them the opportunity to develop their techniques without "outsiders" either influencing their styles or appropriating them. While this isolation angle is tangential to my work here, it may be useful for other researchers to delve into further.[12]

However, while the mobile DJs never made a successful jump into mass media (a point I will discuss shortly), the scratch DJs were far more adept at wielding these media-based tools of marketing and distribution. The Invisibl Skratch Piklz, in particular, were at the forefront of what marketers today would call "managing their brand." According to Travis Rimando (aka DJ Pone), the Invisibl Skratch Piklz's international success initiated a "paradigmatic change in scratch/battle DJ values" and helped cement their reputation as the world's best-known and most respected scratch crew.[13] Pone explained that while the Piklz's technical innovations, that is, creating new kinds of scratches and DJ routines, are part of their legacy, one of their less obvious contributions was revolutionizing the way scratch DJs marketed themselves and the community at large. Pone recalled meeting Q-Bert for the first time in 1993:

> One of my striking memories of [Q-Bert] was of his constant promotion of himself and his endeavors. We went to a local DJ battle, and when he got on the mic, he was promoting his new battle record, the recently released "Battle Breaks."[14] We later went to Kevvy Kev's show at KZSU . . . and again, after scratching live, he got on the mic and gave his same spiel on "Battle Breaks." His proactive and aggressive approach to marketing, unlike that of many other scratch/battle DJs, is yet another distinguishing point about him [countering] the stereotypical image of a scratch/battle DJ [as] an antisocial recluse who prefers to be locked up in a bedroom, practicing.

In other words, Q-Bert and this emergent community of scratch DJs helped transform the image of turntablists from introverted "bedroom DJs" into public figures who began to appear in television commercials, music videos, and motion pictures.[15] DJ Shadow (Josh Davis) also credited the Invisibl Skratch Piklz with dissolving the shroud of secrecy around scratch techniques. In Doug Pray's documentary *Scratch*, Shadow explains: "The Piklz were the first to take the secrecy out of DJing because a lot of hip-hop DJing was about . . . not revealing your tricks. I think the Piklz were the first people to just be like, 'Hey, here's exactly how to do what we do. We want you to go out and do it better so we can learn from you.' I think that was such a giant step forward" (Pray 2002).

Shadow lauded the group for making it easier for DJs to learn scratch techniques and contribute to the expansion of the turntablist community. As in the mobile scene, the early scratch DJs mostly learned from

5.2 / FM20 (Furious Minds 2 Observe) performing at the Eco-Rap show in San Francisco, c.1990–1991. Left to right: Richard "Q-Bert" Quitevis, "Mixmaster Mike" Schwartz, "DJ Apollo" Novicio. These three DJs met when all three were in mobile crews (Live Style, Hi Tech, and Unlimited Sounds, respectively) before forming their own, seminal scratch DJ crew, which went by several names—FM20, Shadow DJs, and Rocksteady DJs—before they settled on the Invisibl Skratch Piklz. Photo courtesy of Apollo Novicio.

one another—both communities originated within specific local spaces where peer-to-peer training and observation were key. However, by the mid- to late 1990s, through videos, websites, and other resources, the Invisibl Skratch Piklz and others created a body of knowledge that other DJs, regardless of their locations, could access. Within a few years, competitive scratch DJs began to emerge in new cities, states, and countries where DJing had rarely found a major foothold previously.[16] As a result, the various streams of turntablist-oriented media content created a shared knowledge base that was bolstered by events and competitions that helped gather like-minded participants from around the world. Just as mobile showcases created opportunities for pilgrimages for most of the 1980s, the scratch scene had its own events that encouraged travel, contact, and collaboration in ways that began to build a global community of scratch DJs. The mobile DJ scene, successful as it was in its own right, never came close to having that same kind of reach.

Things Fall Apart / The Unraveling of the Mobile Scene

Turntablism created an incredibly tight yet vast community of like-minded adherents internationally, especially by the end of the 1990s. Moreover, turntablists also tended to organize themselves into crews, thus continuing and borrowing the crew structure—and its homosocial and communal identity attractions—from the mobiles. At the same time, while turntablism encouraged a communal bond between fellow participants, their relationship to the audience was significantly different from that of their mobile counterparts.

Case in point: how DJs were meant to interact with audiences became a central point of tension within the Invisibl Skratch Piklz. According to DJ Apollo, he and Q-Bert disagreed over the crew's purpose—Apollo wanted the group to retain parts of their mobile crew heritage by continuing to mix at clubs and parties, but Q-Bert saw the future of the group as that of a virtuosic, artistic musical group. Apollo recollected: "[Q-Bert] was really against us [saying] 'Well, all you guys are, are club DJs.' And we were like 'Nah, it's incorporating everything.... We don't wanna just be the hard core elite, we want to do [mix at parties] too.' ... He never saw it that way."[17] This conflict in opinion represented more than just a difference in personal views; it also reflected a fundamental shift within the DJ community during the first half of the 1990s.

Scratching was quickly evolving into a practice distinct from other hip-hop scenes, to say nothing of a wider pop music landscape. Mobile crews had often plugged into larger cultural worlds, overlapping with dance crews, family parties, school events, live music, record labels, and radio stations. In contrast, though scratching was undoubtedly becoming a more visible part of the larger pop mainstream—found in advertising, television, cinema, and so on—the scratching community was becoming more insular as its participant base grew.[18] In Bill Brewster and Frank Broughton's *Last Night a DJ Saved My Life*, they compare turntablists with a "cryptic cult" and argue that the impact of scratch DJing was to distill "the essential elements of hip hop DJing ... until it became an art form almost completely detached from its original dance floor function.... At times, though, these scratch DJs seemed in danger of becoming obsessed hobbyists, competing against each other in increasingly esoteric competitions" (1999: 257). Brewster and Broughton overstate their concerns to some extent—the scene may have been insular, but turntablists were far from monastically self-isolating; scratch DJing advanced a sprawling, global industry, complete with its own recordings, record labels, and schools.[19] However, they are accurate in noting that much of turntablism moved away from DJ traditions inherently connected to dance floor culture. If mobile crews shared a symbiotic relationship with their audiences, turntablists often fell closer to the conventional idea of art or musical performance, where there were clearer separations between performer and audience. As I noted earlier, that disconnection from the dance floor was perhaps the fundamental difference between scratch and mobile DJs—it was not just a stylistic difference but rather spoke to the raison d'être of each expressive form. It is little wonder that older mobile crews dismissed scratching, while emergent scratch DJ crews had less interest in spinning for parties.

This difference in purpose created a fundamental—if less obvious—organizational change: compared to mobile DJs, scratch DJs can travel light. Clients do not book turntablists for their sound system, let alone lighting rigs (the latter serve little purpose in a scratch performance). Moreover, promoters usually booked scratch DJs into bars or nightclubs where sound systems came preinstalled. The most a turntablist might need to bring would be a pair of turntables, a mixer, and a handful of records to scratch with (if even that). Such a rig can be easily handled by a single person; support crews need not apply.

Moreover, a single scratch DJ's performance is usually measured in minutes, not hours. Therefore, there is no need to bring crates of heavy records; a single bag of records is sufficient. Freed from these kinds of logistical burdens, the scratch crews that formed were made up largely of members who were all DJs rather than the conventional mobile structure, which had one or two DJs supported by everyone else.

This last point is crucial. Scratch crews allowed each member to pursue his or her own expressive potential, and by doing so, intensified the focus on the individual. Part of this was based on logistics: the traditional mobile battle pitted crew against crew, but scratch battles tended to be more between individuals. Jazzy Jim observed, "If you look at the kids that were [DJing], we wanted attention. The kids who started the mobile DJs, we really wanted to be good but also basically wanted attention, we wanted to be a star. With the scratching, I think people saw the opportunity to be a bigger star."

This rise in the popularity of scratch DJing lured many younger DJs out of the mobile crews. Shortkut, who began his DJing career as part of the Just 2 Hype mobile crew, recalled that transition: "I wasn't there anymore to do gigs with [Just 2 Hype]. I didn't expect to focus on [scratching] but I got so deep into it, especially going to New York for the first time, by myself. I saw the bigger picture outside of just the mobile scene." By the early 1990s, more and more DJs were following in Shortkut's footsteps, especially with the rising national prominence of scratch crews such as the Invisibl Skratch Piklz, Bullet Proof Scratch Hamsters, Beat Junkies, and others.

Plotted on a timeline, the decline of the mobile DJ scene certainly coincides with the rise of turntablism, but rather than seeing the relationship between the two through some kind of zero-sum equation, it is more useful to consider how scratch DJing was one of several forces chipping away at both the membership and logical necessity of mobile crews. Moreover, those forces were not always external to the mobiles; some of the most detrimental factors arose because of the successes of the mobile scene itself.

Recall that part of the popularity of the mobile crews rested on the way they catered to their peers, creating venues for music and dancing at a time when Filipino youth audiences were not being actively courted by more mainstream clubs. Likewise, radio stations employed major club DJs like Cameron Paul but were not initially tuned into the mobile scene. However, by the end of the 1980s, the prominence of the showcases and general popularity of the mobiles prompted a reevaluation on the part of club and radio industry gatekeepers. The savvier ones began hiring and booking DJs from out of the mobile crews as a way to tap into their fan bases.

For example, radio stations like San Francisco's KMEL and KSOL/KYLD began to hire DJs from the mobile crews to host shows or mix on air.[20] That included Jazzy Jim from Skyway Sounds (KYLD), Ultimate Creations' Genie G (KYLD), and Glen Aure from Boys of Superior Style (KMEL). Perhaps the best known of this cadre is Rick Lee of Styles Beyond Compare, who has been a DJ at KMEL since the 1990s and whose radio IDs always mention his crew affiliation.

This change in opportunity was bittersweet for some. Throughout the 1980s, some of my respondents felt as if they had been passed over because of race. "You had to be white to move into the big radio stations," suggested Kim Kantares. While he was a longtime DJ for the smaller AM station KPOO throughout the 1980s, Kantares tried to get DJ work through KDIA and KSOL—both larger commercial stations that, like KPOO, programmed soul music. Despite his extensive background in radio, however, Kantares found himself shut out of both stations: "Even KDIA, KSOL, they laughed at us. Especially me, man, trying to get on KSOL. They were like, 'It won't work,' and then two months later, 'DJ White Guy,' Cameron Paul, is in the mix, and he's playing hip-hop." Kantares would eventually break through that glass ceiling; by the beginning of the 1990s, Kantares had gone to work at KSOL's rival, KMEL. However, Kantares and other DJs felt that as Filipino Americans, their racial difference contributed to their marginalization from mainstream media companies in the 1980s. Yet, while that marginalization partially fueled the drive toward creating the mobile scene as something that Filipino Americans could lay claim to, as the scene's growth garnered mainstream attention, it also meant that the institutions that had previously shunned those DJs would now play a role in undermining the scene, however unintentionally.

Nowhere was this better illuminated than in the nightclubs. If mobile crews originally came into prominence because they could replicate the discotheque experience "at home," the nightclubs eventually realized the inverse was true too: by hiring DJs from the mobile crews, they could tap into the larger crowds that followed those personalities. By the early 1990s, club promoters began to cherry-pick talent from the different mobile crews. Spintronix's Jay dela Cruz recalled, "The DJs and DJ Crews that played for little or no money wanted to finally get paid! That's why there was a surge to start up party promotion groups, most of them [by former DJs]. With several promotion groups going after the same target market, your competitive edge was hosting a party at a club—it added so much credibility to your party. And, the club and bar owners were hip to this money . . . they opened their doors to these folks." The expansion of the mobile scene into the clubs was long overdue and, on first glance, should have represented a second life for the mobile DJs. However, one unintended consequence of this shift toward hosting parties in clubs and bars was an adverse effect on the crews instead. Kong stated this problem clearly: "Before, people rented halls like the Irish Center. The Irish Center has nothing but some big rooms, so then you have to get guys like Jay [dela Cruz] to bring [Spintronix] to supply the sound system, the lighting, and of course, the DJs. Now promoters, they just rent a club that already has the sound, the lighting, and things like that." As with the scratch DJs, the increase in mix DJs working in nightclubs effectively eliminated the mobile crew's logistical function in moving and installing equipment. Dela Cruz cited this trend in explaining the decline in mobile activity, giving one example with a popular promoter named Chuckles: "He'd have five DJs from five crews spin in a club and the equipment would already be there. There was no need for a mobile DJ to come and set up their stuff." *Tales of the Turntable* curator Melanie Caganot added: "I think it became a matter of convenience because now you could get paid two or three hundred dollars for playing a couple of hours by just bringing your records. You didn't have to lift these huge plates or rent a van or break your back, bring all this truss. The club already had it." Caganot drew attention to another advantage to doing club work: economic incentives. Before, money earned at a gig was usually split between the members of the crew. Nightclub and radio money did not have to be shared, however, thus improving a DJ's earning potential. As a result, throughout the early 1990s, the appeal of big, expensive, troublesome hall parties waned in favor of the relative simplicity—but lucrativeness—of club and radio work.[21]

In summation, by the early 1990s, DJs could command more attention, prestige, and money by themselves than with a crew. Moreover, as DJs found themselves in the situation where they could now get gigs on the strength of their personal reputations, the power of the crew's name waned. Crews might still have offered DJs a sense of local community, but the money and status offered by gigging solo were also strong. Says Pardorla, "I think it's a lot about individualism. With a DJ group, the most famous guy is always going to be the guy behind the turntable and then it takes six other guys to support him—carry the equipment, hook everything up, do the lighting. You're part of a group as opposed to being an individual." This is one of the reasons why, for example, Ultimate Creations ultimately disbanded. Despite the success and reputation of the crew, Gil Olimpiada says that as Gary "Genie G" Millare gained more solo work in the late 1980s, it created tensions with the crew: "[It] started fading '87, '88, '89. Just people going different ways and stuff. People getting different jobs. Gary, when he was hot at the time, people offered him to start DJing clubs and different events. My brother Jose didn't like it, because the way our group was formed, we were like a small family. [His philosophy was] 'We play as one, you don't branch out and try something else.' I was really supportive of Gary. [I would tell him] 'Go for it, it's all you. But if you can get us some gigs, go for it.'" Similarly, Derrick "D" Damian recalled that when he broke away from his Daly City mobile crew, Just 2 Hype, in 1994, "I told [crew partner] Larry [Cordova], 'I'm going to go solo. If you see my name on a flyer and it doesn't say Just 2 Hype, it's not because I'm disrespecting you guys, it's more [that] I'm doing my own thing. You guys are my first and only crew and I'll keep you guys close to heart, but I got to do my own because I can't do weddings. All the guys are old now and it's like, I can't be lugging equipment, doing all these gigs by myself.' He understood and he gave [his] blessing." It is telling that Damian assumed that his crew colleagues would have expected him to include Just 2 Hype on his individual flyers—even working solo, DJs were still expected to include their crews as part of their identity. Therefore, when Damian spoke of gaining Cordova's "blessing," what he meant was that Cordova was effectively permitting Damian to forge a new identity for himself, disconnected from his roots with the crew. These breaks with convention were not just relevant to the crew's business model—since they were not being included in Damian's marketing: symbolically, they also represented a "letting go" of the once omnipresent communal crew identity so central in the mobile scene. DJs were, in a sense, outgrowing the crews, and as they left, the crews found their membership steadily whittling away.

This was part of a larger pattern of internal challenges facing many crews. By the early 1990s, the mobile scene was ten years old, and though crew members might have been as young as thirteen when they started, their aging into adulthood often meant that other commitments would force their attention away from DJing: college, military, work, or family. This is precisely what happened to Sound Explosion. Says cofounder Rafael Restauro, "We weren't doing as many gigs by then. We were getting older, we had all gotten out of high school, you know. Everybody was getting into the working field."

It was not just the DJs who were getting older, seeking new opportunities; the audience was aging as well. "Hall parties were thought to be 'played out' or for teeny boppers (at least in my circles)," dela Cruz suggested. "As my generation got older, the next step was naturally the club, bar scene. During this time, we were in our twenties . . . ready for the club legally." After years of sneaking into clubs, DJs and their fans were now old enough to get into these venues without subterfuge, a rite of passage of sorts. Hall parties became seen as more of a teenage activity, creating another generational split within the DJ audience.

Moreover, the traditional hall parties were in trouble on their own. The end of the eighties brought with it an upsurge in violence at hall parties. Said Jazzy Jim, "As this mobile DJ [era] was dying down, it was the era when the young kids and the gangs started getting back into it, and that caused the trouble at the gigs." Expression's John Francisco concurred: "You were catering to these younger crowds, problems came with them as well, so that's when the police came in. It became harder and harder to actually get venues." As Francisco suggested, this escalation in violence and police involvement made owners of previously DJ-friendly venues more wary of allowing parties to be thrown in their spaces. This was another compelling force that pushed the parties from the halls into clubs. Sound Sequence's Burt Kong observed, "I think the police, they crack down a lot harder on private parties . . . whereas it's so easy to rent a club." Clubs and bars usually provided their own security, thus assuming both the cost and liability from the DJs, yet another way in which club work became a more attractive option for individual DJs.

Meanwhile, back within the crews themselves, recruitment for younger members seemed like a lesser priority, even as older members were "aging out." In most crews, no matter how big they grew, the founding staff still constituted the key leadership. While this may have provided stable guidance and a core identity over the years, as those individuals became older and more involved with other commitments and interests, it meant that there was little or no future leadership to hand the crew's management off to. Only in rare instances did you see some kind of "passing of the guard"—for example, Orlando Madrid took over leadership of Non-Stop Boogie after all the original founders had left. In most cases, though, crews slowly atrophied, member by member. Midstar's Ray Viray shares what is a typical anecdote about how crews ended: "It was slowly. The group didn't talk and split up. There was no verbal, 'It's over.' It just faded away and stopped."

Outside of the DJing world, the early 1990s also saw other cultural activities competing for attention from Filipino American youth, none perhaps more powerful than the emergent import car racing and customization scene. Based initially in Southern California and fueled by the (relative) affordability of compact Japanese auto models such as the Honda Civic, Acura Integra, and Toyota Supra, the import car scene had made its way up to the Bay Area by the early 1990s (Namkung 2004: 162). This scene also organized itself around crews, investing time and expense into tweaking both the mechanical and aesthetic attributes of import cars and competing with one another in both illegal street races and organized racetrack events.

There are no hard numbers to quantify how many Filipino American youth became involved in the import car scene, but among my respondents, the competition for attention between the scenes weighed quite heavily on their minds. Both older and younger DJs saw the import car scene as siphoning off youth who might otherwise have gotten into DJing instead. Said dela Cruz, "Instead of buying records, turntables, and equipment, they're buying mufflers, stickers, and cars." DJ Pone joked, "About 95 percent of the mobile crews that I was aware of in my generation—as soon as they got their Honda, it was over," suggesting that potential DJs fled the scene to get involved in the import car community instead.

As with scratch DJing, the rising popularity of the import car scene may have been related to how it elevated individual status *alongside* promoting a collective identity. Racers were still organized into crews, but within them each member could express himself or herself creatively (so long as you had a car). Pardorla observed, "At least with the import car scene, if you have six of your friends and each and every one of them could have a single car that looks totally different from the next one, you could have your own fifteen minutes of fame." In this way, the car crews retained the supportive camaraderie that comes with being in a collective yet still gave individuals the opportunity to attain social status on their own.

Adding to this, whereas DJing is more about the transformation of *permitted* private spaces (family homes, school gyms, social and church halls) car culture leans more toward the claiming of public space in the most visual of ways—driving down the street or parked in a lot—regardless of having permission to do so or not. If anything, the contested nature of cruising and street racing, both of which have led to any number of municipal laws designed to curtail or outright ban the practices, introduces a level of volatility and danger—and thus excitement—into car cultures (import or otherwise) that has no real parallel in DJing (mobile or otherwise).[22] Along these lines, similar to the way the DJing community allowed young men to experience and express particular forms of masculinity, car customization and racing also have a long history with myriad forms of gender performance in the United States, especially in symbolizing a kind of mechanized form of masculinity that connotes power, danger, sexuality, and of course literal and figurative mobility (see Best 2006, chapter 3). Both scenes offered a similar allure, but car racing and customization could offer a different, and perhaps more dramatic, experience of public realm performance.

Import car customization and racing carried a high price for entry—purchasing and modifying a car required a massive capital outlay—but that also meant the car crews were more likely to compete for members from the same middle-class communities from which the mobile crews emerged.[23] Both activities necessitated disposable family incomes, not to mention those aforementioned requisite two-car garages that came with suburban houses. (Just to reiterate this: over the course of the 1980s and 1990s, perhaps no single cultural space was more important to Filipino American youth culture than the garage.)

The history and legacy of the import car scene within Filipino (or Asian) America is far too broad a topic to adequately address here; suffice it to say, that scene deserves its own studies.[24] For now my point is that as a dominant cultural activity for the generation of Filipino American youth in the 1990s and beyond, the racing scene was another important force that drew the interest of teens who might otherwise have gone into mobile DJing.

So far, I have discussed forces both internal and external to the mobile crews that point to a weakening of communal ties that helped to slowly unravel the mobile scene. However, behind the question of "what happened to the mobile crews?" lies another: "What *did not* happen to the mobile crews?" More specifically, "What did not happen that *could have* extended or expanded the scene's lifespan or popularity?" The history of popular music in the United States is rich with examples of regional DJ and party scenes that eventually transcended their local roots and attained national, if not global, stature: hip-hop out of the South Bronx, the Chicago house scene, techno music out of Detroit, et alia. How did these other DJ-led scenes "make the leap" in ways that the Filipino American mobile DJ scene did not?

In Jennifer Lena's *Banding Together*, she argues that most U.S. pop musics fall into one or more "genre forms" during the course of their growth: avant-garde, scene-based, industry-based, traditionalist (2012: 28–52).[25] For example, for a major musical style such as hip-hop, the trajectory begins with a small, local, and largely unknown style (avant-garde), then it grows more vibrant and popular yet still remaining "underground" (scene-based), then it draws the attention of corporate record labels looking to profit from and exploit the growing popularity of the genre (industry-based). In some cases, such as hip-hop, the industry phase ignites a backlash that leads to a revival of a form considered traditionalist, in an attempt to "restore" the genre to an earlier, preindustry state.[26]

The mobile DJ crews had the most in common with the "scene-based" form: an "intensely active, but moderately sized group of artists, audience members, and supporting organizations" that help codify conventions of performance and appearance while also pursuing "stylistic innovations" via "charismatic leaders" (Lena 2012: 33–34). However, the mobile scene departed from the trajectory of other music scenes in one key way, and perhaps this made all the difference.

Part of what helps define a scene is the creation and proliferation of different kinds of genre-based *media*: from fanzines to independent record labels to—in modern times—genre-inspired websites and social media collectives. This is precisely what was missing in the mobile DJ scene. They generated personal media: business cards, flyers and posters, performance recordings passed hand to hand, photographs shared with crew members. But the mobile scene lacked a *mass* media component: no newsletters or fanzines, no coverage by local or ethnic press, and most ironically for a DJ-based scene, very few self-produced records.

Consider for a moment: how do we know about most music genres to begin with? While it is certainly possible to experience new genres via live performance, we normally hear a new music style via some kind of mass mediated form: a song on the radio, a video on television or the Internet, a recording played at a friend's house. The history of American pop music in the twentieth century is inseparable from the history of the recording industry: the ability to record, manufacture, and distribute music is what helps constitute the "popular" part of "pop music." That is not to discount genres that have a strong live performance component, be it Dallas polka festivals, Los Angeles warehouse raves, New Orleans second line brass bands, or Washington DC go-go. Yet all these genres, however niche, still have some kind of recording component that allows these musics to travel, to reach potential fans outside the immediate geographic range of the genres' home bases, and that at the very least announces the existence of these musical communities to a wider public (not to mention record labels).

Recordings are also key sources of both economic capital and social status, helping to bring in new participants and extend the life span of a scene. New York's hip-hop scene of the late 1970s shared some key similarities with the Bay Area mobile scene of the early 1990s. For one, hip-hop also began as a predominantly DJ-led party scene, first arising in the Bronx borough of New York City in the early to mid-1970s. What started with park and basement parties, centered on Jamaican-inspired mobile sound systems, eventually transitioned into uptown nightclubs and discotheques by the late 1970s. What is often overlooked in the standard narrative of hip-hop's rise is that the genre came close to dissolving by the end of the 1970s. The similarities here to the mobile scene are striking: as early hip-hop DJs began to move away from mobile sound systems and toward more lucrative nightclub gigs, the scene suffered (Fricke and Ahearn 2002: 181).[27] As cultural historian Jeff Chang chronicles it, there was a moment around 1979 when "hip-hop was a fad that was passing. 'I called it the Great Hip-Hop Drought,' says [DJ] Jazzy Jay. 'Everybody started fleeing away from hip-hop'" (2005: 128).

What altered hip-hop's decline was a recording: "Rapper's Delight," by the Sugarhill Gang, the first major rap music hit and a catalyst in moving hip-hop from a local, street culture to a global phenomenon. Obviously, the transition from a party scene to a recorded medium is a profound transformation; as the idiom goes, some things get lost in translation.[28] The act of recording is an act of commodification, literally and figuratively packaging what used to be a musical experience that could only be enjoyed "live" and now making it replicable and consumable in a mass market (and thus, more exploitable). However, the introduction of a recording element also infuses DJ-led scenes with the necessary economic and social capital to extend their life spans and expand their communities.

Veterans of the mobile crews *did* eventually produce recordings by the waning days of the scene.[29] Most prominently, by 1993–1994, Images Inc.'s Francisco Pardorla helped found Velocity Records, which produced recordings for the Filipino American singer Buffy, while Spintronix's Kormann Roque helped establish Classified Records, best known for its own Pinay diva, Jocelyn Enriquez.[30] Both Enriquez and Buffy released songs in the freestyle dance tradition, one of the key styles associated with the mobile scene. Both experienced modest success, especially Enriquez, who eventually was signed by Tommy Boy, one of the leading dance and hip-hop labels of the 1980s.[31] However, these developments came "too little, too late" for the mobile scene. There was no significant attempt to create more or other labels, nor was there interest on the part of other, bigger labels to tap into the talent and energy of the mobile scene. While the scene's overall lack of a recording component was simply one of many factors contributing to its decline, it is easy to imagine that a more robust shift into record production—whether independently run or via industry investment—would have had a major impact on the scene's overall life span.

Jennifer Lena describes "mechanisms of inertia" that "inhibit, derail, or otherwise modify a musical style's transitions." Those include "1) the absorption of artists into other styles . . . 2) various forms of resistance to expansion, including both planned obsolescence of some styles and the incompatibility of a style's genre ideal with the promotional machinery of the U.S. record industry and 3) racist exclusion" (2012: 86). One could argue, for example, that in the mobile scene, younger DJs ended up being "absorbed" into other styles, whether that meant scratch DJ crews or club and radio gigs, both of which were detrimental to the crew structure.

However, the mobile scene's failure to move into a recording phase was not just an issue of losing members to competing scenes; it also came about because so many participants began and ended their mobile careers while still in their teens, lacking sufficient training in either the technical side of record recording and production or the business side of pressing and distribution. Perhaps more important, though, they also lacked older community members who possessed such experience. It is telling that Roque had no role models or mentors to lead him through the challenges of running Classified. He wrote in an email: "We read books like *This Business of Music* and *How to Start an Independent Record Label*. None of us had any prior experience in working at a record label or *having access to being able to shadow other record labels*. We just went with the flow and learned along the way" (emphasis mine).[32]

Importantly, Roque noted that beyond simply lacking experience in working at a label, he and his friends were not aware of local labels where they could "shadow" personnel to help learn those skills; they had to rely on mass market books and guides instead. This highlights the fact that the Bay Area, unlike Los Angeles and New York, has never been a major center of the American recording industry, let alone for recordings catering to Filipino Americans. As Roque also noted, "we didn't even know any Filipino-run labels at the time. . . . Personally, I was inspired by Russell Simmons and Rick Rubin and the whole Def Jam story," referring to the origins of the famed hip-hop label in a New York University dorm room (see Adler and Charnas 2011).

Filipino American rock and jazz artist Eleanor Academia discusses these kinds of limitations in describing the challenges facing her own career. She told interviewer Theo Gonzalvez:

> The Filipino American community is still at an emerging level from knowing how to pull all this together to help launch a solo artist's career successfully in a major way. You are left on your own to find your way. You live both in the wilderness and the jungle. You are in the wilderness because there are no peers from whom you can get professional

> support at the same level; and you are in the jungle faced with a lot of people who recognize your talent, but don't have a structure to systematically get the word out about you properly. (Gonzalvez 2007: 62)

Though Academia was talking about her own difficulties launching a solo career in the mid- to late 1980s, her observations just as easily apply to the challenges facing the mobile crews in trying to build on their local popularity so as to attain a larger stage.[33]

Compounding this issue was that even among the few local dance labels that might have embraced mobile DJs as remixers or producers—as happened in other DJ-centric scenes—there seemed to be little to no awareness of the thriving mobile scene taking place beneath their proverbial noses. As noted earlier in this chapter, it took radio stations and club owners the better part of a decade to catch wind of the scene, but it seems that the local labels never did. For example, I was able to speak with John Hedges, one of the key people behind the popular San Francisco dance music label Megatone. Their records were a major part of the Bay Area club scene in the 1980s, and as Hedges told me via an email conversation, "we mostly promoted to major club jocks around the country," meaning that Megatone had a close relationship to DJs working in nightclubs. However, when I asked if he—someone living in the Bay Area and professionally connected to its DJ community—was aware of the Filipino mobile scene, he replied: "Sorry to say, no." Admittedly, this is just one instance, but I think it is telling that even though mobile DJs were almost certainly playing records by Megatone artists such as Sylvester, those DJs did not enter into the awareness of the label itself.[34]

However, it was not only record labels who had little awareness of the scene. If scene-based genres generally help create or inspire a cadre of supportive media producers (writers, critics, documentarians, etc.), this never significantly materialized with the mobiles, either inside or outside that community. The overall invisibility of the scene to Bay Area news media was especially striking. For example, I approached several journalists who were actively writing on music and entertainment during the 1980s, and like Megatone's Hedges, they had little to no awareness of the mobile scene. Joel Selvin was the longtime music critic for the *San Francisco Chronicle* (the main paper of record in the Bay) throughout the entire 1980s and 1990s, and he told me in an email: "That whole Filipino thing took place outside anyone's notice. . . . I was only the vaguest bit aware of it."

I also spoke to Emil Guillermo, another longtime Bay Area journalist, who was the entertainment reporter for the local NBC affiliate, KRON, from 1984 to 1988. Guillermo never reported on the scene either, though he did at least know about it via his distant cousin, Peter Sugitan, one of the founders of Oakland–Alameda's Ladda Sounds. As Guillermo put it, "you had to be part of the [Filipino] community [to know about the scene]. I'm able to tell you about this because it was part of a grassroots scene and the grassroots included my relatives." However, Guillermo never reported on it himself, nor did he recall any other member of the press doing so. A similar vacuum existed within the budding community of Filipino American–centric filmmakers and documentarians. While many focused on the older, *manong* generation of Filipino immigrants, little was done to document the cultural lives of Filipino American youth of that same 1980s era.[35]

While I do not think these factors rise to the level of what Lena describes as "racist exclusion," this kind of media invisibility seems like a subset of the larger social marginalization faced by Filipinos across major U.S. institutions: economic, political, cultural, and otherwise. In the end, as talented and capable as they were, mobile crews existed within a largely self-contained bubble, hidden from the "outside" world. Though the scene was able to enjoy tremendous success, over the long haul it meant that as crews slowly withered away, there were few opportunities for external forces to pump in new lifeblood via added capital or new personnel.

Contrast this with DJ Pone's observations of how well scratch DJs managed their media profiles and marketed their own records. Bay Area turntablists like the Invisibl Skratch Piklz and Bullet Proof Scratch Hamsters (later renamed Space Travelers) began to release their own "battle records" as early 1992–1993.[36] Within a few years after that, a spate of scratch-based albums, as well as instructional and performance videos, began to become readily available.[37] And, technologically speaking, the scratch DJs had the good fortune to see their scene begin to peak just as the Internet was transforming the dissemination of audio and video across the world.[38]

In summation, over the early 1990s, the mobile crews became challenged by both internal and external mechanisms of inertia that (1) gradually weakened their purpose and appeal, (2) drew off younger members to competing cultural activities, and (3) left many crews incapable of (or uninterested in) replacing those members who were aging out. Finally, whether a consequence of insufficient media skills within the scene or an invisibility to those outside it, the scene never evolved the kind of recording component that often gave other DJ-led scenes new life. The mobile DJ crews had a remarkable, ten-plus year run in the Bay Area, but despite how well it thrived in that time, its momentum waned, and by the mid-1990s the scene was a faint shadow of its former self, with many of the major crews gone and few new ones coming in to replace them.

Of course, mobile DJing never vanished entirely. Some of the biggest crews, including Ladda Sounds, Spintronix, and Styles Beyond Compare, continue to pursue lucrative mobile work around the Bay Area. Other former mobile DJs who kept their equipment, such as Orlando Madrid from Non-Stop Boogie, still hire themselves or their equipment out for gigs even if they no longer have an organized crew supporting them. Unlimited Sounds' Anthony Carrion, as another example, started a savvy business operating photography studios that cater to events, such as weddings, by offering packages that include photo, video, *and* DJ services.

However, while mobile DJing survived, the cultural scene organized around mobile DJ crews did not. There are no longer large-scale battles or showcases that highlight and promote the scene. Independent party promoters or venues, not DJ crews, run the major parties in the Bay. Most important, the very "crew" concept has become an anachronism. DJs still organize themselves into affiliations at times, especially in conjunction with a promotions company, but the phenomenon of mobile crew as surrogate family and fraternity no longer exists in any widespread fashion among the Bay Area's DJs.

Yet traces linger. Apart from the fact that mobile DJ services still proliferate throughout the Bay Area, an increasing number of DJs are returning to the dance floor culture that the mobile crews once cultivated. While this does not represent anywhere near a wholesale return to the dominance of the mobile crews, it does suggest that some of that era's influences continue to thrive, especially among former mobile DJs themselves.

Conclusion / Echo Effects

C.1 / Flyer for the 2006 "Tribute 2 Bay Area Mobile DJs" party in San Francisco, hosted by Dave "Dynamix" Refuerzo and Jon "Shortkut" Cruz. Beginning in the mid-2000s, veterans of the mobile scene began mounting "throwback" parties in honor of the mobile era. This party featured members from several different mobile crews across the Bay Area, vintage lighting rigs, and a fog machine. Courtesy of Dave Refuerzo.

In April 2003, the Triple Threat DJs, made up of Apollo, Shortkut, and Vinroc (Vincent Punsalan), reenacted a classic mobile-era hall party at San Francisco's DNA Lounge. They wanted to capture the old atmosphere of those parties, needing—in Shortkut's words—"fog machine, helicopter lights, all that" (Reines 2003). However, lacking much of that equipment themselves, Triple Threat took a page from the old alliances of the showcase era and reached out to none other than Orlando Madrid, the former Sounds of Success leader, borrowing from his cache of lighting, truss, and equipment to properly set up their staging.

All three Triple Threat members are renowned for their turntablist exploits. Apollo—along with Q-Bert and Mixmaster Mike—was part of the original world champion, Rocksteady DJs in 1992. Shortkut was one of the core members of the Invisibl Skratch Piklz. Vinroc was a two-time individual world champion in turntablism before moving from New Jersey to the Bay Area to help form Triple Threat.[1] However, all three got their start doing mobile DJ work in the 1980s, and in a curious "full circle," their restaged hall party was a reaction against what they saw as the doldrums of DJing in the early 2000s. Shortkut explained, "We're just tired of the scene. . . . It's the same DJs, same music. [We wanted to bring back] that feeling to go to a hall party back then, and once you walk in, you see this crazy ass setup, it's on some rock shit. We just felt, damn, that's missing and it was something that brought the kids together back then too. I'm sure the new kids probably won't understand what the hell is going on, but it's definitely a twist."

Formed in 1999, Triple Threat are not a mobile crew in any traditional sense. The trio do not travel with their own equipment (most of the time they do not even travel with records).[2] Their performance circuit is usually nightclubs or large-scale music events, not church parties and school dances. However, each member's history in the mobile scene intimately influences his DJing craft. Triple Threat are, first and foremost, made up of dance floor DJs, spinning a mix of hip-hop, reggae, house, and R&B in clubs around the world. In contrast to turntablism's performance art approach, separating audience from artist, Triple Threat aspire to connect with their audience in the classic "DJ as orchestrator of collective effervescence" mode that I mentioned in the introduction. With their combined experience, Triple Threat are expert in knowing how to build a floor. Apollo noted the relevance of his mobile background in prioritizing that connection with the audience: "Before we were turntablists, we used to be mobile DJs. . . . People forget about that style. New kids that are just picking up on [DJing] nowadays, they just go straight into the battle stuff and the trick stuff. Which is cool, you know—to each his own. But we feel like you shouldn't forget the basic fundamentals of DJing either. Because you miss out on an important part of it if you don't go through that step" (Reines 2003). His identification of mixing as a "fundamental" DJing skill reinforces the aesthetic values of the mobile era. It was nonstop disco mixing that inspired most of the mobile era's DJs to even pick up the craft to begin with, lured in by the potential to affect audience mood and energy. Apollo implicitly critiques one of the outcomes of the turntablist era when he says that new DJs "just go straight into the battle stuff and the trick stuff," suggesting that those DJs treat mixing as unimportant and therefore never acquire that skill.[3] In contrast to the attitude that scratching requires a higher level of artistic ability than mixing, Apollo said, "Making the crowd move and making the people move on the dance floor is as much as an art form as turntablism. Scratching is a little bit more technical, but everything else is an art form as well, whether you're playing breaks or playing a club."[4]

Triple Threat are one of several prominent hybrid crews that bring together the aesthetics and skill sets of both the mobile and turntablist communities.[5] As DJs who have been important players in both eras,

Apollo, Shortkut, and Vinroc have the experience and perspective to advance their own vision of what DJing practice should embody. Though all three boast exceptional turntablist skills, they are equally, if not more, concerned with their ability to connect to their audience on a visceral level, feeding off its energy and channeling that verve back out to the dance floor through their mixing.

The trio are not revivalists, hoping to revive or kickstart a new mobile era. In "graduating" from the mobile crews, they seek something that very few mobile DJs ever achieved: making a full-time living as DJs. That means performing daily, not just on weekends, and traveling internationally to book high-fee gigs. However, what a group like Triple Threat emphasizes is that today's DJs should remember the key skills and values of the past generation. For them, the mobile era taught them how to connect with other people through music performance, a chemistry that Apollo feels is in danger when younger DJs forget about the "fundamentals" of DJing. For Triple Threat, their re-created hall parties offer a taste of the nostalgic to today's crowds, but they also demonstrate the power in the bond between DJs and audience—for the past, in the present, and for the future.

Triple Threat's first reenacted mobile party came just as I was in the finishing stages of wrapping up primary research for my dissertation (which became the basis of this book). That party felt like an apt event for narrative closure, a "full circle" moment, if you will. However, as convenient a place as that would have been to end the story of the mobile scene, the veterans of the scene had other ideas.

In 2005, I attended the twentieth anniversary party for Spintronix, which drew hundreds of old mobile DJ personalities.[6] Then, in February 2006, I went to a "Tribute 2 Bay Area Mobile DJs" party (figure C.1). In more recent years, Francisco Pardorla, once a key part of the showcase-sponsoring AA Productions as well as Images Inc., has put together a series of parties with names such as "Classic Old School," inviting mobile crew–era talents such as Sound Sequence's Burton "King" Kong, Styles Beyond Compare's Rick Lee, and Ultimate Creations' Gary "Genie G" Millare. A different series of parties in 2010 made this return down memory lane even more specific by billing themselves as "DJs of Imagine Reunions," bringing back DJs from crews who originally performed at Imagines 4 and 5. The "DJs of Imagine 5" party included a curated display case featuring Mark Bradford's original Imagine 5 flyer alongside contest trophies, presumably from the participating crews.

For all their references to the past, these parties and events do not replicate the parties of yore in some keys ways. For one, they are held in more upscale nightclubs and restaurants such as Fremont's Kaenyama, a sushi and teppanyaki restaurant—a far cry from the halls of St. Augustine. In addition, though much of the audio and lighting equipment is vintage—loaned out from the minority of DJs who actually kept their gear—most DJs bring laptops instead of crates of vinyl.[7] And the participants themselves are, of course, older and at a different point in their lives.[8] These events seem to share more in common with high school reunions (not the least of which is that many participants actually knew one another when they were in high school): an excuse to reconnect with old friends, catch up on them and their families, and—as one of Pardorla's other parties was entitled—"Reminisce."[9]

There seems to be a certain generational impulse at play here. When I first began my interviews in the early 2000s, the mobile scene had "ended" less than ten years before. While most respondents held fond memories of that time in their lives, in some cases they had never taken time to reflect on it as adults. More than once, an interviewee would tell me, "You know, no one has ever asked me about this before."[10]

However, these recent reunion parties now appear three decades after the Restauros first assembled Sound Explosion at Balboa High and Mark Bradford began hosting Imagine parties. Whether this is coincidence or not, with that added passage of time there now seems to be a greater desire by veterans of the mobile scene to publicly celebrate the history of that community. To be sure, technology plays a key role here; the ability to reach out to old friends and organize events is heavily facilitated by social media tools, especially Facebook.[11]

Not only have individual members of the mobile era—such as Kong and Pardorla—used the site to post vintage images and flyers from the scene, but there are several Facebook groups and pages dedicated to specific mobile crews, including Oakland's Ladda Sounds, Daly City's Unique Musique, and San Francisco's Beyond the Limit. Notably, these reunion parties seem to be exclusively promoted via Facebook; the DJs of Imagine 5 party invited two thousand site members, and nearly one-quarter of those responded. In 2013 Thudrumble, the DJ company that Q-Bert helped found, announced it was producing a documentary about the mobile scene, tentatively (and coincidentally) entitled "Legions of Boom," and plans on using the fundraising website Kickstarter to cover production costs.

The popularity of these reunion parties and documentaries suggests that they tap into two related impulses. The first is what I suggested before—the "high school reunion" desire to reconnect with old friends and acquaintances. However, more than just facilitating an opportunity for individuals to rebuild old bonds, these reunion parties also seem like an attempt to reconvene a sense of community, to remind people of the mobile scene as it once was, and to encourage the living memory of the scene, its accomplishments, and its people. In the years between the end of the mobile crews and this recent cluster of reunion parties, most members of the mobile scene have taken different paths in school, work, family, and so on. Mobile DJing has ceased to be a dominant, organizing force in their lives.[12] However, what survived—and what these reunion parties are both tapping into and promoting—is the power of connection once forged in that scene. If the showcases of yore once provided a reason for them to connect across geographical and cultural distances, then the contemporary parties provide these middle-aged adults a means by which those communal ties and camaraderies can be reawakened and made meaningful again.

There is also a literally new generation in the mix here: the children of the original mobile DJs. That includes some young children born during the course of my research, including Cameron Paul Rivera, son of Spintronix's Dino Rivera—obviously named after the famed Studio West icon.[13] In 2012 I heard from Rene Anies of Electric Sounds, who wrote to tell me: "My 15 year old spins now. He's done a couple of 21-over clubs and he's doing teen events at various clubs . . . passing the torch!" Anies's son isn't alone; other respondents mentioned that their records and/or equipment had been "passed down" to numerous younger cousins or nephews (notably, I don't recall nieces or female cousins being beneficiaries, however).

Anies's son was one of the first—and I doubt the last—cases of a parent-to-child DJ lineage, and I asked Rene if either he or his wife, former Go-Go's DJ Daphnie Anies, nudged their son toward picking up DJing. Rene replied: "[He] did it on his own. . . . I'm the designated roadie now. He's still [learning] about sound, but he mixes well. Trained him to blend instead of cut mix." That last part is notable, since Rene is explaining that he's training his son how to DJ using the nonstop disco mixing style that dominated the early mobile era rather than "cut mixing," the more common, hip-hop-influenced style that many DJs use today.[14]

C.2 / Royce "DJ Devarock" Anies, San Francisco, 2014. Royce is an active DJ and the son of two mobile scene participants, Rene Anies of Electric Sounds and Daphnie Gambol Anies of the Go-Go's. Photo courtesy of Royce Anies.

Even if his son picked up DJing on his own, Anies is mentoring him in the values of DJ aesthetics that he himself first learned over thirty years ago. The DJ landscape that this younger Anies will find himself participating in will look very different from his mother and father's era, but just as Daphnie and Rene were part of a wave that transformed DJing in the Bay Area, it will be intriguing to imagine what the next generation might accomplish within their own cohort. After all, the original mobile DJ scene happened within a limited mediascape, one in which the Bay Area's mainstream media outlets all but ignored or missed recognizing the scope of the scene beneath their figurative noses. Though young Filipino Americans today have hardly reached parity in their access to conventional media, they have shown themselves—alongside other youth of color—to be quite adept at using the do-it-yourself tools of social media as platforms of musical creation, collaboration, and distribution (Kun 2010; Tongson 2010). Meanwhile, the popularity of DJing seems no less resonant today than it was in the 1980s. Perhaps these scions of the mobile scene might forge their own kinds of community via musical production and participation—a continuing cycle as the turntables spin on.

The Next Set

One of my favorite parts of DJing is thinking about what song to play next. Much like the act of writing, where I play with fitting words and sentences together to form coherent ideas, I enjoy the process of sequencing songs together in hopes of forming a compelling mix. As I stressed in the introduction, these decisions all go into how you build a floor. Choose wisely and you bring the crowd to climax. Choose poorly and you risk deading the floor.

Every act of song selection is also, inversely, an act of abandonment. Choosing to play one song means choosing *not* to play countless others, and I have often felt as much regret over the songs I did not play as enjoyment from the ones I did. To put it another way, every mix I ever created has been haunted by the songs I left off.

Now that I have reached the end of my writing process, I feel similar sentiments. My choices of topics and themes inadvertently highlight—to me at least—those paths not taken. Like all writers, I made those decisions out of practical concerns for time, length, and narrative, but it does not erase the nagging feeling that comes with choosing one direction and then staring down the other forks and imagining where they might have led.

This feeling is especially acute because so little work has been done on the mobile scene. When I first began this research in 2001, I was aware of no other scholars who had studied this community, but I assumed, at the time, that I would simply be "one of the first." Instead, a dozen-plus years later, I remain "one of the only." This has always astounded me, since the mobile DJ scene was neither small in scope nor limited in influence, and the vast majority of participants are easily accessible (and eager to share). I have scraped the proverbial surface: asked a select and relatively small set of questions for a community, scene, and movement that is ripe for far greater exploration and examination. In wrapping this book up, I want to highlight several potential areas for future scholarship, both as reminders to myself and as suggestions to colleagues and peers.

First, it may seem odd that a book about DJs, written by a music scholar-journalist-DJ, does not include an extensive engagement with the actual *music* being played in the scene. I mention songs and artists tangentially, but for the most part, there is no analysis of what these song choices "mean," and certainly this could be a rich topic for exploration.[15] Why, for example, did these DJs gravitate toward specific genres, especially freestyle, new wave, and hip-hop? If, as Simon Frith wrote, "our experience of music—of music making and music listening—is best understood as an experience of this self-in-process," then what do DJ playlists from this scene say about the "self-in-process" that both DJs and their audiences were creating (Frith 1996a: 109)? If we treat those playlists as a text, what can a "read" reveal of the kinds of social and cultural affiliations and allegiances these young people may have sought?

My only caution with following this line of thought—and perhaps one reason I intuitively avoided this topic—is that the musical choices DJs make are rarely purely "their own." Since mobile DJs fundamentally provide a service, their tastes in music are always a negotiation of sorts with their audience's desires. For most DJs—myself included—a "dream" gig is one where "we can play whatever we want" *and* the audience is enthralled by those choices. The important dynamic here is not the freedom of choice but rather the validation by the audience. Any DJ at any gig can technically play "whatever he or she wants": they are on the turntables, it is their records. But if the audience dislikes their choices, it is hard to derive much pleasure from the experience. If you truly just wanted to play the records you wanted to hear, you could do so in the comfort of your bedroom.

However, DJing—as a performative and interactive act—requires an audience. Therefore, an exploration of musical choice says at least as much about who a DJ is playing to and what their tastes are as about the DJ herself or himself. As a text, the playlist reflects that dialectical process between DJ and audience and needs to be understood and treated as such. Therefore, as an area of future research, it might be as useful to talk to DJs' *fans* about their musical preferences rather than just the DJs themselves.

Second, though I tried to talk about some of the salient gender issues in the mobile scene, I missed the opportunity to probe the question of sexuality. For one, insofar as the mobile scene was partially taking its cues from the San Francisco discotheque scene, by extension, it meant they were in some kind of conversation, intentional or not, with the city's prominent gay club and dance music scene. That included the major clubs, such as the Trocadero Transfer and I-Beam, important record stores, such as Aloha and Streetlight, and music labels like Megatone (home to Sylvester, who became a gay musical icon prior to his death in 1988).[16] Likewise, though I focused on the homosociality of mobile crews, I did not explore the role, if any, of homosexual erotic desire within the scene. Though discussions around queerness arose when discussing Mark

Bradford, the focus there was outward, toward an outsider. The topic of same-sex desire *between* people within the scene (whether within crews, between crew members and others, and so on) never arose, and this could be a viable area for future inquiry.[17]

Third, one of the biggest shifts in Asian American studies, especially Filipino American studies, that happened between when I began my fieldwork and when I ended the writing process was the rise of interest in and application of postcolonial theory to cultural analyses. Though I have lightly touched on this throughout the text, it is essential to emphasize how Filipino American immigration and community formation and identity development have been shaped by empire—both Spanish and American—and its influence on Philippine and Filipino American history, society, and diaspora. I feel there is great potential for scholars to apply a postcolonial analysis to this community, especially in helping to frame family settlement patterns, the complexities of Filipino American community and identity in the immediate post-1965 immigrant generations, and perhaps most salient, the "misrecognition" and social invisibility of Filipino Americans of this generation from the dominant American racial discourse and categories of citizenship.[18]

Fourth, as a popular culture scholar, I see mobile DJing as just one activity within a broader spectrum of under-studied Filipino American cultural forms, both before and after the scene's heyday. Recent texts such as Antonio Tiongson Jr.'s *Filipinos Represent* (2013) and Mark R. Villegas, Kuttin' Kandi, and Roderick N. Labrador's *Empire of Funk* (2014) are important examinations of Filipino Americans involved in various hip-hop forms such as scratch DJing, b-boying, graffiti, and MCing, but a wealth of other cultural activities awaiting greater study remains, especially those from the 1970s, such as competitive dance crews, rock and R&B bands, and those oft-mentioned ROTC drill teams in San Francisco high schools. This is to say nothing of how mobile DJing might also fit within a broader discussion of other activities in other eras: traveling Filipino American jazz groups of the early twentieth century, World War II–era dance halls, the phenomenon of collegiate cultural nights, and so on. I feel like we are on the cusp of what will become a fruitful generation of scholarship looking at these, and other, examples of formative cultural activities and communities.

On that note, I want to close by acknowledging, again, my admiration for and astonishment at the cultural scene created by the Bay Area mobile crews, especially in remembering how so many of them were young high school students when they started. The study of youth culture often focuses more on college students, for practical reasons—they are a convenient population for college professors to study—but of course, youth culture exists far beyond campus lines. The Bay Area mobile scene is just one example; we could also include everything from generations of basketball leagues to import car clubs to the budding cohort of YouTube personalities. All are compelling examples of how teenagers can take cultural production and participation into their own hands, just as the mobile DJs did when they laid their hands upon turntables and began to remake their social worlds through them.

C.3 / Venue sign advertising a 1987 showcase, "Summer Showcase III," in Hayward, hosted by AA Productions. Photo courtesy of Francisco Pardorla.

Appendix 1 / Captains of the Field /
San Francisco Drill Teams

In the course of my interviews with mobile crew participants from San Francisco, a curious commonality arose: drill team. Many had been involved in the drill teams of their high schools' Junior ROTC (Reserve Officers' Training Corps).[1] For example, Sound Explosion's Restauro clan and their friend Sam Beltran all initially met and became friends via drill team at Balboa High School. I began noticing similar stories from other San Francisco interviewees, and what gradually emerged was that many mobile crew participants were also active in drill team and that these two activities shared key parallels.

For example, Electric Sounds' Rene Anies, who attended Lowell High School in the city, explained, "Growing up in late seventies, early eighties in San Francisco, ROTC to the Filipino community was like being on the varsity football team. If you were in ROTC and a member of the drill team, and you were, like, commander, you were like the captain of the varsity football team. But that's a story within itself right there. The competition to get in, the competition amongst the other schools, the rivalry was just amazing." The comparison to the "varsity football team" suggests that for young Filipinos at these schools, drill team represented an alternate and parallel social world in which the currency of social capital—popularity, reputation—could be earned. The comparison also hints at the idea that going out for the varsity football team was not a common activity among Filipino students, suggesting that different tracks of social networking existed within these schools.

This point is accentuated by Richard Quitevis (DJ Q-Bert), who also became a member of the drill team at Balboa High. I asked if being on drill team had made him or his friends seem "cooler" to their peers. Q-Bert replied, "Not really, they just thought we just nerds. We would walk around school and they would just laugh like 'Look at these dorks.' But then, everyone in ROTC, if you were in drill team, it was like 'Those guys are cool.' It was like both, nerds and fucking cool." That dichotomy further highlights the idea that, at least in these schools, there was a "dual track" for social capital. Outside of those involved in the ROTC, the drill team was seen as "dorky." But within the ROTC student community, drill team held stature.

Kicks Company's Paul Tumakay, who attended Wilson High School, went a step farther and suggested that joining and participating in the drill team was a means to become more involved in, as he put it, "the Filipino scene": "What got me more into the Pilipino scene was the drill team. At that time . . . the majority of the people involved in the ROTC Drill Team were Filipinos. You had other ethnicities, but the active participants were Filipinos. That paved the way for me to get to know people and [for] doing some other Filipino interests." This has important parallels with the mobile DJ scene, in which participation in mobile parties and events was, in essence, a way one confirmed one's "belonging" to the Filipino American community. At least in San Francisco, drill teams were an earlier means through which Filipino American youth could develop a sense of community identity by participating in a form of cultural performance. At the very least, drill team was a distinctively Filipino American social space. As Willie Sparks, another Balboa alum, put it, "I hung out with a lot of Filipino guys to the point where instead of doing P.E. I went to ROTC and that's where we all hung out."

Finally, it's worth drawing attention to the particular physical appeals of drill team. Tumakay said, "I thought it was really neat, fascinating, how they could coordinate and be as one." That coordination wasn't just an attraction; in the case of Q-Bert, he credits it with helping him later develop his competitive DJing skills: "We would have these routines where there would be three five-minute-long drill team routines and from there, it would take months to prepare and from there, I learned how to make a DMC mix. You practice a certain amount of weeks on a certain little thing that would last, maybe, thirty seconds, and then at the end, you piece it all together and make a composition out of it. From being in that drill team, it taught me how to be a composer.... Subconsciously, I was thinking that." Lest I make too much of this, the influence of drill team on the mobile DJ scene seemed confined largely to San Francisco–based crews; the Daly City school system didn't have drill team, so it's only among those from the San Francisco public schools that drill team appears to have been a common activity among DJs of the late 1970s and early 1980s.

The appeal of the competition aspect aside, the link to drill team—and more specifically, the ROTC—seems relevant given the historical links between the Filipino American community and military service. In the case of the Restauros, Rafael mentioned that his father had worked for the U.S. Army for thirty years. Paul Tumakay's father hadn't been in the military himself, but he respected the military and encouraged his son to explore the ROTC as a result: "I sort of had been encouraged [by] my dad . . . he wasn't in the military, but he knew people in the military, to sort of look at the military with some sort of respect."[2] More research is needed to explore the role of drill team among San Francisco's Filipino American youth of the 1970s and 1980s, but it does appear to have been a distinct feature of their social lives in that era.[3]

Appendix 2 / Born versus Sworn /
Filipino American Youth Gangs

During the course of the 1970s, the Bay Area witnessed the rise of two major kinds of Filipino American youth gangs. The first were offshoots of provincial prison gangs established in the Philippines and then "imported" to the United States during the post-1965 waves of Filipino immigrants. In the Bay Area, three of the larger gangs of this kind included the BNG (Bahala Na Gang), LVM (Luzon Visayan Mindenao, later changed to Luzon Visayan Mobsters), and SS (Sigue Sigue). Filipino teens encountered these gangs either as youth when they lived in the Philippines or through older relatives once in America (Nuevo 2002). For example, Kim Kantares recalled that during his childhood these gangs "were old school gangs that we knew about from the older relatives and brought over. . . . Some of those gang members made it over here and started their own chapters or started to influence a younger cousin or friend in school." Yusef Rashid related a similar set of experiences from his youth as well: "These are hard core, very, very violent and organized gangs in the Philippines. They control all kinds of vice, you know, out of the prisons. So a lot of time . . . the guys who . . . appear to come from maybe middle-class backgrounds, their fathers had authentic gangster backgrounds even if they became successful here. . . . That kind of has a holdover effect." The other type of Filipino youth gang was indigenous to the Bay Area—"homegrown," if you will, instead of "imported." These gangs were often very local—down to the city block—and more numerous. Their names often reflected popular culture influences, inspired by gang culture shown through popular media, as well as high-profile Chinatown gangs of the 1960s (Takagi and Platt 1978: 25–29). Some of these homegrown gangs included ABG (All Brothers toGether) and the Downtown Boys, Frisco Boys, Kearny Boys, Pittsburgh Pinoys, UCB (Union City Boys), and UCP (Union City Pinoys). Kantares, for example, once belonged to a South of Market gang called the Superflys (a direct homage to the influence of blaxploitation film in the 1970s), which later folded into Krux (pronounced as "crooks"), which eventually integrated into the large Downtown Boys gang.

Besides the difference in origin, gangs were also differentiated by the way individuals became members. Rudy Corpuz, a former street dancer from SOMA, now works as a gang prevention counselor in San Francisco's Bernal Heights and at Balboa High School. Having been involved with the downtown gangs of the 1970s, he described a difference between the Filipino youth who joined gangs by circumstance and those who did so by choice. He explained, "We were more born into it, not sworn into it. Like the Tenderloin, that's drug infested, gang infested, whereas in the suburbs I think it was more copycatted."

His delineation between "born" and "sworn" gangsters reflected a sensitivity to the social and class environments that different youth experienced. In downtown neighborhoods like the Tenderloin, gangs formed an integral part of the social environment, whereas in the suburbs, gang culture was less indigenous and more cultivated through emulation. Not surprisingly, the different kinds of gangs also mapped onto the class cartography of Filipino communities. Gangs like Kantares's former Superflys that formed in working-class, urban centers tended to be "born in," whereas the "sworn in" gangs took root in the suburbs, such as the Avenues and Daly City.

This conforms with some of Bangele Alsaybar's findings regarding Filipino street gangs in Los Angeles and what he described as "two dominant gang models in the Filipino American community: the 'urban type' exemplified by the Satanas, and the 'suburban' type, exemplified by the 'BNG'" (1999: 126). Alsaybar described the stylistic differences between the two, suggesting that urban gangs borrowed heavily from Chicano cholo culture in terms of dress and attitude, whereas the suburban gangs "wore GQ-style clothes and drove late-model Japanese cars" (1999: 126).

Though Alsaybar curiously failed to identify BNG as an imported gang from the Philippines (whereas he is very clear in identifying the Satanas as a homegrown gang), his research helps flesh out the importance of the role geographic boundaries play in understanding the complexities of the Filipino gang scene.

In either case, most of the Bay Area Filipino gangs of the 1970s and 1980s lacked the more formal, organized crime interests associated with the Italian Mafia–type gangs of popular lore. Violence between Filipino gangs of this era often was more an expression of machismo or petty jealousy than an offshoot of illicit activities.[1] Though Kantares suggested some of the larger, older gangs, such as the massive Downtown Boys, had more involvement in criminal activities, many other youth gangs were essentially glorified cliques of peers who banded together for protection and intimidation. The underlying idea was that there was safety and power in numbers, and early into the formation of these gangs, there were legitimate reasons for seeking that kind of group protection.

Alsaybar, for example, traced the origins of the Satanas directly to Chicano versus Filipino racial conflict in Los Angeles inner cities. Already organized as a car club, the Satanas also provided Filipino youth with a measure of protection from cholo gangs who targeted Filipinos for persecution (Alsaybar 1999: 123). The same forces were at work in the Bay Area. In Rashid's recollection, Filipino youth in mixed neighborhoods like San Jose's Berryessa had to contend with "the element of hostility towards Filipinos. . . . If you were just a solo Filipino kid, walking around, it wasn't unusual to be accosted by a group of white kids. . . . It was to be expected and even with the Mexicans. Sometimes you caught flak with them and yeah, a lot of times, you know, for security's sake, we tended to actually be in groups." In the Templeton district, at the border of Daly City and San Francisco, open hostilities boiled between Filipino and Chicano youth, a tense situation that Jonathan Cruz (aka DJ Shortkut) remembered. "There was a big rivalry back then. [There were] a lot of the gangs around my hood, Filipinos against the Mexicans or the cholos I should say. The Filipino gangs were LVM, BNG, and all those cats. The cholos would be ESDC—East Side Daly City. There was so much tension . . . down on Mission and Templeton, right on the grocery wall, [was written] 'Flips will die.'" Once a handful of gangs came into creation, that only fueled the creation of even more gangs among the newly arrived immigrant Filipinos. Union City's John Francisco (Expressions Promotions) suggested that "gangs were actually being developed because of the gangs that were already existing. Immigrants that were coming in thought they were getting picked on. [They came] together just so that they could protect themselves. The cycle never ends."

Several of my respondents who participated in youth gang activity confirmed the way the "safety in numbers" mentality was at play, but equally compelling was that gangs gave Filipino youth—especially first-generation immigrants—a sense of belonging and camaraderie at a time when many of them felt marginalized, not just by outright hostility but also by difficulties in adjusting to life in America. Sound Explosion's Rafael Restauro went on to become a sergeant in the San Francisco Police Department and has had considerable experience with Asian youth gangs. His perspective links gang involvement with feelings of alienation and a desire to find community among first-generation immigrants who felt displaced and alone upon arriving in America. Restauro said,

> They weren't accepted, being Asians that didn't speak the American language. . . . They tend to stay with themselves. You have to remember, back when you had the migration of families that come over, the land of opportunity, their parents are working eighteen hours a day to support the family back [in the Philippines] . . . plus support the family here so they don't have that parental supervision that you'd normally get. They're looking to be accepted, to get that comfort, so that's how they turn into their little cliques, and then they got away from the family because the family wasn't here for them, their buddies were their families.

Restauro's analysis includes important considerations of class, noting that oftentimes, working- and middle-class Filipino parents spent so much time in the workplace that they were unable to provide either parental supervision or even basic family life, contributing to a lack of stability that Filipino youth struggled with. This theme was recurrent in my interviews and partially helped to explain why dislocated immigrant youth sought out gangs as informal families, similar to Alsaybar's *barkada* formations.

Importantly, Rashid and Corpuz both observed that these forces were as much at work in the suburbs as in the inner city, and though the socioeconomic conditions may have differed between neighborhoods, the same sense of isolation and dislocation helped spur gang development in both areas. According to Corpuz, "I know a lot of our parents would work two jobs, they'd be working hard and it'd be a lot of neglect. We looked after each other, and I'm talking in the city and the suburbs."

Rashid elaborated further, speaking specifically on how youth from seemingly affluent families would still become gang involved: "I noticed that many of the guys who were involved in gang activities, that kind of gang culture they were actually from well-off families, pretty stable homes or what appeared to be stable homes. I mean . . . I realize that both parents are working and there's not much supervision and that whole sense of 'Wow, all my parents do is work I don't get enough attention.' [Other] people [came] from some serious economic disadvantage, just serious, dysfunctional homes, but I guess dysfunction is everywhere, even if you got a nice home." Rashid was largely skeptical of these middle-class gangs, even though he was willing to accept that dysfunctional home life was as much an issue in more affluent suburbs as in the depressed inner city. For him, it was the *lifestyle* of the gangs that was the additional element that pulled many middle-class youth in. Especially with the imported gangs, Rashid observed that older relatives helped to glamorize gang life, even in the most affluent environments: "Though a lot of these guys who appear to come from stable homes . . . their fathers were actually hoodlums in the Philippines and this has a strong influence. Whenever their uncles would get together, you know playing cards, you know, and drinking what not, they'd start recalling their days of youth, OK, and they would really glamorize it."

As far as gang glamorization, one example close to home for Rashid was how his cousin, after witnessing a drive-by shooting at a local garage party, was actually pulled further into gang life on the basis of the way the people around him reacted to the shooting: "That was a pivotal experience for him . . . it pulled him in. . . . He thought it was glamorous because the way . . . women were reacting . . . he saw how much attention this cat [received]. This cat became like the heroic figure. . . . From that point on, [my cousin] was really fascinated with that kind of street life thing. He actually became quite a hoodlum." These testimonials suggest that a confluence of forces were at work. On one level, immigrant youth felt dislocated and alienated within their social environment. At home, the struggles of their parents to make a living oftentimes left children alone, undersupervised and isolated. Add to this tensions within and from outside their community as newly arrived immigrants dealt with the snobbery of American-raised peers, ethnic conflict in their schools and neighborhoods, and preexisting gangs who persecuted newcomers and outsiders alike. Finally, older, gang-affiliated relatives and popular media helped glamorize the icon of the gangster among youth who chose to be "sworn in" gang members even though their socioeconomic conditions were more privileged than those of the youth who were "born in" to the gang life.[2]

Clearly, there was no single reason why some Filipino youth fell into gangs, but the most powerful overall incentive stemmed from a general atmosphere of displacement. As immigrants or at least children of immigrants, Filipino youth found themselves cast into social environments where they were largely ignored, misunderstood, or marginalized. Though hardly ideal, the gangs were one form of social grouping that provided some youth with a sense of communal identity. By the 1980s, as this book suggests, middle-class young men from this larger community could find that collective solidarity via the mobile DJ crews, but this was not an opportunity or activity universally accessible to all Filipino young men, especially given the class requirements for starting up and running a mobile crew. As I suggested earlier in the book, the gangs and mobile crews may have shared some key similarities as homosocial, male-centric organizations, encouraging shared identity and bonding, but they also ran along parallel and largely separate tracks, usually intersecting only when their respective worlds overlapped spatially at parties and dances.

Notes

Prologue

The narrative of the prologue was adapted from a conversation I had with Dino Rivera, asking him to describe the step-by-step process that goes into planning and executing a gig. In some cases, the adaptation was written directly from quotes Rivera gave me; at other times, I added details based on his testimony but rewrote them for the sake of clarity and narrative consistency.

1. A truss is a modular, metal frame used to support lighting equipment. It can be broken down into smaller component parts for easy storage and assembly. "Helicopters" are spotlights that sit on a spinning platform and revolve, similar to an emergency vehicle siren. "Oscillators" are spotlights that pan across a horizontal plane.

Introduction

1. *Scratching*, aka *scratch DJing* aka *turntablism*, refers to the manipulation of vinyl records and a turntable stylus to create sounds and rhythms. Scratching came out of early hip-hop DJ styles and still shares a close relationship with hip-hop culture and music. While this book discusses the rise of turntablism within the mobile scene, my primary focus is on the mobile crews, not the scratch crews. For the latter, see Tiongson 2013, as his research looks almost exclusively at Bay Area Filipino American scratch DJs of the 1990s, some of whom began in mobile crews but who constituted a distinct and largely separate generation of DJs from the

mobile crews of my study. For more on the general history of scratch DJing, see Pray 2002 and Katz 2012.

2. With "scene," I'm borrowing from Richard Peterson and Andy Bennett's concept of "a focused social activity that takes place in a delimited space and over a specific span of time in which clusters of producers, musicians, and fans realize their common musical taste" (2004: 8). The mobile DJ scene, as I outline it, consisted of the Bay Area mobile DJ crews, their fans, their promoters, and the extended family and community networks that mobile crews intersected with. When I first began this research, I described the mobile scene as a "subculture," via the framework of the term as pioneered by Dick Hebdige (2011). However, in the years during which I revised my work, the notion that the mobile scene was a subculture began to feel less and less appropriate, especially since the classic notion of a subculture is framed through a lens of deviance, that is, it "presumes that a society has one commonly shared culture from which the subculture is deviant" (Peterson and Bennett 2004: 3). That definition didn't fit with a mobile DJ community that—as distinctive as its cultural markers may have been—did not express values that seemed in opposition to or somehow separate from larger Filipino American or Bay Area communities. Hence, the term "scene" is a more flexible idea for explaining the particular cultural formation of the mobile crews. See also Hollows and Milestone 1998: 84 and Huq 2006: 9–24 for two other critiques of the shortcomings of subcultural theory as they apply to DJ- and club-centric music scenes. See MacDonald 2001: 94–95 for a class-based critique of the subcultural model as well.

3. A few articles published after the mobile scene's end mention the mobile crews. See Aaron 1997: 64; Chonin 2001.

4. Chapter 5 discusses the difficulties the mobile DJ community experienced in trying to become record-making.

5. A word about naming conventions in this book: I refer to interviewees by the most appropriate name to use *at the time of our interview*. In other words, since Q-Bert and Apollo, for example, still actively perform under those names, I refer to them by stage name. However, I refer to other former mobile DJs by their legal surnames if they are no longer actively performing full-time.

6. My essay for *American Music* "Between the Notes" (Wang 2001a) encapsulated many of my ideas from this era. However, it was written before my turn toward thinking of music as *productive* of identity rather than merely reflective.

7. A "set" may refer to the block of time a DJ is scheduled for during a party (i.e., "What time is my DJ set at?"). Similarly, a set may also refer to the selection and sequencing of songs that a DJ plans ahead of time or makes up as she or he goes along (i.e., "I had a really good set going, the crowd was feeling it").

8. Reading this quote again makes me think of something art critic Dave Hickey famously wrote: "It's hard to find someone you love, who loves you—but you can begin, at least, by finding someone who loves your love song" (1997: 17).

9. The inverse would be to "dead the floor" or "lose the floor," i.e., unintentionally dispersing a dance floor crowd, usually through a poor song choice (or several

in a row). Deading a floor usually happens far faster than building a floor; the wrong song at the right moment will scatter dancers in stunningly quick time.

10. In the summer of 2013, I attended an event (Kun 2013) jointly sponsored by the Grammy Museum and Red Bull where musician-DJ-bandleader Ahmir "?uestlove" Thompson described how he approaches a DJ set. Thompson shared that he usually requests a three-hour set and he uses that first hour to "gain the trust" of the dancers. The goal, for him, is to eventually gain enough of their trust to allow him to play whatever he wants rather than being constrained by only recognizable "hits" or single genres.

11. Nicolas Bourriaud describes the role of the DJ—as mixer—quite well: "The DJ's work consists both of proposing a personal orbit through the musical universe (a playlist) and of connecting these elements in a certain order, paying attention to their sequence as well as to the construction of an atmosphere (working directly on the crowd of dancers or reacting to their movements). . . . One can recognize a DJ's style in the ability to inhabit an open network (the history of sound) and in the logic that organizes the links between the samples he or she plays" (2002: 32).

12. "Catching the break" means finding a point in a recording's composition—i.e., a break—that you can mix in or out of in a way that doesn't disrupt the overall flow. Many pop songs have a "natural" break around either the choruses or the bridge, and DJs memorize these breaks as a way to strategize when they can mix in a new song.

13. As an aside: also in the summer of 2012, the vodka company Smirnoff published a print and web ad that featured a male "DJ" standing in front of turntables, with an attractive woman looking on, smiling. As many DJs noted on social media sites, the ad was unintentionally comedic since (1) there were no records on the turntable, (2) there was no slipmat—a piece of felt that sits between the record and the turntable and that all DJs use with turntables, (3) the turntables had no needles, (4) there was no DJ mixer, which more or less is what makes DJing possible to begin with, and (5) the power switch for the turntables was visibly in the "off" position. In other words, the ad represented DJing completely inaccurately. However, it's entirely possible that most people didn't notice anything amiss in the ad at all: the image of a DJ standing behind turntables communicates enough information without requiring the mise en scène to be accurate, which says a lot about how ubiquitous this image has become in mass media.

14. To be fair, advertising and popular media are not the only ones that tend to treat DJs as solitary figures; most scholarly texts on DJing culture do the same. A recent exception would be Mark Katz's *Groove Music*, which discusses both the mobile crews and turntablist crews (2012, chapter 5).

15. "Crew" was originally a military term, taken from the French *crue*, meaning "group of soldiers." Its transition into the cultural realm goes back at least as far as usages of the term "dance crew" in the 1940s.

16. Within U.S. urban youth culture, cliques of graffiti writers were among the first to organize themselves as self-described "crews," as this provided an important

distinction from "gangs." See Alsaybar 1993: 236–39; Phillips 1999: 313; Williams and Kornblum 1985: 75.

17. I had initially taken it for granted that the DJs I interviewed referred to their own groups as crews, but when I went back through my transcripts, I noticed a subtle generational difference. More veteran participants, who joined the mobile scene in the first half of the 1980s, tended to say "DJ groups." It was often my younger respondents—from the latter half of the 1980s—who talked about "DJ crews." They were describing the exact same organizational structure, but I suggest that the spreading use of the term "crew" over the 1980s follows the spread of hip-hop's influence on the pop culture vernacular. In hip-hop, the term "crew" is ubiquitous and applies across the culture's myriad forms—graffiti crews, DJ crews, b-boy crews, etc. Therefore, as hip-hop became more popular, it helped proliferate an idea of a "crew" as referring to groups of youth engaged in shared cultural activities. My point here is that even those with a minimal interest or awareness of hip-hop may still end up using the term "crew," as it has become a commonplace term to describe a particular social grouping.

18. A word about this book and hip-hop. One recurrent—and mistaken—assumption made about my research is that it is about "Filipinos and hip-hop." This is erroneous but understandable: hip-hop and mobile DJing existed as concurrent movements, and more to the point, hip-hop's early years in the 1970s involved many mobile DJs. Likewise, many Bay Area mobile DJs gravitated to hip-hop once rap music became ascendant over the course of the 1980s. However, the origins of the mobile scene predate hip-hop's national expansion, and however familiar mobile DJs were with hip-hop records, most crews were equally enamored with other genres such as funk, disco, new wave, and freestyle. Later crews—those that formed in the late 1980s and early 1990s—were more likely to identify with being a "hip-hop DJ crew," but that did not hold for most of the crews that formed earlier. In short, my research was never focused on the topic of Filipinos and hip-hop. Mobile DJing and hip-hop DJing are distinct cultural movements with important overlaps and parallels but cannot and should not be treated as interchangeable. Curiously, even when I have explicitly stated this, people still made that conflation; it was if they couldn't help but assume that anything dealing with Filipinos and DJing must also be about Filipinos and hip-hop. I believe this says much about (1) how DJing is seen as a subset of hip-hop (even in those historical cases where it is not), and (2) how powerfully we associate Filipino Americans with hip-hop. Both, I would argue, are phenomena that can be traced, in part, back to the importance of the mobile scene, insofar as it helped beget the scratch DJ scene, which in turn helped put hip-hop DJing—and the role of Filipino Americans within it—on a global map.

19. I should note that most of my research was on rappers of East Asian descent (Chinese, Japanese, Korean, etc.). Whether their experiences or perspectives offer insight into their Filipino American contemporaries is open to question, as the inclusion of Filipino Americans within a broader Asian American rubric is neither uniform nor uncontested. As Tiongson suggests, that conflation tends to be based

around geography rather than a more nuanced analysis of history and imperialism that could just as easily link Filipinos with other colonized communities such as Chicanos and Puerto Ricans (2013: 58). As it relates here, though, the ethnicity of the rappers is less relevant than the fact that they are rappers, that is, engaged in an art form where identity is often front and center.

20. Pursuing "how?" is a methodological strategy I learned long ago from sociologist Howard Becker, no stranger to the study of cultural communities (1998: 58).

21. One underrated but vastly important role that women had in regard to the scene: they were the main documenters, collecting flyers and photos, organizing them into scrapbooks, etc. Had it not been for their efforts, most of the artwork that currently circulates (including in this book) likely would never have survived. And of course, Melanie Caganot was the first to mount an exhibit around the scene. As I stress throughout, women were underrepresented in the ranks of the DJs, but they were ever-present in other parts of the scene.

22. In fact, a great deal of visual and paper media—flyers, posters, business cards—survives, but most of it resides in people's private archives, a fancier way of saying "collecting dust in their garage." However, since the late 2000s, the rise of social media sites such as YouTube and Facebook has created new forums to share paper and video footage from the mobile era. I created the legionsofboom.com website as a way to help collect and consolidate some of this material.

23. There is no database or mechanism by which one can arrive at a *precise* figure for the total number of mobile crews in the Bay Area. My estimate is based on anecdotal estimates by my interviewees as well as my looking through what physical media survived—business cards, party flyers, etc. An educated—though limited—guess would put that total number somewhere in the range of between 100 and 150.

Chapter 1 / Cue It Up

1. Though the film became more of an emblem—if not a caricature—of late 1970s pop culture and kitsch, it is hard to overstate its impact when it opened. From a cultural point of view, the movie took what had been a largely underground phenomenon—with roots firmly planted in gay, African American, Latino American, and working-class communities—and cemented its crossover to straight, mainstream middle America (Echols 2010). Moreover, as disco had existed for years prior to the movie's release, *Saturday Night Fever* could be seen as more of a capstone than an instigator of disco's popularity. Either way, as Tim Lawrence chronicled, even New York's infamous "law and order" mayor, Ed Koch—not the most likely poster child for celebrating "love is the message"—proclaimed, "The disco and its lifestyle has helped to contribute to a more harmonious fellowship towards all creeds and races" (2004: 38).

2. I focus on San Francisco's nightclubs because they came up the most frequently in my interviews. However, the discotheque explosion in the Bay Area was certainly not confined to just that city.

3. Hedges, an Ohio native, is widely considered the first major disco DJ in the Bay Area, and Paul considered him one of the most important figures in helping popularize New York–style nonstop mixing in the Bay.

4. In speaking to various respondents, I was given the impression that the nightclub scene in San Francisco of the 1970–1980s split along sexuality lines, with some clubs "known" for primarily serving gay patrons while other, so-called "mixed" clubs served both gay and straight patrons. According to a conversation I had with former Studio West DJ Paul John Weber, the club opened primarily as a mixed club, and one potential reason it was so popular was because, after 2 a.m., when cabaret licenses formally ended the legal sale of alcohol, the club could then allow in an eighteen-and-over crowd. In my interview with Cameron Paul, he recalled "leading up to two o'clock in the morning there'd be lines, blocks long, of the minors waiting to get in." (By "minors" Paul meant "under twenty-one," rather than the more conventional "under eighteen" definition of the term.) Paul also added, "They let in a lot younger than that"—a policy, whether official or not, that many of my respondents could also attest to.

5. Cameron Paul himself grew up in Daly City, albeit half a generation ahead of the mobile DJs. He began as one of many white DJs in San Francisco's burgeoning discotheque scene of the late 1970s, but by the end of the 1980s he would command a minimusical empire in the Bay Area—as a major radio DJ for the top-rated "urban" station KMEL FM and founder of Mixx-It Records, which specialized in remixing popular and underground club hits.

6. The fact that most pop music songs feature a "fade out" is itself a product of both technological and aesthetic factors (Cole 2010).

7. Interestingly, the origins of the disco break are open to debate, and the merits of various arguments depend heavily on what is perceived as "proper" disco production. For example, most music historians credit engineer Tom Moulton with being the disco break's creator after he deliberately edited parts of Don Downing's 1974 single "Dream World" to create a longer percussive section that then almost doubled the length of the song as a boon for DJ use (Lawrence 2004: 146). However, others argue that producer Frank Wilson, drawing from his background in gospel, inserted a "break" into Eddie Kendricks's 1972 song "Girl You Need a Change of Mind," which, as Alice Echols describes it, "emptied the track of instrumentation and then gradually built it back up" (2010: 15). Whether Wilson or Moulton deserves credit largely depends on what becomes the most crucial element—the production approach or the end result; and because Moulton deliberately created Downing's break in postproduction, his is usually cast as the true "birth" of the disco break, because it involved a deliberate act of reediting (whereas Wilson's break came in the song's arrangement). This may seem like hair-splitting, but it speaks to how important technology and technique were to defining a particular style.

8. In an earlier *Billboard* issue of 1974, a front-page story focuses on Jane Brinton, "a 24-year-old British girl" and "one-woman discotheque" who set up a mobile DJ service in Los Angeles by "traveling about in an immaculate new VW van

containing her own $12,000 'supersound' unit" (Dexter 1974: 1). I mention this because it demonstrates that even in the earliest days of mobile DJing, there was an impressive amount of creative energy going into the endeavor (not to mention considerable capital).

9. The Jamaican sound system culture—another mobile DJing–based community—offers interesting precedents and parallels. In Norman Stolzoff's (2000) history of Jamaican dancehall history, he notes how the concept of the sound system traveled from peer to peer, as personal encounters (as opposed to mass media dissemination) spread the awareness of the sound system, its technologies, and its potential. One example involved future Merritone sound system operator Winston Blake; he used to travel into Kingston from the Jamaican countryside and came across "Mr. Chin . . . owner of the Sky Rocket sound system. . . . For a country boy like Blake, the sound systems and men who were involved in running them were larger than life. 'I looked at the Kingston sounds like they were gods,' he said. Noting Blake's avid interest, Chin suggested one day that Blake ask his father to start his own sound. He carried this idea back to his father and four brothers in Morant Bay" (47). This anecdote is almost identical to those of my respondents, for whom club DJs were their "gods" who inspired them to bring the inspiration to DJ back from the city to the suburbs.

10. Daly City's motto is "Gateway to the Peninsula." Sarah Jackson, in her essay on Filipino scratch DJs, interprets that motto as "a point of both entry and departure, with city borders that are porous, not impenetrable" (1998: 15).

11. The immigrant families I write about are described by some as the "third wave" and others as the "fourth wave" of Filipino immigration. Those who ascribe to a "fourth wave" model usually separate the students and laborers in the first wave into two distinct though overlapping waves. I use the first form of the "third wave" appellation throughout this book.

12. In an unlikely turn of events, over twenty-five years after it all but disappeared, San Francisco's Manilatown is being reconstructed. That has included the building of a new International Hotel, a residence for low-income seniors with more than one hundred units, that opened in 2005 (Franko 2007).

13. The struggle to save the International Hotel drew much attention to the historical presence of the north-of-Market Manilatown district, but Filipinos in SOMA have a long history as well. The collaboratively authored *Filipinos in San Francisco* suggests Filipino families in SOMA date back to the same 1910s–1920s era in which Manilatown began to take form (Filipino American National Historical Society 2011: 8). Sobredo suggests that a bigger influx arrived with returning Filipino veterans from World War II, married to "war brides"; it's inferred that SOMA residences were more family-friendly than those in Manilatown (Sobredo 1998: 284).

14. There are historical antecedents for similar kinds of secondary migration by Filipino families. In his analysis of Filipino settlement patterns in Los Angeles in the 1920s and 1930s, Benicio Catapusan looked at the wide dispersion of some families away from the main Filipino enclave along downtown LA's First Street. He

surmised that "this wide distribution is due to effort on the part of some of the Filipinos to avoid the First Street life, despised so by the American, and subjected to bad association and disreputable influences. Housing conditions on First Street are very poor, small rooms and fourth-class hotels are about all there is to be had. There is not enough respectable territory there for better social expression. Filipinos who have families certainly will not live in such a congested section. And as a result many are moving into some distant places that will free them from First Street influences" (Catapusan 1934: 8). For the Filipino families connected to the mobile DJ scene, similar reasoning explained their decisions to move from the dense confines of downtown to the more expansive space of the suburbs.

15. In all fairness, while the percentage increase of Filipinos in Marin, Napa, and Sonoma counties was higher than San Francisco's, the absolute number of Filipinos remained small. By 1990, the *combined* Filipino population in those three counties was less than five thousand. In comparison, the Bay Area county with the fourth smallest Filipino population (Contra Costa) still had four times as many Filipinos as Marin, Napa, and Sonoma combined.

16. In older models of immigration settlement patterns, especially as predicted by spatial assimilation theory, immigrant groups first settled in urban ethnic enclaves, then moved to more ethnically mixed suburbs (usually dominated by non-white Hispanic majorities). However, one of the distinguishing facets of Asian immigration in the post-1965 era is that "ethnic enclave" and "suburbs" are hardly mutually exclusive. If anything, one defining feature of post-1965 Asian immigration is its centering on suburban enclaves such as Monterey Park (Los Angeles), Flushing (Queens), and, of course, Daly City (Alba et al. 1999).

17. Two works touch on the pattern of Filipino American local resettlement patterns: Benito Vergara's (2009) monograph on the history of Filipinos in Daly City, *Pinoy Capital*, and Allyson Tintiangco-Cubales's (2009) essay on the Excelsior district in southern San Francisco. The two neighborhoods are less than two miles apart, with Mission Street being one shared thoroughfare. Though there are important differences in them, both have become primary destinations within secondary settlement patterns among Filipino American families. As each author traces, during the post-1965 era the Filipino populations exploded in each area: the Excelsior eventually contained nearly a third of San Francisco's total Filipino population (Tintiangco-Cubales 2009: 112)—the most of any San Francisco neighborhood—and Daly City still has the highest concentration of Filipino Americans of any midsized (or greater) U.S. city (Vergara 2009: 24).

18. See Spigel 2001 for a discussion of how the proliferation of the television industry coincided with, and mutually shaped, the popularization of suburbia as an idealized construct for U.S. public and private family life.

19. According to Tan et al. 1987, upward of 60 percent of television programing in the Manila area in the early 1980s originated from the United States. This is a provocative figure, though I would caution that this says little about the impact of U.S. television in cities and areas besides Manila. Nonetheless, it seems reasonable

to assume that decades of American occupation have given U.S. mass media an outsized presence in the Philippines, throughout the twentieth century.

20. As an aside, there is a vintage photograph of the original Quezon City subdivisions from the 1950s in a *Philippine Star* article on the history of the area (Alcazaren 2011). In a testament to the universality of suburban design, the photograph looks practically interchangeable with that of early American suburbs of the same era, such as Levittown, Pennsylvania (Harris 2010), or Lakewood, California (Waldie 2005).

21. Calvin Welch estimated that of the fourteen thousand lower income homes demolished by the city, barely a third were ever replaced, and even that took more than twenty years (2011: 156). Likewise, Charles Wollenberg opined that the redevelopment efforts in the 1950s and 1960s "probably destroyed more moderate-priced housing than they produced" (1985: 341).

22. The city's downtown development ambitions aimed to achieve three broad goals. First was the modernization of the San Francisco skyline, part of the process that helped erect the now iconic Transamerica Pyramid even as it also helped tear down the International Hotel. Second was the construction of high-rise residential towers (which also went hand in hand with the completion of BART stations in the downtown area). Rodriguez argues that while the city's elite may have resisted new housing construction elsewhere in the city, they more easily embraced the high-rises, as "they reinforced the city's urban identity. The high-rises also buttressed San Francisco's image as *the* center of the Bay Area," even though, as he also points out, "its population declined relative to the other centers in the multicentered metropolis" (1999: 41). Third, the city's image as a "destination center" meant a greater focus on building the tourism industry. Somewhere between 1960 and 1980, tourism grew to become the city's primary industry, and the construction of large, towering hotels—all in the downtown–SOMA area—furthered that goal (Wollenberg 1985: 330). The controversial "Golden Gateway" mixed commercial and residential complex, built from the 1960s through the 1980s, was a hat trick of sorts, as it created new high-rises to serve all three goals (Scott 1985: 290).

23. According to Allyson Tintiangco-Cubales, these economic pressures were among the key factors that drove many Filipino families toward more suburban neighborhoods, both in the city (the Excelsior district, for example) and beyond city limits (2009: 112).

24. As a side note: Laguerre argues that the downtown Manilatown was created through "housing discrimination, poverty, and the fact that most of [the residents] were single men" (2000: 83), but other testimonials suggest that the latter two may have been more powerful reasons than housing restrictions. The Filipino American National Historical Society's history *Filipinos in San Francisco* states that following World War II, Filipino Americans able to benefit from the provisions of the GI Bill "began to buy homes in the Richmond and Sunset districts on the west side, *despite white-only racial covenants*. Others moved from the SOMA southward into the Mission, Bernal Heights, Excelsior–Outer Mission, Crocker-Amazon, and Visitacion

Valley neighborhoods and Daly City" (9; emphasis mine). Tintiangco-Cubales also notes that Filipino families began settling in that neighborhood "as early as the 1950s" (2009: 113). Therefore, while it may be true that housing discrimination funneled residents toward Manilatown, it seems that some middle-income Filipinos had housing options elsewhere. It may be valuable for future scholarship to explore the extent to which Filipinos were and were not subject to discrimination in the Bay Area housing market before (and after) the Fair Housing Act of 1965.

25. San Leandro, just south of Oakland, achieved minor notoriety as a white flight haven when *Newsweek* profiled some of its white residents in a 1969 cover story, "The Troubled American: A Special Report on the White Majority" (Copeland 2006: 12).

26. Daly City's white population made up nearly 90 percent of all residents in 1970 but declined by one-third by 1980, slipping another 11 percent by 1990 and then seeing a 27 percent drop by 2000. Daly City's Latinos—once the second largest ethnic group in the city—have grown in absolute numbers, but as a proportion of the city's population, they have held steady, while Asians (presumably most of whom were Filipino specifically) grew to become the city's largest ethnic group—both proportionately and in relative numbers—by 1990 (Bay Area Census 2012). The city's African American population increased tenfold, from 1 percent in 1960 to nearly 11 percent in 1980, before declining back down to 5 percent by 2000 (De Graaf 2001: 419–21). De Graaf attributes this rise and fall to several factors, including the end of legalized housing discrimination practices that opened up affordable homes in the newer, less expensive (though farther flung) suburbs as well as displacement by incoming Latino and Filipino residents.

27. In the neighboring Excelsior district, Tintiangco-Cubales suggests that Filipino American families flocked there for similar reasons: the establishment of Filipino American businesses, churches, and other community institutions (2009: 113).

28. Dela Cruz specifically cited a 1983 news story that aired in New Jersey about the Filipino community reaction to the assassination of Benigno "Ninoy" Aquino. The story featured footage from a Mass held at St. Andrews Church in Daly City. These kinds of institutions were part of the evolving set of local, Filipino-specific entities and services that became a draw for Filipino families. Besides churches, they also included groceries, restaurants, social organizations, etc.

29. "The Avenues" refers to the Richmond and Sunset districts. Because of their geographic proximity and demographic similarities, there's an understandable impulse to fold the Excelsior and Vistacion Valley neighborhoods together with Daly City to create a kind of mega-Filipino district, but for working families there were still key differences in which side of the border you lived on. Tintiangco-Cubales suggests that the Excelsior is well served by a location "close to public transportation for the commute to downtown, where many blue- and white-collar jobs were located" (2009: 112). Indeed, both the BART trains and the city's MUNI bus-and-rail system run through the Excelsior. In contrast, Vergara discusses how moving to Daly City often resulted in a geographic "isolation imposed by the spatial layout,"

requiring "a nearly total reliance on motorized transportation, either public or private, but mostly the latter" (30). This came about largely as a result of the city's urban planning matrix, laid out in the 1940s and 1950s, which created many streets that sprawl across the city's hilly terrain but also disperse a population in a pattern that makes it prohibitively expensive for public transit to adequately service (29–30).

30. Father Bitanga offered one other—I presume half-joking—explanation for the movement to Union City–Fremont in particular, including from Daly City: "After Daly City, Union City opened also. Now Daly City is foggy, Filipinos do not like the fog there, cold. When Union City was opened, they left Daly City and went to Union City with sprawling houses and the weather is just perfect."

31. San Francisco's lower median family income was only true for this time period. In the past twenty years, incomes have risen dramatically, and based on the 2010 American Community Survey, San Francisco now would be number three on that list, behind Fremont and San Jose.

32. The garage's duality as both "in and out" can be seen in the common purposes it serves for families. The things we don't want "inside" our house we store in the garage: boxes of old toys or bags of used clothing. But likewise, the things we don't want to leave "outside" also end up *in* the garage: cars and bicycles, sharp tools.

33. By "organized parties" dela Cruz is referring to regularly scheduled parties (usually weekly or monthly), organized by DJs or party promoters and held in nightclubs. As chapter 5 discusses, the eventual emergence of organized parties, starring mobile crew DJs, was one force that helped bring about the end of the mobile era. In contrast, there were the "daytimer" bhangra parties in London in the middle and late 1980s. They got their name from the fact that they were held during daytime hours, ostensibly as a way for South Asian teens to attend them without disapproving parents finding out (Manzoor 2012). The daytimer scene makes for an interesting contrast with the mobile scene in a few ways. First, the mobile scene partially formed because Filipino American youth lacked existing club spaces of their own; family support—as I stress—was key to the mobile scene's success. The daytimer scene partially formed because South Asian British youth lacked existing familial support; daytimer clubs and raves came about to meet their needs. One might see these two youth scenes as coming forth from opposite catalysts, but both share a commonality as creative adaptations to societal limitations. Huq notes that though the interest of the British press in the daytimer phenomenon quickly passed by the late 1980s, they still happened up through at least the early 2000s (2006: 70).

34. Lest I paint too positive a picture here, let us be clear: ephemeral forums are always about compromises made in the face of deprivation. The very ephemerality that these bands in Southeast LA must contend with contrasts with "established forums" devoted to practice and performance that other communities enjoy: music schools, concert halls, etc. The musicians in Leal's research engaged in "guerrilla

conversions" of private and abandoned spaces because local, civic infrastructure was incapable or unwilling to do more.

35. In one sense, mobile crew venues were always temporary—and therefore ephemeral in that sense—but in comparison with the on-the-fly transformations necessary for Southeast LA bands to find a space to rock out in, mobile crew venues in the 1980s weren't as threatened with the danger of being literally and figuratively policed by law enforcement or disgruntled citizens and neighbors. Mobile crews transform venues they are invited into, and these are often spaces that are dependably available for their use, unlike Leal's ephemeral forums, which always carry some implicit instability and unpredictability.

36. BART: Bay Area Rapid Transit, the local subway line; MUNI: a San Francisco–specific bus and light rail system.

Chapter 2 / Team Building

1. See chapter 1 for a longer discussion of nonstop mixing.

2. Many of my respondents' families first moved to the United States in or immediately after 1972, presumably fleeing the Philippines to avoid political persecution or, at least, to seek a more stable environment. See Espiritu 1995: 20.

3. See appendix 1 for more on the drill team connection.

4. This form of promotion prefigures so-called street team squads employed by radio stations and record labels, who sent out sound system vans into local neighborhoods to help promote brand awareness for these companies.

5. The role of social network density in influencing the growth of music scenes is discussed extensively by Nick Crossley (2008, 2011). See, in particular, Crossley 2008: 103.

6. As chapter 3 discusses, a lower social network density of Filipino American family and community nodes would also mean a lower or more uneven rate of "gig distribution," which in turn would make it harder for nascent crews to find the necessary business to stay afloat.

7. I clearly am drawing from Pierre Bourdieu's (Bourdieu and Wacquant 1997) theories on forms of capital, but I have adapted them to the particular logics of the mobile scene. Those include economic capital (money), symbolic capital (reputation and status), social capital (family- and community-based networks), and cultural capital (DJing skills and equipment).

8. It is also worth noting that Carrion's perk—free food—is a form of economic capital.

9. As with Carrion, it is notable that Kong seems ambivalent or possibly reluctant in acknowledging the importance of social status, as he first compares himself and his peers to "world champs" but one sentence later downplays comparisons to "movie stars." These are different metaphors—sports versus cinema—but practically speaking, they are just variations on an identical theme.

10. Roque, alongside all of the other Spintronix founders, attended Westmoor,

a public high school in Daly City. However, the strong Catholic influence in Filipino American families meant that many of his peers attended local private Catholic schools, hence "private school girls."

11. In other music scenes, this relationship between male stars and female fans is commonly described through the derisive terminology of "groupies," aka "girls who follow pop stars or members of rock groups, often in the hope of deliberately provoking sexual relations with them" (Hilts et al. 2003: 237). However, in the mobile scene interviews the term "groupie" barely arose, and even when it did, the deployment of it tended to be gender-neutral and nonsexual in implication. To my respondents, groupies could be men or women, and while the term suggested a certain level of fawning fandom, their use of the term lacked the kind of misogynistic derision that exists toward groupies in other music scenes. I am uncertain if this implies that mobile DJs had a different relationship to female fans, or if the minimal use of the term was a strategic choice of vernacular by middle-aged family men recalling their teenage years, or something else, only that my respondents almost never spoke about female fans in the scene through any language that could be construed as intentionally demeaning.

12. When I asked Daphnie Anies if any one of the Go-Go's had wanted to form a crew as a way to meet men, she practically scoffed in her reply: "That's funny. That was not the intention for our group. Most of us were spoken for or getting away from dating."

13. It is not unusual, for example, to hear DJs complain about events being "a sausage fest," i.e., "too many men, not enough women." There is a general belief that a party with too few women is a failure, and many clubs and parties offer free admission to women, since their presence is believed to attract paying male patrons. In less obvious ways, the presence of women may also moderate latent homophobic anxiety in otherwise homosocial settings (see Coates 2007: 84; Sedgwick 1985: 25).

14. Party crews and DJ crews are similar though not necessarily synonymous. In the way Alsaybar describes them, they might also be party promotions crews, who throw parties, but not all party crews necessarily include DJs (though many do). Most of the existing literature, both academic and popular, dealing with the Filipino party crews is focused on Southern California. Besides Alsaybar, see also De Leon 2004 and Slovick 2007.

15. Electric Sounds' tensions with one street gang, LVM, took on tragic proportions when crew member "Tiger" Tapia was shot to death by the gang members during a DJ gig in the early 1980s.

16. See appendix 2 for a longer discussion of the role Filipino youth gangs played in the Bay Area during the 1970s. See also Alsaybar 1999 for his discussion of how some Filipino gangs in Los Angeles transformed into "party crews" by the 1990s.

17. Nancy MacDonald, in her study of graffiti crews, came to a similar realization when a respondent suggested to her: "Instead of questioning why more women don't do it, maybe we should question why men do?" (2001: 96).

18. Though there is worth in thinking through the parallels between graffiti crews and DJ crews, it must be noted that one major difference is that graffiti's status as quasi-legal or, oftentimes, completely illegal confers a different kind of status—especially related to masculinity—than does a legal, less controversial activity such as DJing.

19. This contrast—between the bodily abandonment of the dancer and the mental presence of the DJ—would be useful in expanding the discussion around the "mind-body split" in popular music as spearheaded by the likes of Frith 1996b, chapter 6, and McClary and Walser 1994.

20. At the same time, the absence of Filipinos in American mass media complicates the ways these youth would have been confronted with an idealized masculinity, modeled in popular culture. In discussing the role of masculinity among heavy metal bands and fans, Robert Walser argues that "this constituency . . . is a group generally lacking in social, physical, and economic power but besieged by cultural messages promoting such forms of power" (1993: 109). While I don't doubt that male youth of all persuasions are likely impacted, to some degree, by what Walser calls "an obligatory masculinity" circulated through various social channels, he's still largely talking about a white constituency, on both ends of that dialogue. However, with recognizable Filipino faces and bodies missing from the model of "obligatory masculinity," I believe it is harder to ascertain how Filipino American youth would have felt a specific pressure to live up to an ideal that did not even seem aware of their existence. Moreover, questions of "powerlessness" have to be weighed against the economic power most of these youth enjoyed, coming from comfortable middle-class families, and arguments of social isolation have to be balanced against the demographic presence they had in both school and neighborhood.

21. For more on the complexities of contemporary Filipino American masculinity, see Shimizu 2012: 123–38 and Capino 2010: 139–50. Both authors use Gene Cajayon's movie *The Debut* (2000) as a way to interrogate how masculinity, race, and class are wound together through the lead protagonist, Ben Mercado.

22. Anies noted that the second floor, above the ROTC basement, was where more recently arrived Filipino students hung out: "We used to call them the Second-Floor FOBs [fresh off the boat]. That's where the Filipinos were segregated." I took the "segregation" here to refer to a self-imposed separation rather than anything externally enforced.

23. Like many crews, their membership was informal and dynamic. During my interview with them, they argued over who was in the group and who wasn't—depending on who you asked, the Go-Go's either had seven, eight, or nine members.

24. The following section is based on the opinions and testimonials of the Go-Go's members, but I could not verify or corroborate these stories with members of Young 'N' Tough as I was unable to track any of them down.

25. "Using a tape" meant that a crew substituted a prerecorded set for a live mix, the DJ equivalent of lip-synching a vocal performance and trying to pass it off as live.

26. There is also no indication that the "98 percent of DJs have a penis" claim was empirically verified.

27. Even in older DJ and club scholarship with otherwise excellent discussions about gender in club cultures, gender issues *within the ranks of DJs themselves* are minimally addressed. For example, the topic only merits a passing mention in Sarah Thornton's *Club Cultures* (1996), despite the comprehensive quality of the book overall, and though Kai Fikentscher's *"You Better Work!": Underground Dance Music in New York City* (2000) has substantive chapters on both DJ culture and the gender identities in club spaces, there is no discussion about the gender of DJs. Even Simon Reynolds in *Generation Ecstasy*, which went further than most in addressing the issue, still limited it to a single paragraph, writing: "The presence of women on the dance floor is not reflected by the proportion of women in the ranks of professional DJs. . . . This has a lot to do with the homosocial nature of techno: tricks of the trade are passed from mentors to male acolytes. DJ-ing and sample-based music also go hand in hand with an obsessive 'trainspotter' mentality: the amassing of huge collections of records, the accumulation of exhaustive and arcane information about labels, producers, and auteurs" (1999: 274). There are exceptions to this in older texts, including Tricia Rose's *Black Noise* (1994) and Joseph Schloss's *Making Beats* (2004), but again, these are the exceptions.

28. Cohen argues that masculine normativity in rock music scenes is partially replicated in the music itself: "The music does, however, contribute to the continual process through which categories of men, male and masculine are produced, contested and redefined, and rock and pop have typically involved exploration of both behavior and ideas concerning gender and sexuality" (1997: 21).

29. Unlike in the 1980s, since at least the late 1990s, DJ schools and academies do now exist.

Chapter 3 / Unlimited Creations

1. As noted in the introduction, developing a database for mobile crews is highly dependent on crews being aware that attempts to collect that data exist and their willingness to participate. My guess is that my database, at present, includes less than half the number of total crews that formed, and even that estimate may be too large.

2. Insofar as DJing can be seen as a form of service sector labor that produces no physical product but rather an experience, it may be worthwhile for scholars to explore how contemporary DJs and musicians fit into Maurizio Lazzarato's concept of immaterial labor (1996). This is largely underexplored territory, though Andrew Lison does invoke immaterial labor in discussing DJs who spin "minimalist techno," given how the spinning of techno music increasingly happens via digital DJing solutions, thus mirroring the technological processes by which the music itself is created (2011: 213).

3. I want to carefully note: Kelley is referring to primarily inner-city youth,

whose economic choices were likely more limited than the suburban youth covered in my study. DJing, while an attractive choice for reasons already discussed, was both a privileged choice and not the only one available to educated, middle-class teenagers.

4. Adjusted for inflation, a scale of $100–$200 in 1983 would be equivalent to earning $230–$470 in 2013.

5. The relatively low profit potential in the mobile scene—combined with its marginalization from mainstream venues such as nightclubs—made the concept of "selling out" all but absent from my interviews. Selling out—the idea that one would trade artistic integrity for financial gain—is a common tension in pop musical culture (Rhodes and Westwood 2008), including other club-based scenes (Thornton 1996: 122) but was seemingly not a major issue in the mobile DJ scene. Though interviewees might have complained about other crews "not paying dues" by having their equipment gifted to them by their families, none of my respondents levied a charge that another DJ or crew had "sold out" their credibility. I believe one reason for this absence is that selling out is typically understood as the "incorporation" of a subculture into commodity status (Hebdige 2011: 95–96), but this presumes such a conversion is even possible to begin with. Since the mobile scene existed—for most its history—under the radar of the rest of society, there were few, if any, possibilities for commodification to easily exist. For example, no one was approaching mobile crews to appear in, say, a McDonald's ad or to endorse a clothing brand. I speculate that debates around selling out likely were more manifest in the scratch DJ era, given that the national and global prominence of DJs from that community made commodification more possible than for their mobile predecessors.

6. Interestingly, several of the most prominent DJ-led scenes also have deep ties to immigrant communities. Tim Lawrence discusses how the growth of the New York discotheque scene in the 1970s was intimately tied to both Italian American club owners and DJs (2004: 53); George Lipsitz chronicles how the evolution of Jamaican sound system culture included key personnel who came out of Jamaica's Chinese immigrant community (2007: 44). In turn, it was that same Jamaican sound system tradition that became key in powering hip-hop's birth in the South Bronx of the 1970s, especially via key pioneering figures such as Kool Herc, Afrika Bambaataa, and Grandmaster Flash—all three children of West Indian immigrants (Rubin and Melnick 2007: 183). Unaddressed in these accounts and histories, however, is how DJs coming from middle-class immigrant communities might have enjoyed particular advantages in attaining and distributing capital—especially through family- and community-based networks—to the benefit of a cultural activity as capital-dependent as DJing. As this section details, the Filipino American mobile scene absolutely depended on those very networks to help distribute the necessary capital to support a scene made up of dozens and dozens of different crews.

7. In general, my respondents were very reluctant to say anything critical of

any other crews or DJs *by name*. They were not reluctant to talk about negative incidents or behavior, but there was something about actually naming the crew or DJ that made them uncomfortable. I took this as politeness arising out of the age of my respondents at the time of our interviews (i.e., they were in their thirties and forties), but it is possible that had I interviewed them when they were younger, and still involved in the mobile scene, they would have exhibited less reticence toward "naming names."

8. "Paying dues" is a common value system in many musical communities, though what the phrase means changes depending on context. For example, in João Vargas's study of jazz musicians, "paying dues" means participating in "jam sessions" that act as a "substantial site for learning, developing, and establishing social connections" (2008: 324). In Joseph Schloss's study of hip-hop producers, "paying dues" is displayed through looking for used vinyl records (i.e., "digging") rather than sampling from compact discs (2004: 110). In most instances, though, "paying dues" involves some level of hardship that demonstrates, to others within a scene, that newer participants have gone through the same laborious rituals that they had to.

9. As Choi has remarked to me, he feels odd that he now rubs shoulders with wealthy, powerful clients, given that he grew up as the son of immigrants and spent part of his troubled teen years living in group homes.

10. One scene included in Filipino American filmmaker Gene Cajayon's film *The Debut* was an extended dance sequence orchestrated by a Filipino mobile DJ.

11. A debut is a coming-of-age celebration for Filipinas, usually held around the eighteenth birthday. A fictional debut is at the narrative center of *The Debut*; mobile DJs play a small side role during the debut itself.

12. To be sure, family and community groups were not the only source of economic capital; so were independent party promoters, a group I discuss in chapter 4.

13. Spring examines how the "underlying complex" that supported the techno scene in "Rushton" began to unravel when, for example, a key venue owner decided against supporting a local precinct alderman for reelection. The city official retaliated by directing local police to set up DUI checkpoints close to the bar, thus intimidating would-be partygoers out of attending (2004: 61). Spring's essay highlights the fragility of scenes that, even at the height of their success, often depend on a delicate social balance to sustain them. Weaken even a single pillar, and the entire structure of the scene may be subject to eventual collapse.

14. A trio of distinctly different studies highlights the importance—and diversity—of how social networks function within different music scenes. In discussing the ability of a regional (non-Western) music style to enter the global marketplace, Andrew Leyshon, David Matless, and George Revill argue that "the discovery, nurture, and recording of artistic talent is a transactional, information-rich, and highly discursive process. As a consequence, local social networks are critical to global success" (1998: 11). However, they would identify the key social networks as including A&R (artist and repertoire), staff, music publishers, and entertainment attorneys,

among others. These may be essential personnel to a music scene that is dependent on the production and distribution of physical merchandise or product, but these same players would have little function within musical communities that produce no physical product (such as the mobile DJ scene). In contrast, in Mari Yoshihara's study of Asian and Asian American classical musicians, she discusses how aspects of a person's background such as "access to familial and social networks . . . constitute a form of currency in mainstream society and affect one's class location in important ways" (2007: 133). In this case, "social networks" refers to the kind of "who you know" social capital that is derived from family, personal, and professional relationships that abet the Asian musicians—especially immigrant Asian musicians—in their endeavors to find work in the United States. This is more of an informal network, closer in relation to the networks in the mobile scene. Finally, also see DeWitt 2008, chapters 2 and 5. Even though, musically, there's not much in common between the Zydeco and Cajun music of DeWitt's study and the urban contemporary dance music most relevant in the mobile DJ scene, there are unexpected parallels in the ways both scenes depend on immigrant settlement patterns and tightly knit family- and community-based social networks for the long-term viability of their respective music professionals.

15. Besides some of the aforementioned studies looking at the role of social capital in music scenes (Crossley 2008; DeWitt 2008; Spring 2004; Thornton 1996), there is an interesting parallel between the family and community networks supporting the mobile DJ scene and another, largely immigrant network supporting a nonmusical cultural endeavor: Indian Americans and spelling bees. In a 2010 article in *Slate*, Ben Paynter profiles the Indian American–founded North South Foundation, a national circuit for spelling bee contests, involving seventy-five chapters, what Paynter describes as both "a minor-league spelling bee circuit" and a "nerd Olympiad for Indian-Americans." Because the foundation helps to identify, train, and support prospective spelling bee contestants, the children who participate in these activities improve their competitive odds at the annual Scripps Spelling Bee. Indeed, the winners of both the 2010 and 2011 Scripps contests were foundation "alumni," and in 2010, 11 percent of the Scripps contestant field came through the foundation (even though Indian Americans represent only 1 percent of the total U.S. population; Paynter 2010). While there are surely many differences between the Filipino American mobile scene and the Indian American spelling bee circuit, what I find notable about both is that they undermine the assumption that some purely cultural influence can explain the predominance of each respective group in their area of cultural activity and instead bring attention to the kind of structural and social capital advantages necessary for such advancement. There is also a parallel in the importance of peer-to-peer inspiration, though unlike the media invisibility of the mobile crews, in the case of Indian American spelling contestants, the successes of previous winners have been well documented in mass media, especially in the 2002 documentary *Spellbound*, which chronicled the eventual championship of Indian American Nupur Lala at the Scripps contest that year. Paynter quotes the

foundation's founder, Ratnam Chitturi, regarding the film's impact: "The parents were just excited. They saw that it was a possibility [to win the National Spelling Bee]."

Chapter 4 / Imaginings

1. In Sarah Thornton's work on club cultures, she eschews the term "subcultures" in favor of "taste cultures," given the importance of "shared taste in music" to the reasons people go to clubs to begin with (1996: 3).

2. A "biter" refers to someone who is unoriginal and can perform only by copying—aka biting—someone else's style.

3. Several respondents claimed to have known people whom Bradford had abused, but in all cases, they refused to share names with me (and none admitted being abused themselves). As far as I know, however, no one ever reported Bradford to the authorities. One respondent suggested that this happened prior to the intense mass media focus on childhood sexual abuse and therefore people at that time took Bradford's actions less seriously than how similar behavior might be addressed today.

4. For example, Dell Farinas of San Francisco's Chilltown Crush Crew stated that Bradford approached him and others in his crew: "He would try to bribe us, try to buy us records for sexual favors. A lot of the kids were young and naïve. They were easy prey." Farinas used language similar to Alvair's, describing Bradford as "basically a child molester." I collected other "off the record" testimonials that also allege similar, harassing behavior on Bradford's part.

5. The Juice Crew took its name from a group of New York rappers organized by producer Marley Marl that included well-known, late-1980s rappers such as Biz Markie, Roxanne Shante, Kool G Rap, and Big Daddy Kane.

6. Another unexpected outcome was how the rise of showcases increased the role of women within certain crews, not as DJs but as MCs. Especially with the growing popularity of rap music and hip-hop culture, crews began to use designated MCs to introduce their DJs during battles and showcases, tasking them with raising the energy of the audience. MCs were meant to get the crowd "hyped," using call-and-response shouts, witty rhymes, and other forms of audience interactions. In comparison to the subordinate status of "lady DJs," MCs could take a more central and visible role within a crew, and that included Daphnie Anies of the Go-Go's, Jocelyn "Lady J" Castillo of Sound Sequence, and Melanie Caganot, curator for the *Tales of the Turntable* exhibit, who was a well-known fixture in the mobile scene as rapper Lani Luv. Ultimately, more research needs to be done to properly document this phenomenon, but it does strike me as an important way in which women found a visible role in the liminal space that literally sat between the turntables and dance floor.

7. Alviar's father had roots in U.S. naval service, though in the United States he worked as a mail office clerk. Her mother was a nurse. Alviar's family reached Union

City in the early 1970s, having followed a familiar route of secondary migration stops via cities with large naval bases: first in Portsmouth, Virginia, then Alameda, California, and finally to Union City just as new subdivisions were being built there.

8. Alviar told me that Bradford harbored racist sentiments toward African Americans, allegedly once asking her why she wanted to invite "those Black creatures" to her parties. However, the differences of her parties from Bradford's were likely beyond just personal prejudices, given the demographic profile of the regions.

9. Northern Soul was a scene predicated heavily on record rarity. DJs built playlists around distinctly mid-1960s, Motown-influenced styles of R&B, but rather than focus on the giants of the era—the Miracles, Marvin Gaye, the Supremes—the groups that had failed became the fuel for Northern Soul obsessives. Intrepid DJs visited the United States and scoured record stores for singles by forgotten, small-time acts. The more obscure the songs the higher the prestige, and as the Northern Soul scene evolved, fans from across Great Britain would flock to venues such as Blackpool's Mecca or the Wigan Casino to hear the latest discoveries. See Brewster and Broughton 1999: 88–91; Hollows and Milestone 1998; Nowell 2011.

10. "Translocality" has become a popular concept in pop music studies since the mid-1990s; Peterson and Bennett use it to refer to scenes that are "local [but] are also connected with groups of kindred spirits many miles away" (2004: 8–9). The mobile scene, in my opinion, shares some elements of translocality, insofar as collective travel to musical events is often cited as a bonding force in creating a translocal scene. However, most other examples of translocal music scenes involved the trade and sharing of recordings and other physical media, artifacts that did not exist in the mobile scene.

11. Dame Cruz is a pseudonym as my respondent requested anonymity.

12. Sarita See invokes the term to refer to the Filipino diaspora and its diversity in "region, religion, language, class, sexuality, and race that intersects unevenly with a history of plural colonialisms and migration patterns" (2009: 141).

13. When Tumakay suggests that at DJ parties "you have to behave in a certain way," it recalls Will Straw's observations that "bringing together the activities of dance and musical consumption, the dance club articulates the sense of social identity as embodied to the conspicuous and differential display of taste" (2004: 92). This counters the ideal that dance floors allow for total freedom from self-consciousness or conventional rules of behavior, yet in Tumakay's example he is suggesting that the conventions at these dance parties actually helped facilitate contact between different cliques, thus assisting in the formation of community.

14. See Nadal 2010 for other first person narratives about Filipino American identity.

15. Pardorla's testimonial also reinforced the point that Filipino American DJs, at that time in the 1980s, simply did not exist in any mass mediated forum. As noted in the introduction, the social and racial marginalization and invisibility of Filipino Americans would have been especially acute in the 1970s and 1980s. Even though mainstream U.S. pop culture was replete with images of DJs, thanks to

shows like WKRP and movies such as *Saturday Night Fever*, few would have included Asian or Filipino characters. Therefore, these peer-to-peer encounters created by mobile crew parties would have been one of the only ways that any young Filipino Americans would have seen a DJ who looked like themselves or came from the same backgrounds.

16. David Henry Hwang's play *FOB* (1980) delves into similar tensions within the Chinese American community.

17. Daphnie Anies, recounting the social geography of Balboa High, alluded to a similar separation between the "Second-Floor FOBs" and the "cool" Filipinos who hung out in the ROTC basement.

18. Bangele Alsaybar's study (1999) of both Filipino youth gangs and "party crews" in Los Angeles is also a worthwhile comparison. Both geography and age separate his study subjects from mine, but the Filipino fraternity-derived party crews of his research share key similarities with the mobile crews in terms of function and purpose. (The main difference was that party crews could exist without DJs being members; mobile crews, by definition, included at least one DJ.) Alsaybar opines that in contrast to the self-conscious "Pinoy pride" of Filipino youth gangs, the party crews tended to avoid conspicuous displays of ethnicity (119, 132). He theorizes that as Filipino youth moved further away from the immediate experience of immigration, especially among those born in the United States, the desire to hold on to a cultural identity as Filipinos faded as well. That left them open to other forms of social and cultural identification, not always based directly on ethnicity or heritage. As he puts it, "today's crews aspire for multiple and overlapping identities . . . based on the appropriation of mainstream popular music genres like hip[-hop] and anglo American technological symbols like cars and drag racing" (132–33). As noted, his work may be more relevant to thinking about shifting identity alliances for those who entered into the mobile scene in its later years, as opposed to my research subjects, who tended to be older participants.

19. When I interviewed Alviar in 2002–2003, she was still using her promotions background to help sponsor local community events and activities for her children's schools, but she left the DJ world behind when she stopped actively promoting.

20. Imagine 20 was billed as a "20th anniversary" party, though technically it would have been the twentieth Imagine-billed event, as opposed to the twentieth year of events. Between party numbers eleven to twenty, I was only able to find a flyer for Imagine 16 (1989); it is possible the "missing" Imagines were those held in Southern California.

21. A "gyro" is a breakdance move where the dancer executes a standing cartwheel.

22. I spoke with journalist Jinni Bartolome, who covered the Bradford murder at the time in 1992. She explained to me that a suspect was never arrested and the main "person of interest" was a twenty-one-year-old Filipino American man, originally from Daly City, who people in the community believed had fled to the Philippines to avoid speaking to the police. Over the years, I have heard many rumors around Bradford's death—that he was murdered by a jealous ex-lover, that he was

killed over a drug deal or excessive debts. Conspicuously, though, no one I spoke to suggested there was communal remorse over his passing despite his outsized presence in the scene. Bartolome speculated that ultimately, what people respected were Bradford's accomplishments more than the man himself.

Chapter 5 / Take Me Out with the Fader

1. The video of this battle has become urban legend within the mobile community; several of my respondents mentioned having Q-Bert's part of the battle recorded on an *n*th-generation VHS dub. That part of the video does indeed exist—it has been on YouTube since at least 2010—but a smaller number of people also claim to possess the full battle, including Jazzy Jim's half; however, this full video has yet to reenter the digital public domain.

2. For more on the history of scratching, see Doug Pray's excellent documentary *Scratch* (2002) and read Mark Katz's *Groove Music* (2012).

3. In Pray's *Scratch*, there is a funny and poignant montage of testimonials by different DJs, including Mixmaster Mike, all talking about first seeing "Rockit" performed.

4. For more on the history of beat-juggling, see Katz 2012: 116–21.

5. For a list of songs that have sampled "Impeach the President," see the website Rap Sample FAQ, http://the-breaks.com/search.php?term=impeach+the+president&type=4.

6. The scratch crew headed by the core of Apollo, Mike, and Q-Bert went under a variety of names beginning in the late 1980s. These included FM2O, the Shadow DJs, and Rocksteady Crew. Eventually, in 1995, they settled on Invisibl Skratch Piklz, a name that lasted until their dissolution in 2000.

7. The War Memorial is a park located near the border between Daly City and San Francisco. In the early 1980s, it became a popular site for youth into b-boying and other street dance styles.

8. Interestingly, like many of the Balboa's early mobile DJs, Q-Bert was also a member of the school's prestigious ROTC drill team. In fact, in my interviews with him, Q-Bert credited his training in drill team routines as benefiting his later mastery of scratch routines, since both required a highly synchronized set of physical movements to be performed within a limited time frame. See appendix 1.

9. Once the Invisibl Skratch Piklz organized formally in 1995, their ranks included other former mobile DJs, including Just 2 Hype's Shortkut, Sound City's D-Styles, and Second To None's Yoga Frog.

10. FM2O was a Filipino American hip-hop group featuring two MCs—FMD and H2O—and the three DJs. Though the name originally came from the rappers, most of the media attention focused on the FM2O DJs, especially after Q-Bert became the American DMC champion in 1991. For a digital dubbing of the 1992 episode of the local Bay Area television show *Home Turf* that spotlights the FM2O DJs, see YouTube video posted July 26, 2007, www.youtube.com/watch?v=5zfCbxLWZt4.

11. That name change is especially important—Rocksteady is the name of the

most vaunted b-boy crew in the United States, originally founded in the early 1980s in New York. Rocksteady's leader, Crazy Legs, then imparted the Rocksteady name unto Apollo, Mike, and Q-Bert after seeing them perform in New York, not only embracing the three in a gesture of bicoastal solidarity but also solidifying their legitimization within the hip-hop world. It also suggested that the community these DJs belonged to was an emergent, national hip-hop one versus the local Bay Area mobile scene. These were not massive breaks by themselves but, rather, small points of divergence that, over time, contributed to the separate development of a scratch DJ scene.

12. In my estimation, the relative isolation of Bay Area scratch DJs during the 1980s was a competitive boon, because it allowed DJs like Q-Bert, Apollo, and Mixmaster Mike to develop styles through a long-term process in which their experimentations in technique and style were not being actively observed and appropriated by others. Insofar as one primary way that DJing styles "traveled" was through direct peer-to-peer interaction and observation, the isolation the Bay Area turntablists enjoyed meant that by the time Q-Bert entered into his first national competition in the early 1990s, his styles were so distinct that it helped him stand out against a crowd of East Coast and European DJs in which cross-pollination of styles had created (unintentional) similarities. While technical skill is one marker by which DJs are judged, the more nebulous category of "unique style" is even more valuable in terms of symbolic capital, and while isolation alone does not guarantee the development of unique style, it can be one vital precondition.

13. One of the major paradigm shifts their victory engendered was the devaluing of body tricks. From that point onward, their success set a new standard in technical, scratch proficiency that future DJs were expected to meet.

14. A "battle record" is a vinyl LP designed specifically for scratch DJs to use in competitions. Most times, these records contain short vocal snippets, drum patterns, and other sounds that are ideal for scratching. Instead of bringing in a dozen records, each with a single sample, the battle record included many possible tools in a single source. This created a custom consumer product created by and for scratch DJs. See Katz 2010: 128 for more on battle and breakbeat records.

15. The term "bedroom DJ" is popularly used to refer to DJs who spend much of their time sequestered at home, practicing. Most DJs practice extensively in private, but turntablism is well suited to that isolation because many of the styles one has to learn can only be achieved through constant training and practice.

16. For example, at the turn of the millennium, China had no real DJ tradition to speak of—in a city like Shanghai, with over seventeen million residents, there were no stores that even sold vinyl records. Yet in 2002 China held its first national DMC contest, attracting over a dozen competitors. The contest was won by Shanghai's Gary Wang, aka DJ V-Nutz, a DJ who learned the craft while working in Tokyo in the 1990s. In our conversations, Wang (no relation) credited the importation of scratch DJ videos into China as a major way by which aspiring Chinese DJs are now learning how to mix and scratch.

17. When I asked Q-Bert for his side of the story, his email reply confirmed the basics of Apollo's recollection: "We both love each other like brothers . . . but [yes], i wanted to do more skratching as an instrument and he wanted to do party rockin stuff at that time."

18. As I was working on revisions for this book in 2011, I saw a preview for the animated film about dancing penguins *Happy Feet 2*. In the "teaser" preview, there is one point where a penguin—performing a sanitized version of Justin Timberlake's "Sexy Back"—walks on-screen and makes a scratching motion with her flipper, coinciding with a moment in the soundtrack where a scratching "zigga zigga" sound can be heard. While there is no turntable present in the scene, the gesture—and accompanying sound—felt intuitively obvious, as if anyone watching (children included) would simply understand "that penguin is scratching."

19. There are several scratch academies, including ones based in New York and London. In the Bay Area, the International DJ Academy opened in 2003, led by Alex Aquino, a Filipino American entrepreneur who began with Unlimited Sounds and in the early 1990s managed several members of Invisibl Skratch Piklz prior to the crew's formal incorporation.

20. Both KMEL and KSOL were leading urban contemporary stations, and for many years fierce competitors. Eventually KSOL changed call letters to become KYLD in the mid-1990s, though both continued to operate with a successful, popular urban contemporary format. They have ceased to be true competitors, however—in the late 1990s, both stations were bought by radio conglomerate Clear Channel. Notably, Jim Archer, aka Jazzy Jim, formerly of San Jose's Skyway Sounds, became a program director at both KMEL and KYLD, another example of how alums of the mobile scene continue to play leading roles in the Bay Area's music community.

21. Just 2 Hype's Derrick Damian mentioned that many of the DJs at one popular nightclub party—City Nights—drew the Filipino American crowds but, from his perspective, didn't hire enough Filipino DJs: "A lot of the non-Filipinos, like Rick Lee, Jose Melendez, Jazzy Jim, no offense, but what kind of irked me, they'd be doing all the City Nights but it'd be all of our people: it'd be all the Filipina girls, Filipino people but it wasn't Filipino DJs and that shit made me mad. Why these guys, where are all the Filipino DJs?"

22. Best (2006, chapter 2) discusses the relevance of cruising culture among young Chicano and Latino Americans, and while I wouldn't conflate the latter's experiences with that of young Filipino Americans, the idea of cruising as a way of building and marking community identity seems highly relevant to both groups.

23. In Gene Cajayon's film *The Debut* (2000), there is a short scene about the "import car conspiracy," with the suggestion being that car customization and racing is a consumerism-based distraction from greater social justice issues.

24. For more on the Asian American import car racing scene, see Kwon 2004 and Namkung 2004. For more on car racing and cruising in general, see Best 2006.

25. With "genre," Lena is departing from the way that term is typically used in pop music conversations. We usually think of genres—rock, hip-hop, jazz, classical,

et alia—as referring to a musical style or idiom. However, for Lena, to talk about hip-hop as a genre, for example, does not just refer to its stylistic and aesthetic attributes. Rather, she defines genres via a more sociologically grounded perspective, describing them as "systems of orientations, expectations, and conventions that bind together industry, performers, critics, and fans in making what they identify as a distinctive sort of music" (2012: 6). In other words, a genre is a social construction arising out of a community of interactive, like-minded participants. That definition doesn't negate the way a genre label also functions as a shorthand for various stylistic elements, but it does foreground the importance of human social activity in constructing (or challenging) genre lines.

26. Obviously, not all genres follow this trajectory—polka, for example, never enjoyed an industry-based phase, while Lena argues that jazz fusion made it from avant-garde up through scene and industry-based forms but didn't reach a traditionalist stage (2012: 68).

27. Grandmaster Flash tells the story of how DJ Hollywood "changed the whole game" by booking multiple nightclub parties in a single night and increasing his income threefold as a result. Flash says, "This made the sound system a dinosaur" (Fricke and Ahearn 2002: 179).

28. As both Jeff Chang (2005) and Dan Charnas (2010) detail, some of the biggest names in the New York hip-hop party scene, *pre*-"Rapper's Delight," had no interest in cutting a record because they didn't see how hip-hop—then an exclusively party-based culture—could translate onto a recording. Sylvia Robinson, of Sugar Hill Records, initially wanted star DJ Lovebug Starski to help cut what would eventually turn into "Rapper's Delight," but he declined (Fricke and Ahearn 2002: 179). Likewise, Grandmaster Flash, another major DJ on the scene, had no interest in recording himself or his crew, the Furious Five, until *after* "Rapper's Delight" became a massive hit (Chang 2005: 129).

29. I am referring specifically to the Filipino American scene here. There are other examples of Bay Area mobile DJs moving into the record-making end of the business, in particular, DJ EFX of Mind Motion—a Latino American crew in the Bay Area—released a twelve-inch single, "Just Freakin'," in 1988 on the Def Turntable imprint. However, these are all exceptional cases rather than anything normative for any of the Bay Area mobile scenes.

30. Enriquez began her career as a member of a high school singing group that called itself the Pinay Divas (Wong 2004: 244).

31. The fact that Enriquez initially recorded in Latin freestyle—a genre pioneered by East Coast Latino artists but adopted far and wide—made sense given her and Classified's connection to the mobile scene, but it inadvertently created a controversy early in her career. As Elizabeth Pisares recounts, because the cover art of Enriquez's debut album, *Lovely*, partially obscured her face and because her first single, "I've Been Thinking of You," included a Spanish version (as a way to tap into the Latino buying audience), some Filipino Americans accused Enriquez of trying to "pass" as Latina rather than Filipina (Pisares 2006: 176). To only complicate things further,

when Enriquez was signed to Tommy Boy and released the house music–influenced "A Little Bit of Ecstasy" in 1998, she was then accused of trying to pass as African American. In both cases, her critics pointed at both the musical styles and marketing art as "evidence" of Enriquez's desire to pass as anything but Filipina (178).

32. The mobile scene did, however, serve as a training ground for *some* of these teenagers to later pursue careers in professional sound and lighting engineering and technology.

33. Eleanor Academia, in particular, had far more resources to draw from in her own career, having been mentored by Quincy Jones and signed to major labels such as Epic and Columbia. Yet despite that, her description of the "wilderness and the jungle" facing Filipino American artists suggests that there has been a massive gulf between individual achievement and community and systematic resources.

34. The focus of Megatone—and likely any other significant dance labels in San Francisco—was on nightclub DJs, not mobile DJs. According to Hedges, the label's practices created a divide between the camps via their distribution system: Megatone serviced major nightclub DJs directly, whereas mobile DJs received Megatone releases through "record pools," i.e., third party promoters to whom labels would send their releases in order to then be distributed to DJs within the pool. For Megatone at least—and likely for other labels too—nightclub DJs were seen as more valuable, thus pushing their awareness of the mobile scene and its DJs further to the margins.

35. In Rolando Tolentino's essay "Identity and Difference: 'Filipino/a American' Media Arts," he suggests that among the Filipino American media arts community of the 1980s, most were fixated on "social problems encountered by Filipino immigrants," specifically the "retrieval of the history of male pioneers, placing them in the nexus of U.S. national history" (2002: 119). Given that focus, there may have been little interest in the cultural activities of Filipino Americans two generations *younger* than the subjects of documentaries such as Linda Mabalot's *Manong* (1978), Curtis Choy's *The Fall of the I-Hotel* (1983), or Naomi De Castro's *In No One's Shadow: Filipinos in America* (1988). Interestingly, though, on the tail end of this first period of Filipino American media arts, Tolentino briefly mentions a 1993 narrative short, *Diary of a Gangsta Sucka*, which satirizes a suburban Pinoy teenager's fascination with the gang "lifestyle." *Diary* was written and directed by one of my respondents, John Castro, who grew up in San Jose and was briefly a member of a mobile crew that, according to what he told me, "disbanded before we ever agreed on a name."

36. The Bullet Proof Scratch Hamsters were a mostly Latino and white crew, based in Daly City. Though best known as turntablists, their members also originated in mobile crews.

37. Bomb Hip-Hop Records' 1995 release *Return of the DJ* was an early, seminal release that showcased turntablist talent across the United States. Filipino American DJs are well represented on the album: Mixmaster Mike, the Invisibl Skratch Piklz, LA's DJ Babu and the Beat Junkies (1995). Beginning that same year and

through 1996, Billy Jam, a local Bay Area DJ, began videotaping scratch DJ performances, at his home, for his show *Pirate Fuckin' Radio*. Beginning in 1999, he released these performances on CD and VHS on his Hip Hop Slam imprint under the title *The Shiggar Fraggar Show*.

38. There is a tempting desire to contemplate "what if?" scenarios, such as "what if YouTube had existed during the mobile era and something like the Imagine showcases could have been simulcast around the world?" But while such a difference in media technology could certainly have impacted the mobile scene, one would also have to consider whether the scene could or would have formed the way it did had there been other outlets for personal expression via the Internet and social media. In any case, my firm impression from interviewing mobile scene participants is that there are few regrets as to how everything played out.

Conclusion

1. Vinroc, like Apollo and Shortkut, is Filipino American; he got his start with a Jersey City mobile crew named 5th Dimension.

2. Full-time, professional DJs such as Triple Threat were quick to adopt the Rane Corporation's Serato Scratch Live, a digital DJing system that debuted in 2004. Scratch Live allows DJs to integrate digital music files within a conventional turntable setup, thus combining the convenience of digital technology and tried-and-true practices of analog DJing. See Carpenter 2005 and Katz 2012: 220.

3. I interviewed Triple Threat in 2001, and we engaged in a lively conversation about the fact that many of today's DJs learn scratching but do not possess a fundamental knowledge of nonstop mixing, even from the technical basics of beat-matching (Wang 2001c).

4. "Breaks" refers to older funk, soul, jazz, and rock songs on which much of hip-hop's sound was based.

5. Triple Threat are one of many hybrid scratch–party DJ crews out there. In Los Angeles, their counterparts are the Beat Junkies, who have among their ranks prominent Filipino American DJs such as Babu, Rhettmatic, Icey Ice, and Symphony, as well as former Invisibl Skratch Piklz members D-Styles and Shortkut. Like Triple Threat, the Beat Junkies came out of LA's mobile crews and then excelled during the scratching era. Also like Triple Threat, since retiring from active turntable competition in 1998, the Beat Junkies have focused mostly on returning to spinning at clubs and parties, integrating their skills as both mixers and scratchers (De Leon 2004; Wang 2002).

6. Spintronix held their twenty-fifth anniversary party in 2010 and have since commissioned a video documentary about the history of the crew.

7. At the 2006 "Tribute 2 Bay Area Mobile DJs" party, I noticed that the most important accessory that most of the participating DJs had with them was a portable external hard drive that stored their "digital crates" of records. That way, instead of having to bring computers, they could all plug into the same shared laptop.

8. At the very least, no one attending the reunion parties is trying to revive the fashions of the 1980s.

9. Arguably, one of the earliest of these "back in the day" parties, the Agenda DJ Showcase, was held in 1996 in San Francisco. The flyer for that party read "in 1984, assemblies of the DJ groups came together and brought to the Bay Area the DJ Showcase . . . 12 YEARS LATER . . . THEY RETURN."

10. The obvious exception to this was Melanie Caganot's 2001–2002 exhibit *Tales of the Turntable* at the San Mateo County History Museum, but as groundbreaking as that was, it likely only reached a slice of the former mobile community. (It is intriguing to consider how awareness/attendance of that exhibit might have turned out had social media sites like Twitter and Facebook existed then.)

11. Myspace, which was the dominant platform in the mid-2000s, drew some of these mobile veterans, but from my observation, the ascendance of Facebook has made the greatest difference.

12. At least one respondent—Ken Anolin, formerly of Fusion—told me that our interviews were one reason he decided to start DJing again. I do not mention this to be self-aggrandizing; it just strikes me that the power of revisiting the past can be enough to reignite interest in practices previously left fallow.

13. Rivera's partner in Spintronix, Jay dela Cruz, named his own son Derek Jordan dela Cruz, aka D.J. dela Cruz. Suffice it to say: not a coincidence.

14. Cut-mixing means that the DJ "cuts" in new tracks with minimal blending or beat-matching. Quick-mixing, for example, is a form of cut-mixing.

15. It was never a conscious decision, at least in the beginning, to forego "a music chapter," but when I finished the initial draft of the book, I realized I didn't have one and contemplated adding one on, since it seemed like an odd absence. However, my friend and colleague Joseph Schloss counseled me to reflect on why, intuitively, it had not occurred to me to make this topic part of my research agenda from inception. And in doing so, I realized that my interest in this topic was never about the music; it was about the community of DJs: how they came together, why they stayed together, what forces helped them rise and fall. Music may have been a central part of their craft, but it was secondary to the other factors and forces that helped address the evolution of the mobile scene and its relationship to the Filipino American community in the Bay Area.

16. For more on the history of the San Francisco club scene, see Diebold 1988. For more on Sylvester, see Echols 2010, chapter 4.

17. I owe a debt to Christine Balance, who suggested that beyond discussing the presence and absence of homosexual desire in the mobile scene, it would also be worth exploring whether a covert heterosexist, normative logic operated within the scene, one in which queerness—within the crews—was erased and avoided.

18. In particular, I think of what Karen Tongson has written about Filipino American suburban settlement positing these neighborhoods as "a repository for the subjects scattered by the United States' latent imperial ambitions in the twen-

tieth century, and as a consequence of the nation's collusion with other imperial projects during earlier ages of empire" (2011: 13–14).

Appendix 1

1. Besides Sound Explosion's members, other drill team participants included Rene Anies (Electric Sounds), Willie Sparks (Non-Stop Boogie), Daphnie Anies (the Go-Go's), Paul Tumakay (Kicks Company), and Richard "Q-Bert" Quitevis (Live Style Productions).

2. In line with the discussion of sexual capital in chapter 2, Tumakay also said that part of his interest in ROTC was "the females, they looked really nice in their uniform and if you wanna get to know them, then you gotta fit with the crowd, so to speak."

3. Notably, the ROTC drill teams at both Balboa and Lowell became embroiled in hazing controversies in 1994: senior commanders were accused of practicing physical hazing against junior members. Though reports did not identify the three junior members specifically as Filipino, it is likely (based on surname) that they were. It is unclear if the senior members under investigation were also Filipino American. See Hatfield 1999; Lutz and Bartlett 1995: 36.

Appendix 2

The history and import of Bay Area Filipino youth gangs remains an important area for future research. What I have included in this appendix was based on conversations that arose in the course of conducting research related to the rest of the book. In the end, I felt the material in both this and appendix 1 were too tangential to warrant inclusion in the main book narrative yet still had enough merit to include here, as addenda.

1. Corpuz and Rashid both suggested that the import of crack culture into the inner city elevated violence between gangs, as the drug industry gave gangs an economic incentive to battle one another.

2. Alsaybar suggested one additional factor. He argued that among second-generation, American-born Filipino youth, gang involvement was also a way for youth to "feel a sense of 'Pinoy Pride'"—in other words, for them to secure a sense of ethnic identity through the gangs (1999: 125). While Alsaybar makes a convincing argument for this additional attraction, my own data neither fully support nor refute this analysis. For the most part, none of my respondents who were either gang members themselves or were at least familiar with the scene cited ethnic pride as a compelling reason why youth became involved in gangs.

References

Books and Articles

Aaron, Charles. 1997. "Turning the Tables." *Spin*, March, 63–65.
Adler, Bill, and Dan Charnas. 2011. *Def Jam Recordings: The First 25 Years of the Last Great Record Label*. New York: Rizzoli.
Alba, Richard, and Nancy Denton. 2005. "Old and New Landscapes of Diversity: The Residential Patterns of Immigrant Minorities." In *Not Just Black and White: Historical and Contemporary Perspectives on Immigration, Race, and Ethnicity in the United States*, ed. N. Foner and G. Fredrickson, 237–61. New York: Russell Sage Foundation.
Alba, Richard, John Logan, Brian Stults, Gilbert Marzan, and Wenquan Zhang. 1999. "Immigrant Groups in the Suburbs: A Reexamination of Suburbanization and Spatial Assimilation." *American Sociological Review* 64(3): 446–60.
Alcazaren, Paulo. 2011. "The Suburbs of Quezon City." *Philippine Star*, August 6. www.philstar.com/modern-living/713377/suburbs-quezon-city.
Alsaybar, Bangele. 1993. "Satanas: Ethnography of a Filipino American Street Brotherhood in Los Angeles." MA thesis, University of California, Los Angeles.
Alsaybar, Bangele. 1999. "Deconstructing Deviance: Filipino American Youth Gangs, 'Party Culture,' and Ethnic Identity in Los Angeles." *Amerasia* 25(1): 116–38.
Ancheta, Angelo. 2006. *Race, Rights, and the Asian American Experience*. New Brunswick, NJ: Rutgers University Press.
Austin, Joe. 2001. *Taking the Train: How Graffiti Art Became an Urban Crisis in New York City*. New York: Columbia University Press.

Balance, Christine. 2007. "Intimate Acts, Martial Cultures: Performance and Belonging in Filipino America." PhD diss., New York University.

Bartolome, Jinni. 1992. "Police Seek Filipino in Promoter's Death." *Philippine News*, October 28–November 3, 1, 11.

Bay Area Census. 2012. Metropolitan Transportation Commission and Association of Bay Area Governments. www.bayareacensus.ca.gov.

Becker, Howard. 1982. *Art Worlds*. Berkeley: University of California Press.

Becker, Howard. 1998. *Tricks of the Trade: How to Think about Research While You're Doing It*. Chicago: University of Chicago Press.

Best, Amy. 2006. *Fast Cars, Cool Rides: The Accelerating World of Youth and Their Cars*. New York: New York University Press.

Bonus, Rick. 1996. "Cartographies of Filipino American Ethnicity." In *Filipino American Architecture, Design, and Planning Issues*, ed. A. Ubalde, 171–95. Los Angeles: Flipside.

Bonus, Rick. 2000. *Locating Filipino Americans: Ethnicity and the Cultural Politics of Space*. Philadelphia: Temple University Press.

Bourdieu, Pierre, and Loïc Wacquant. 1992. *An Invitation to Reflexive Sociology*. Chicago: University of Chicago Press.

Bourdieu, Pierre, and Loïc Wacquant. 1997. "The Forms of Capital." In *Education: Culture, Economy, and Society*, ed. A. Hasley, H. Lauder, P. Brown, and A. Wells, 47–58. London: Oxford University Press.

Bourriaud, Nicolas. 2002. *Postproduction*. New York: Lukas and Sternberg.

Brewster, Bill, and Frank Broughton. 1999. *Last Night a DJ Saved My Life: The History of the Disc Jockey*. New York: Grove.

Capino, Jose. 2010. *Dream Factories of a Former Colony: American Fantasies, Philippine Cinema*. Minneapolis: University of Minnesota Press.

Carpenter, Susan. 2005. "Enter the Digital Rage." *Los Angeles Times*, August 4, E4.

Catapusan, Benicio. 1934. "The Filipino Occupational and Recreational Activities in Los Angeles." MA thesis, University of Southern California.

Chang, Jeff. 2005. *Can't Stop, Won't Stop: A History of the Hip-Hop Generation*. New York: Picador.

Charnas, Dan. 2010. *The Big Payback: The History of the Business of Hip-Hop*. New York: New American Library.

Chonin, Neva. 2001. "Turning the Tables: Vibrant Bay Area DJ Culture Celebrated in Clubs, Museum." *San Francisco Chronicle*, September 27. www.sfgate.com/bayarea/article/Turning-the-tables-Vibrant-Bay-Area-DJ-culture-2873777.php.

Coates, Norma. 2007. "Teenyboppers, Groupies, and Other Grotesques: Girls and Women and Rock Culture in the 1960s and Early 1970s." *Journal of Popular Music Studies* 15(1): 65–94.

Cohen, Sara. 1997. "Men Making a Scene: Rock Music and the Production of Gender." In *Sexing the Groove: Popular Music and Gender*, ed. S. Whiteley, 17–36. New York: Routledge.

Cole, Tom. 2010. "You Ask, We Answer: Why Do Some Songs Fade Out at the End?" *Record*, October 7. www.npr.org/blogs/therecord/2010/10/07/130409256/you-ask-we-answer-why-do-some-songs-fade-out-at-the-end.

Connell, John, and Chris Gibson. 2003. *Sound Tracks: Popular Music, Identity and Place*. New York: Routledge.

Cook, Dave. 1995. "Filipino DJs of the Bay Area [Why Are They So Successful?]." *Davey D's Hip Hop Corner*. www.daveyd.com/filipinodjs.html.

Copeland, Brian. 2006. *Not a Genuine Black Man: My Life as an Outsider*. San Francisco: MacAdam/Cage.

Crossley, Nick. 2008. "Pretty Connected: The Social Network of the Early UK Punk Movement." *Theory, Culture and Society* 25(6): 89–116.

Crossley, Nick. 2011. *Towards Relational Sociology*. New York: Routledge.

De Graaf, Lawrence. 2001. "African American Suburbanization in California, 1960 through 1990." In *Seeking El Dorado: African Americans in California*, ed. L. De Graaf, K. Mulroy, and Q. Taylor, 405–49. Los Angeles: Autry Museum of Western Heritage.

De Leon, Lakandiwa. 2004. "Filipinotown and the DJ Scene: Cultural Expression and Identity Affirmation of Filipino American Youth in Los Angeles." In *Asian American Youth: Culture, Identity and Ethnicity*, ed. J. Lee and M. Zhou, 191–206. New York: Routledge.

DeWitt, Mark. 2008. *Cajun and Zydeco Dance Music in Northern California: Modern Pleasures in a Postmodern World*. Jackson: University of Mississippi Press.

Dexter, Dave, Jr. 1974. "British Femme Runs Mobile Disco in LA." *Billboard*, November 2, 1, 12.

Diebold, David. 1988. *Tribal Rites: The San Francisco Dance Music Phenomenon 1978–88*. 2nd ed. Northridge, CA: Time Warp.

Durkheim, Emile. 2003. "The Elementary Forms of Religious Life." In *Emile Durkheim: Sociologist of Modernity*, ed. M. Emirbayer, 109–21. Malden, MA: Blackwell.

Echols, Alice. 2010. *Hot Stuff: Disco and the Remaking of American Culture*. New York: Norton.

Eljera, Bert. 1996. "Filipinos Find Home in Daly City." *Asianweek*, May 3.

Elwood, Philip. 1967. "Psychedelic Rockers: Musical Revolutionaries." *Billboard*, May 6, SF-6–SF-9.

España-Maram, Linda. 2006. *Creating Masculinity in Los Angeles's Little Manila: Working-Class Filipinos and Popular Culture, 1920s–1950s*. New York: Columbia University Press.

Espiritu, Yen Le. 1995. *Filipino Lives*. Philadelphia: Temple University Press.

Espiritu, Yen Le. 1997. *Asian American Women and Men: Labor, Laws and Love*. Thousand Oaks, CA: Sage.

Fikentscher, Kai. 2000. *"You Better Work!": Underground Dance Music in New York City*. Hanover, NH: University Press of New England.

Filipino American National Historical Society, Manilatown Heritage Foundation, and Pin@y Educational Partnerships. 2011. *Filipinos in San Francisco*. Charleston, SC: Arcadia.

Flannigan-Saint-Aubin, Arthur. 1994. "The Male Body and Literary Metaphors for Masculinity." In *Theorizing Masculinities*, ed. H. Brod and M. Kaufman, 239–58. Thousand Oaks, CA: Sage.

Franko, Kantele. 2007. "I-Hotel, 30 Years Later—Manilatown Legacy Honored." *San Francisco Chronicle*, August 4. www.sfgate.com/bayarea/article/I-Hotel-30-years-later-Manilatown-legacy-3416119.php.

Fricke, Jim, and Charlie Ahearn. 2002. *Yes Yes Y'all: The Experience Music Project Oral History of Hip-Hop's First Decade*. New York: Da Capo.

Frith, Simon. 1996a. "Music and Identity." In *Questions of Cultural Identity*, ed. P. du Gay and S. Hall, 108–28. Thousand Oaks, CA: Sage.

Frith, Simon. 1996b. *Performing Rites: On the Value of Popular Music*. Cambridge, MA: Harvard University Press.

Gober, Patricia. 1999. "Settlement Dynamics and Internal Migration of the U.S. Foreign-Born Population." In *Migration and Restructuring in the United States: A Geographic Perspective*, ed. K. Pandit and S. Withers, 231–49. New York: Rowman and Littlefield.

Gonzalves, Theodore. 2007. *Stage Presence: Conversations with Filipino American Performing Artists*. San Francisco: Meritage.

Gonzalves, Theodore. 2010. *The Day the Dancers Stayed: Performing in the Filipino/American Diaspora*. Philadelphia: Temple University Press.

Habal, Estella. 2007. *San Francisco's International Hotel: Mobilizing the Filipino American Community in the Anti-eviction Movement*. Philadelphia: Temple University Press.

Habal, Estella. 2011. "Filipino Americans in the Decade of the International Hotel." In *Ten Years That Shook the City: San Francisco 1968–1978*, ed. C. Carlsson, 126–40. San Francisco: City Lights Foundation Books.

Hakim, Catherine. 2010. "Erotic Capital." *European Sociological Review* 26(5): 499–518.

Harris, Diane, ed. 2010. *Second Suburb: Levittown, Pennsylvania*. Pittsburgh: University of Pittsburgh Press.

Harrison, Anthony. 2009. *Hip Hop Underground: The Integrity and Ethics of Racial Identification*. Philadelphia: Temple University Press.

Hatfield, Larry. 1999. "S.F. Prep Coach Fired over Hazing Incident." *San Francisco Examiner*, April 7. www.sfgate.com/news/article/S-F-prep-coach-fired-over-hazing-incident-3089502.php.

Hebdige, Dick. 2011. *Subculture: The Meaning of Style*. New York: Routledge.

Hedman, Eva-Lotta, and John Sidel. 2001. *Philippine Politics and Society in the Twentieth Century: Colonial Legacies, Post-colonial Trajectories*. New York: Routledge.

Hickey, Dave. 1997. *Air Guitar: Essays on Art and Democracy*. Los Angeles: Art Issues.

Hilts, Janet, John Shepherd, and David Buckley. 2003. "Groupies." In *Continuum Encyclopedia of Popular Music of the World*, pt. 1, 237–38. New York: Continuum International.

Hing, Bill Ong. 1993. *Making and Remaking Asian America through Immigration Policy, 1950–1990*. Stanford, CA: Stanford University Press.

Hing, Bill Ong. 2004. *Defining America through Immigration Policy*. Philadelphia: Temple University Press.

Hodkinson, Paul. 2004. "Translocal Connections in the Goth Scene." In *Music Scenes:*

Local, Translocal, and Virtual, ed. A. Bennett and R. A. Peterson, 131–48. Nashville: Vanderbilt University Press.

Hollows, Joanne, and Katie Milestone. 1998. "Welcome to Dreamsville: A History and Geography of Northern Soul." In *The Place of Music*, ed. A. Leyshon, D. Matless, and G. Revill, 83–103. New York: Guilford.

Huq, Rupa. 2006. *Beyond Subculture: Youth and Pop in a Postcolonial World*. New York: Routledge.

Jackson, Kenneth. 1987. *Crabgrass Frontier: The Suburbanization of the United States*. New York: Oxford University Press.

Jackson, Sarah. 1998. "Bay Area 51." Unpublished paper.

Jamero, Peter. 2006. *Growing Up Brown: Memoirs of a Filipino American*. Seattle: University of Washington Press.

Katz, Mark. 2010. *Capturing Sound: How Technology Has Changed Music*. Berkeley: University of California Press.

Katz, Mark. 2012. *Groove Music: The Art and Culture of the Hip-Hop DJ*. New York: Oxford University Press.

Keast, Darren. 2000. "Feeling Mighty Real: How Disco Changed the Face of Local Dance Music." *SF Weekly*, August 16. www.sfweekly.com/sanfrancisco/feeling-mighty-real/Content?oid=2139568.

Kelley, Robin D. G. 1997. *Yo' Mama's Disfunktional!* Boston: Beacon.

Kim, Jodi. 2010. *Ends of Empire: Asian American Critique and the Cold War*. Minneapolis: University of Minnesota Press.

Kun, Josh. 2010. "Eastern Promise—YouTube Helps Legaci's Breakout." *New York Times*, June 20. www.nytimes.com/2010/06/20/arts/music/20legaci.html.

Kun, Josh. 2013. "Art of the Crossfade." Public presentation, Grammy U, Santa Monica, July 24.

Kwon, Soo Ah. 2004. "Autoexoticizing: Asian American Youth and the Import Car Scene." *Journal of Asian American Studies* 7(1): 1–26.

Laguerre, Michel S. 2000. *The Global Ethnopolis: Chinatown, Japantown and Manilatown in American Society*. Houndmills, UK: Palgrave Macmillan.

Lawrence, Tim. 2004. *Love Saves the Day: A History of American Dance Music Culture, 1970–1979*. Durham, NC: Duke University Press.

Lazzarato, Maurizio. 1996. "Immaterial Labor." In *Radical Thought in Italy: A Potential Politics*, ed. P. Vimo and M. Hardt, 133–47. Minneapolis: University of Minnesota Press.

Leal, Jorge. 2011. "The Ephemeral Forums of South East Los Angeles." Presentation at Experience Music Project Pop Conference, Los Angeles, February 25.

Lena, Jennifer. 2012. *Banding Together: How Communities Create Genres in Popular Music*. Princeton, NJ: Princeton University Press.

Leyshon, Andrew, David Matless, and George Revill. 1998. "Introduction." In *The Place of Music*, ed. A. Leyshon, D. Matless, and G. Revill, 1–30. New York: Guilford.

Lipsitz, George. 2007. *Footsteps in the Dark: The Hidden Histories of Popular Music*. Minneapolis: University of Minnesota Press.

Lison, Andrew. 2011. "Postmodern Protest? Minimal Techno and Multitude." In *Between the Avant-Garde and the Everyday: Subversive Politics in Europe from 1957 to the Present*, ed. T. Brown and L. Anton, 201–18. New York: Berghahn Books.

Liu, John, Paul Ong, and Carolyn Rosenstein. 1991. "Dual Chain Migration: Post-1965 Filipino Immigration to the United States." *International Migration Review* 25(3): 487–513.

Lowe, Lisa. 1996. *Immigrant Acts: On Asian American Cultural Politics*. Durham, NC: Duke University Press.

Lutz, Catherine, and Lesley Bartlett. 1995. *Making Soldiers in the Public Schools: An Analysis of the Army JROTC Curriculum*. Philadelphia: American Friends Service Committee.

MacDonald, Nancy. 2001. *The Graffiti Subculture: Youth, Masculinity and Identity in London and New York*. Houndmills, UK: Palgrave Macmillan.

Maira, Sunaina. 2002. *Desis in the House: Indian American Youth Culture in New York City*. Philadelphia: Temple University Press.

Manzoor, Sarfraz. 2012. "Strictly Bhangra: How Daytimers Got Young British Asians Dancing." *Guardian*, April 10. www.guardian.co.uk/music/2012/apr/10/strictly-bhangra-daytimers-british-asians.

Maramba, Dina. 2008. "Immigrant Families and the College Experience: Perspectives of Filipina Americans." *Journal of College Student Development* 49(4): 336–50.

McClary, Susan, and Robert Walser. 1994. "Theorizing the Body in African American Music." *Black Music Research Journal* 14(1): 75–84.

Mendoza, Susanah. 2002. *Between the Homeland and the Diaspora: The Politics of Theorizing Filipino and Filipino American Identities*. New York: Routledge.

Nadal, Kevin, ed. 2010. *Filipino American Psychology: A Collection of Personal Narratives*. Bloomington, IN: AuthorHouse.

Namkung, Victoria. 2004. "Reinventing the Wheel: Import Car Racing in Southern California." In *Asian American Youth: Culture, Identity, and Ethnicity*, ed. J. Lee and M. Zhou, 159–76. New York: Routledge.

Nowell, David. 2011. *The Story of Northern Soul: A Definitive History of the Dance Scene That Refuses to Die*. London: Anova.

Nuevo, Miramon. 2002. "Life in Terrorville." *Philippine News* 42(7), October 2–8.

Olaveson, Tim. 2004. "'Connectedness' and the Rave Experience: Rave as New Religious Movement?" In *Rave Culture and Religion*, ed. G. St. John, 83–104. New York: Routledge.

Olson, Mark. 1998. "'Everybody Loves Our Town': Scenes, Spatiality, Migrancy." In *Mapping the Beat: Popular Music and Contemporary Theory*, ed. T. Swiss, J. Sloop, and A. Herman, 269–89. Oxford: Blackwell.

Paul, Cameron. 2006a. "Cameron Paul Tells All." August 27, 2006. Myspace.com, June 18, 2008.

Paul, Cameron. 2006b. "Friday, January 27, 2006." *Cameron Paul & Mixx-It* (blog). http://mixx-it.blogspot.com/2006/01/ive-chosen-first-tracks-which-will-be.html.

Paynter, Ben. 2010. "Why Are Indian Kids So Good at Spelling?" *Slate.com*, June 2. www.slate.com/id/2255622/.

Pechansky, Alan. 1974. "Mobile Discos: From Nursing Homes to Country Clubs." *Billboard*, October 2, 48, 52.

Peterson, Richard A., and Andy Bennett. 2004. "Introducing Music Scenes." In *Music Scenes: Local, Translocal, and Virtual*, ed. A. Bennett and R. A. Peterson, 1–16. Nashville: Vanderbilt University Press.

Phillips, Susan. 1999. *Wallbangin': Graffiti and Gangs in L.A.* Chicago: University of Chicago Press.

Pisares, Elizabeth. 2006. "Do You (Mis)Recognize Me: Filipina Americans in Popular Music and the Problem of Invisibility." In *Positively No Filipinos Allowed: Building Communities and Discourse*, ed. A. Tiongson Jr., E. Gutierrez, and R. Gutierrez, 172–98. Philadelphia: Temple University Press.

Pisares, Elizabeth. 2011. "The Social Invisibility Narrative in Filipino-American Feature Films." *Positions: East Asia Culture Critiques* 19(2): 421–37.

Poschardt, Ulf. 1998. *DJ Culture*. London: Quartet Books.

Putnam, Robert. 2001. *Bowling Alone: The Collapse and Revival of American Community*. New York: Simon and Schuster.

Reines, Dan. 2003. "Styles upon Styles: The Bay Area's Triple Threat DJs Bring All Records to the Party." *SF Weekly*, May 14. www.sfweekly.com/sanfrancisco/styles-upon-styles/Content?oid=2148037.

Reynolds, Simon. 1999. *Generation Ecstasy: Into the World of Rave and Techno Culture*. New York: Routledge.

Rhodes, Carl, and Robert Westwood. 2008. *Critical Representations of Work and Organization in Popular Culture*. New York: Routledge.

Rodriguez, Joseph. 1999. *City against Suburb: The Culture Wars in an American Metropolis*. Westport, CT: Praeger.

Root, Maria. 1997. *Filipino Americans: Transformation and Identity*. Thousand Oaks, CA: Sage.

Rose, Tricia. 1994. *Black Noise: Rap Music and Black Culture in Contemporary America*. Hanover, NH: University Press of New England.

Rubin, Rachel, and Jeffrey Melnick. 2007. *Immigration and American Popular Culture: An Introduction*. New York: New York University Press.

Schloss, Joseph. 2004. *Making Beats: The Art of Sample-Based Hip-Hop*. Middletown, CT: Wesleyan University Press.

Scott, Mel. 1985. *The San Francisco Bay Area: A Metropolis in Perspective*. 2nd ed. Berkeley: University of California Press.

Sedgwick, Eve. 1985. *Between Men: English Literature and Male Homosocial Desire*. New York: Columbia University Press.

See, Sarita. 2009. *The Decolonized Eye: Filipino American Art and Performance*. Minneapolis: University of Minnesota Press.

S.F.U.S.D. (San Francisco Unified School District). 2002. Information about Our Schools. http://orb.sfusd.edu/schdata/schdata.htm.

Shimizu, Celine. 2012. *Straightjacket Sexualities: Unbinding Asian American Manhoods in the Movies*. Stanford, CA: Stanford University Press.

Slobin, Mark. 1993. *Subcultural Sounds: Micromusics of the West*. Middletown, CT: Wesleyan University Press.

Slovick, Sam. 2007. "The Fil-Am Invasion." *LA Weekly*, August 8. www.laweekly.com/2007-08-09/music/the-fil-am-invasion/.

Sobredo, James. 1998. "From Manila Bay to Daly City: Filipinos in San Francisco." In *Reclaiming San Francisco: History, Politics, Culture*, ed. J. Brook, C. Carlsson, and N. Peters, 273–86. San Francisco: City Lights Books.

Spigel, Lynn. 2001. *Welcome to the Dreamhouse: Popular Media and Postwar Suburbs*. Durham, NC: Duke University Press.

Spring, Ken. 2004. "Behind the Rave: Structure and Agency in a Rave Scene." In *Music Scenes: Local, Translocal, and Virtual*, ed. A. Bennett and R. A. Peterson, 48–63. Nashville: Vanderbilt University Press.

Stolzoff, Norman. 2000. *Wake the Town and Tell the People: Dancehall Culture in Jamaica*. Durham, NC: Duke University Press.

Straw, Will. 1997. "Sizing Up Record Collections: Gender and Connoisseurship in Rock Music Culture." In *Sexing the Groove: Popular Music and Gender*, ed. S. Whitely, 3–16. New York: Routledge.

Straw, Will. 1999. "Authorship." In *Key Terms in Popular Music and Culture*, ed. T. Swiss, 199–208. Malden, MA: Blackwell.

Straw, Will. 2004. "Systems of Articulation, Logics of Change: Communities and Scenes in Popular Music." In *Popular Music: Critical Concepts in Media and Cultural Studies*, ed. S. Frith, 79–100. New York: Routledge.

"Tacky into the Wind." 1964. *Time*, February 28. http://content.time.com/time/magazine/article/0,9171,873851,00.html.

Takagi, Paul, and Tony Platt. 1978. "Behind the Gilded Ghetto: An Analyses of Race, Class, and Crime in Chinatown." *Crime and Social Justice* 9: 2–25. www.socialjusticejournal.org/pdf_free/09Takagi-Platt.pdf.

Takaki, Ronald. 1989. *Strangers from a Different Shore*. New York: Penguin.

Tan, Alexis, Gerdean Tan, and Alma Tan. 1987. "American TV in the Philippines: A Test of Cultural Impact." *Journalism Quarterly* 64(1): 65–144.

Thornton, Sarah. 1996. *Club Cultures: Music, Media and Subcultural Capital*. Middletown, CT: Wesleyan University Press.

Tintiangco-Cubales, Allyson. 2009. "Building a Community Center: Filipinas/os in San Francisco's Excelsior Neighborhood." In *Asian America: Forming New Communities, Expanding Boundaries*, ed. H. Ling, 104–28. Piscataway, NJ: Rutgers University Press.

Tiongson, Antonio, Jr. 2013. *Filipinos Represent: DJs, Racial Authenticity, and the Hip-Hop Nation*. Minneapolis: University of Minnesota Press.

Tolentino, Rolando B. 2002. "Identity and Difference in 'Filipino/a American' Media Arts." In *Screening Asian Americans*, ed. P. Feng, 111–32. New Brunswick, NJ: Rutgers University Press.

Tongson, Karen. 2010. "Analog Acoustics: Echoes of the Subject from Rin on the Rox to 'Glee.'" Presentation at Experience Music Project Pop Conference, Seattle, April 17.

Tongson, Karen. 2011. *Relocations: Queer Suburban Imaginaries*. New York: New York University Press.

U.S. Census Bureau. 2007. "Asian/Pacific American Heritage Month: May 2007." March 1.

Vargas, João. 2008. "Exclusion, Openess, and Utopia in Black Male Performance at the World Stage Jazz Jam Sessions." In *Big Ears: Listening for Gender in Jazz Studies*, ed. N. Rustin and S. Tucker, 320–47. Durham, NC: Duke University Press.

Vergara, Benito, Jr. 2009. *Pinoy Capital: The Filipino Nation in Daly City*. Philadelphia: Temple University Press.

Viesca, Victor. 2012. "Native Guns and Stray Bullets: Cultural Activism and Filipino American Rap Music in Post-riot Los Angeles." *Amerasia Journal* 38(1): 113–42.

Villegas, Mark R., Kuttin' Kandi, and Roderick N. Labrador, eds. 2014. *Empire of Funk: Hip Hop and Representation in Filipina/o America*. San Diego: Cognella.

Waldie, D. J. 2005. *Holy Land: A Suburban Memoir*. New York: Norton.

Walser, Robert. 1993. *Running with the Devil: Power, Gender, and Madness in Heavy Metal Music*. Middletown, CT: Wesleyan University Press.

Wang, Oliver. 2001a. "Between the Notes: Finding Asian America in Popular Music." *American Music* 19(4): 439–65.

Wang, Oliver. 2001b. "Mobile Madness: A New Exhibit Looks at the History of Filipino American DJs." *San Francisco Bay Guardian*, October 3.

Wang, Oliver. 2001c. "Three's the Magic Number." *Blu*, May.

Wang, Oliver. 2002. "Hooked on Sonics." *LA Weekly*, August 14. www.laweekly.com/2002-08-22/music/hooked-on-sonics/.

Wang, Oliver. 2006. "These Are the Breaks: Hip-Hop and AfroAsian Cultural (Dis)Connections." In *AfroAsian Encounters: Culture, History and Politics*, ed. H. Raphael-Hernandez and S. Steen, 146–66. New York: New York University Press.

Wang, Oliver. 2007. "Rapping and Repping Asian: Race, Authenticity, and the Asian American MC." In *Alien Encounters: Popular Culture in Asian America*, ed. M. Nguyen and T. Tu, 35–68. Durham, NC: Duke University Press.

Wang, Oliver. 2014. "Getting Schooled: Lessons from Researching Filipino American Mobile DJ Crews." In *Empire of Funk: Hip-Hop and Representation in Filipina/o America*, ed. M. Villegas, K. Kandi, and R. Labrador, 37–42. San Diego: Cognella.

Welch, Calvin. 2011. "The Fight to Stay: The Creation of the Community Housing Movement in San Francisco, 1968–1978." In *Ten Years That Shook the City: San Francisco 1968–1978*, ed. C. Carlsson, 151–62. San Francisco: City Lights Foundation Books.

Williams, Terry, and William Kornblum. 1985. *Growing Up Poor*. San Francisco: Lexington Books.

Wolf, Diane. 1997. "Family Secrets: Transnational Struggles among Children of Filipino Immigrants." *Sociological Perspectives* 40(3): 457–82.

Wolfe, George. 1996. "Bring In 'da Noise, Bring In 'da Funk." *Playbill*, April.
Wollenberg, Charles. 1985. *Golden Gate Metropolis: Perspectives on Bay Area History*. Berkeley: Institute of Governmental Studies, University of California, Berkeley.
Wong, Deborah. 2004. *Speak It Louder: Asian Americans Making Music*. New York: Routledge.
Yoshihara, Mari. 2007. *Musicians from a Different Shore: Asians and Asian Americans in Classical Music*. Philadelphia: Temple University Press.

Recordings, Plays, and Films

Cajayon, Gene (dir.). 2000. *The Debut*. Motion picture. Los Angeles: Sony Pictures.
Castro, John (dir.). 2003. *Diary of a Gangsta Sucka*. Short film.
Choy, Curtis (dir.). 1983. *Fall of the I-Hotel*. Video recording. San Francisco: Crosscurrents Media and National Asian American Telecommunications Association.
Deep Concentration. 1998. Various artists. Audio recording. Om Records.
De Leon, Lakandiwa, Dawn Mabalon, and Jonathan Ramos (dirs.). 2001. *Beats, Rhymes and Resistance: Pilipinos and Hip-Hop in Los Angeles*. Video recording. Los Angeles.
Enriquez, Jocelyn (performer). 1994. "I've Been Thinking of You." On 12-inch single. Audio recording. Classified Records.
Evans, Faith (performer). 1995. "You Used to Love Me." On 12-inch single. Audio recording. Arista Records.
Gang Starr (group). 1989. "DJ Premier Is in Deep Concentration." On *No More Mr. Nice Guy*. Audio recording. Chrysalis Records.
Grandmaster Flash (performer). 1981. "The Adventures of Grandmaster Flash on the Wheels of Steel." Audio recording. Sugar Hill Records.
Hancock, Herbie (performer). 1983. "Rockit." Audio recording. Columbia Records.
Hwang, David Henry (dir.). 1980. *FOB*. Play.
Leva, Gary (dir.). 2008. *The Legion of Doom: The Pathology of the Super Villain*. Short film. Los Angeles: Warner Home Video.
Portugal, Ramon, III (dir.). 2006. *Spin Doctors: A Profile of a Bay Area Deejay Crew*. Video recording. Daly City, CA. www.youtube.com/watch?v=vfP1poeHtc4&e.
Pray, Doug (dir.). 2002. *Scratch*. Motion picture. New York: Palm Pictures.
Return of the DJ. 1995. Various artists. Audio recording. Bomb Hip-Hop Records.
Reynolds, Malvina (songwriter). 1962. "Little Boxes." Recorded by Pete Seeger on "Little Boxes," 7-inch single, 1963. Columbia.

Index

AA Productions, 61, 99, 107–9, 122–23, 127, 154, 108–9, 122–23, 154–55; "Summer Girls Showcase," 122–23
Academia, Eleanor, 147–48, 198n33
"Adventures of Grandmaster Flash on the Wheels of Steel, The," 129
Agenda DJ Showcase, 200n9
Alba, Richard, 40
alliances between crews, 27–28, 105–7, 152
Alsaybar, Bangele, 64, 168–69, 170, 185, 193n18, 201n2
Altered Images, 98
Alviar, Arleen, 61, 104, 107–8, 109, 123, 191–92nn7–8, 193n19
Anicete, Candido, 33
Anies, Daphnie, 46, 90, 156–57, 185n12
Anies, Rene, 62, 65, 74, 156–57; on the role of DJs, 55, 58
Anolin, Ken, 20, 68, 102, 104, 200n12
Apollo (DJ). *See* Novicio, Apollo
Apostol, Leila, 46, 72
Archer, "Jazzy" Jim, 106, 126–27, 137, 138, 141, 146, 194n1, 196nn20–21

Aure, Glen, 138
Austin, Joe, 17
authorship of mixes, 73, 102–3

Balance, Christine, 44, 45, 200n17
Balboa High School, 168; as a birthplace for crews, 55–56, 105, 132, 155; and ROTC, 70, 163, 164, 193n17, 194n8, 201n3; shows taking place at, 50–52, 54–55, 89, 100
Bambaataa, Afrika, 68, 188n6
Barkada, 64, 65, 170
Bartolome, Jinni, 90, 193–94n22
Bautista, Renel, 50–54
Beat Junkies, 122, 138, 198n37, 199n5
Becker, Howard, 91, 177n20
Beltran, Sam, 50–55, 163
Beyond the Limit, 90, 97, 98–99, 105, 155
Billy Jam (DJ), 198–99n37
Bitanga, Father Fred, 39, 41, 183n30
Bomb Hip-Hop Records, 198n37
Bonifacio, Alvin, 33
Bourriaud, Nicolas, 175n11

Bradford, Mark: business practices of, 58, 96–98, 100–101, 107, 112, 123–24, 154–55; death of, 124, 127, 193–94n22; personal life of, 100, 103–4, 159–60, 191nn3–4, 192n8

Brewster, Bill, and Frank Broughton, 74, 136–37

Buffy, 146

Bullet Proof Scratch Hamsters, 138, 149, 198n36; as Space Travelers, 149

Caganot, Melanie "Lani Luv," 89–90, 191n6; on battles, 105–6; on club work, 140; on Imagine, 101–2; and *Tales of the Turntable*, 25, 126, 177n21, 200n10

Cajayon, Gene, 186n21, 189n10, 196n23

Canson, Paul "Pauly Tek," 102, 123

capital: cultural, 103, 184n7; economic, 43, 57, 81, 90, 101, 143, 145–46, 179n8, 184nn7–8, 188n6, 189n12; erotic, 60–63, 77, 201n2; social, 81, 86–87, 90–93, 132, 145–46, 163–64, 184n7, 190nn14–15; symbolic, 57–60, 68, 69, 83, 84, 101–3, 184n7, 195n12

Carp, Mickey, 33

Carrion, Anthony, 13, 30–33, 56, 59, 60–61, 88, 101–2, 106, 131, 150, 184nn8–9

Castillo, Jocelyn "Lady J," 191n6

Castro, John, 89, 198n35

Catapusan, Benicio, 179–80n14

Celis, Amy, 70–75

Chang, Jeff, 146, 197n28

Charnas, Dan, 197n28

Chilltown Crush Crew, 18, 101, 191n4

Choi, Moe "Choimatic," 86–87, 189n9

Choy, Curtis, 198n35

Chuckles, 129–30

City Lights, 60, 117–18

Classified Records, 146, 197n31

Cohen, Sara, 65, 76–77, 187n28

Colma, 42

competition between crews, 66–67, 100–101, 102–5, 107, 126–27, 195nn12–14

Cordova, Larry, 140–41

Corpuz, Rudy, 168, 170, 201n1

Cosmix Sounds, 15, 74

Creative Madness, 27, 106

Crossley, Nick, 92, 184n5

Cruz, Dame, 111–12, 113–14, 192n11

Cruz, Jonathan "Shortkut," 10, 11, 130–31, 137, 138, 152, 154, 169, 194n9, 199n1, 199n5

Daly City, 26, 30–31, 109, 165, 178n5, 179n10; crews of, 27, 97, 100, 103, 105, 106–7, 123, 130, 132, 155, 198n36; history of, 37, 38–40, 41–42, 180n17, 182–83nn26–30; local landmarks, 18, 80, 83, 194n7; on the map and travel around, 36, 110, 115, 169; parties in, 45, 89, 102

Damian, Derrick "D," 68, 83, 140–41, 196n21

Danville, 50–51

Davis, Josh "Shadow," 134

decline of the mobile crew scene, 140–50

dela Cruz, Jay, 32, 42, 119, 143, 200n13; and his work with Spintronix, 5, 46, 58, 61, 63, 87, 88, 89, 102, 139–41, 183n33

dela Cruz, Patrick, 90, 98–99, 105

Denton, Nancy, 40

Diary of a Gangsta Sucka, 198n35

disco, 30–33, 35, 176n18, 177n1

Disco Mix Competition (DMC), 130, 133, 164–65, 194n10, 195n16

Disco Tech Limited, 55, 72, 74

Dizon, Liza, 72

DJing techniques, 4–5, 67–68, 153, 175nn11–12; beat-juggling, 130–31, 194n4; beat-matching, 9, 199n3; blend mixing, 9; building the floor, 12–15; collective practice of, 16–18; cut-mixing, 200n14; disco break, 34; quick-mixing, 9, 127; scratching, 9, 11, 25, 122, 127, 128–38, 149, 153, 173–74n1, 176n18, 188n5, 195nn2–3, 195n6, 195n8, 195nn12–14, 195n16, 196nn18–19, 199nn2–3; slip-cueing, 33; tandem mixing, 133

"DJ Premier in Deep Concentration," 67

"Don't Stop the Madness" (Imagine 7).
  See Imagine
Dreamscape, 102
Dr. Funk, 50, 54
drill team, 50, 51, 160, 163–65, 194n8, 201n1
D-Styles (DJ), 194n9, 199n5
Dumlao, Rebecca, 72–74, 75
Durkheim, Emile, 13–14

economics of the scene, 5, 52–54, 56,
  80–86, 88, 90, 140, 150, 154
Electric Sounds, 55, 56, 62, 65, 72, 74, 88,
  110, 132, 185n15
Elwood, Philip, 37
Enriquez, Jocelyn, 146, 197–98nn30–31
Eternal Sound Productions, 100
ethnic/racial identity, 177n1,
  189–91nn14–15, 197–98n31, 198n35;
  DJ Apollo on, 20, 42, 120; DJing and
  the creation of community within,
  113–14, 115–22, 188n6; and home
  life, 19–22; interacting with gender,
  69–70; and marginalization, 138–39,
  149, 169–70, 186n20, 192–93n15,
  196n21, 198n33; marketing outside
  of a single, 107–9; in school, 21; self-
  identity and, 201n2
Expressions Entertainment, 123, 126–27

Fair Housing Act (1965), 41, 182n24
family and community support, 2, 56–57,
  75–76, 81–86, 87–93, 120–21, 184n6,
  188n6; perceptions of crews within
  their communities, 83–84, 174n2
Farinas, Dell, 101, 191n4
female participation in the mobile DJ
  scene, 109–10, 177n21; as consumers,
  54, 60–62, 77, 88, 185n11, 185n13,
  187n27; as creators, 61–62, 70–77,
  191n6; Daphnie Anies on, 61–62,
  70–74, 75, 191n6; exclusion from, 22,
  66; sexual politics of the dance floor,
  62–63
Flannigan-Saint-Aubin, Arthur, 66–67
Foreplay. See Expressions Entertainment
Francisco, John, 26, 103, 117, 123, 126–27,
  141–42, 169–70

Fremont, 21, 25, 36, 38, 40, 42, 47, 62, 75,
  108–10, 114, 155, 183n30
Fresh Beats Incorporated, 102
Frith, Simon, 11–12, 114, 159
Fusion, 20, 102, 104
Futuristic Sounds, 18, 100–101

Gambol, Daphnie. See Anies, Daphnie
Gang Starr, 67
garage parties, 4, 35, 43–47, 57, 64, 88, 90,
  114, 144
Genie G (DJ). See Millare, Gary
Geronimo, Henry "G," 100–101, 104
Glew, Sarah, 83–84
Go-Go's, the, 46, 55, 61–62, 70–75, 100,
  102, 186nn23–24
Gonzalvez, Theo, 147–48
Gramlich, Amy, 70–75
Grandmaster D.S.T. (DJ), 129
Grandmaster Flash (DJ), 129, 188n6,
  197nn27–28
Grandwizard Theodore (DJ), 128–29
Grasso, Francis, 33–35
Guillermo, Emil, 149

Hakim, Catherine, 60
Hancock, Herbie, 129
Harrison, Anthony, 122
Hedges, John "Johnny Disco," 32, 148,
  178n3, 198n34
Hercules, 42
High Energy, 98
High Tech Soundz, 132
Hip Hop Slam, 199n37
Hodkinson, Paul, 111
Hollows, Joanne, 111
homosociality, 63–65, 68, 70, 77, 196n17

Images Inc., 25, 27–28, 57–58, 63, 81,
  97–98, 106, 108, 154
Imagine, 96, 100–102, 103–4, 112,
  123–24, 193n20; Francisco Pardorla
  on, 97, 98; Imagine 1 ("Let the Music
  Play"), 100; Imagine 5, 154–55;
  Imagine 6, 96; Imagine 7 ("Don't Stop
  the Madness"), 96–99; Imagine 8,
  106; Imagine 20, 123–24, 193n20

Immigration Act (1965), 37, 51
"Impeach the President," 130–31, 194n5
import car scene, the, 142–44, 196nn23–24
Invisibl Skratch Piklz, 10–11, 122, 134–36, 138, 149, 152, 194n6, 194n9, 198n37; as Furious Minds 2 Observe (FM2O), 133, 135, 194n6, 194n10; as Rocksteady Crew, 133, 152, 194n6, 194–95n11; as the Shadow DJs, 194n6

Jackson, Kenneth, 44
Jackson, Sarah, 179n10
Jamaican sound system culture, 84–85, 145, 179n9, 188n6
Javier, Kristine, 74
Jazzy Jim (DJ). See Archer, "Jazzy" Jim
Juice Crew, the, 106, 191n5
Just 2 Hype, 11, 68, 74, 130, 137–38, 140–41

Kantares, Kim "KK Baby," 39, 45, 46, 138–39, 167, 168, 169
Katz, Mark, 74, 129, 174n1, 175n14, 194n2
Kelley, Robin, 82, 187–88n3
Kicks Company, 35
Kong, Burton "King," 19, 27, 59, 89, 106–7, 139, 142, 154, 155, 184n9
Kong, Melanie. See Caganot, Melanie "Lani Luv"
Kool Herc (DJ), 68, 188n6

Ladda Sounds, 97, 149, 150, 155
Lani Luv (MC). See Caganot, Melanie "Lani Luv"
Lawrence, Tim, 14, 177n1, 188n6
Lazzarato, Maurizo, 187n2
Leal, Jorge, 46, 183–84nn34–35
Lee, Rick, 138, 154, 196n21
Legion of Boom, 27–28, 106–7, 126–27
Lena, Jennifer, 77, 91, 144–45, 146–47, 149, 196–97nn25–26
"Let the Music Play" (Imagine 1). See Imagine
liminal forums, 44, 47, 112, 191n6
"Little Bit of Ecstasy, A," 197–98n31

"Little Boxes," 37, 41
Liu, John, 38
Live Style Productions, 11, 56, 105, 126–27, 132
Livingston, Theodore, 128–29
Los Angeles, 38, 46, 64, 122, 168, 193n18
Lowell High School, 55, 163, 201n3

MacDonald, Nancy, 67, 185n17
Madrid, Orlando, 55, 72, 82–83, 85, 88, 131, 142, 150, 152
Maira, Sunaina, 62
Manor Music, 2, 4, 18, 83–84
Maramba, Dina, 75
Marcos, Ferdinand, 51
masculinity, 23, 65–70, 74, 143, 186n18, 186nn20–21, 187n28
Megatone, 148, 159, 198n34
Mendoza, Susanah, 122
mentorship, 16, 76, 104–5, 130, 157, 187n27
Midstar Productions, 27, 33, 42, 86, 97, 106, 142
Miguel, Chris, 2–5, 102
Milestone, Katie, 111
Millare, Gary "Genie G," 85, 96, 97, 98, 138, 140, 154
Mixmaster Mike (DJ). See Schwartz, Michael "Mixmaster Mike"
mobility: immigration, 31, 37–41, 51, 84, 179–80nn14–17; as metaphor, 112, 116; practical aspects of production and, 3–4, 5, 16–18, 57, 137, 141, 199n7; Rene Anies on, 88, 110, 115; and social mobility, 58–60, 65, 76, 84; traveling to gigs, 14–15, 35, 50–55, 59, 75, 88, 109–10, 136, 184n35, 192n10; traveling to parties, 47, 99, 110–14, 183n33
Monsayac, Jeremy "Uprise," 113, 115
Music Masters, the, 50
music scenes, definition of, 77, 93, 145, 174n2, 189nn13–14, 190n15

Negro, Joey, 34
nightclubs, 14, 34, 67, 139–40, 153, 177n2, 178n4, 188n6; Broadway Power and Light, 32; City Disco, 32; Dance

Your Ass Off, Inc., 32; financial lure of, 139–40, 145–46, 188n5, 197n27, 198n34; The Firehouse, 50–51; I-Beam, 32; The Mineshaft, 32; Oil Can Harry's, 32; The Palladium, 32, 35; and scratching, 137; Studio West, 30, 31, 32–33, 35; Trocadero Transfer, 32; underage club admission, 30, 32; as youth space, 46

Nite Lime, 75, 109

Non-Stop Boogie, 33, 55, 56, 73, 82, 131, 142, 150

Northern Soul, 111, 192n9

Novicio, Apollo, 11, 89, 130, 132–33, 174n5; work and technique of, 131, 136, 152–55, 194n6, 194–95nn11–12, 196n17

Oakland, 36, 57, 97, 108, 149, 155, 182n25

Olimpiada, Gil, 58, 112–13, 140

Olimpiada, Jose, 58, 98, 140

Ong, Paul, 38

Oroc, Chris "Babu," 129, 198n37, 199n5

Pardorla, Francisco, 143, 146; on being part of a crew, 63; on DJing, 57–58, 60, 81, 117–18, 131–32, 140, 192n15; on the Legion, 28, 106–7

Paul, Cameron, 32–33, 56, 118, 138, 139, 178nn3–5

peer-to-peer observation and growth of mobile DJing, 56–57, 76, 80–84

Pinole, 42

Pirate Fuckin' Radio, 199n37

Pisares, Elizabeth, 21, 197n31

Pray, Doug, 134, 194nn2–3

Punsalan, Vincent "Vinroc," 152–55, 199n1

Putnam, Robert, 91

Q-Bert (DJ). *See* Quitevis, Richard "Q-Bert"

queerness, 32, 100, 104, 159–60, 177n1, 178n4, 185n13, 200n17

Quitevis, Richard "Q-Bert," 10–11, 56, 155–56, 194n8, 201n1; and competition, 126–27, 152, 164–65, 194n1, 194n10; on role models, 76; working with other DJs, 105, 132–34, 136, 194n6, 194–95nn11–12, 196n17

Racho, Suzie "Suzie Q," 15, 74

radio, 33, 83, 136, 138–39, 140, 147, 148, 178n5, 184n4, 196n20

Raggawinos, the, 123

"Rapper's Delight," 146, 197n28

Rashid, Yusuf, 45, 110, 114, 167, 169, 170–71, 201n1

Ravipudi, Sanjeev, 8–9

Recania, Leila, 46, 72

recordings and the lack thereof, 145–50, 189n14, 192n10

Refuerzo, Dave "Dynamix," 21, 47, 121

Restauro, Edward, 50–55, 163

Restauro, Rafael, 50–55, 83, 84, 118–20, 141, 163, 165, 170

Restauro, Ricky, 50–55, 163

Return of the DJ, 198–99n37

Reynolds, Malvina, 37, 41

Reynolds, Simon, 13, 187n27

Rhettmatic (DJ), 199n5

Rimando, Travis "Pone," 120, 134, 143, 149

Rivera, Dino, 2–5, 80, 85, 88, 102, 119, 156, 173

Robinson, Sylvia, 197n28

"Rockit," 129, 132, 133, 194n3

Rodriguez, Joseph, 110, 114, 116, 181n22

Roque, Kormann, 4, 57, 60, 119, 129, 146, 147, 184–85n10

Rose, Tricia, 76, 187n27

Rosenstein, Carolyn, 38

ROTC (Reserve Officers' Training Corps), 163, 186n22, 193n17, 201n1

Ruaro, Rebecca, 72–74, 75

Sacramento, 110, 132

Samson, Brian "MC Fly," 105, 115

San Bruno, 42

San Diego, 38

San Jose, 21, 26, 36, 42, 45, 47, 54, 89, 108, 110, 122, 169

San Mateo, 96–97

Saturday Night Fever, 30, 32, 177n1, 192–93n15

Schloss, Joseph, 187n27, 189n8, 200n15
Schwartz, Michael "Mixmaster Mike," 11, 132–33, 152, 194n3, 194–95nn11–12, 198n37
Second To None, 102, 107, 123
Seeger, Pete, 37
Selvin, Joel, 148
Seoul Brothers, 19
Serato Scratch Live, 199n2
Shadow (DJ). *See* Davis, Josh "Shadow"
Shiggar Fraggar Show, The, 199n37
Shortkut (DJ). *See* Cruz, Jonathan "Shortkut"
showcases, 23, 99–102, 104, 105, 107–9, 112–13, 116, 122–24, 126–28, 138
Skyway Sounds, 106, 126–27
Slobin, Mark, 17
Sound Explosion, 50–56, 70, 119–20, 141, 155
Sound Sequence, 19, 27, 59, 74, 97, 106, 191n6
Sounds of Success, 55, 72
Sound Syndicate, 126–27
Sparks, Willie, 55, 164, 201n1
Spintronix, 2–5, 18, 46, 57, 60, 63, 87–88, 102, 103, 105, 106, 150, 154, 199n6
Spring, Ken, 91, 189n13
Stockton, 110
Stolzoff, Norman, 84–85, 179n9
Straw, Will, 68–69, 76, 192n13
street gangs, 65, 69, 167–72, 193n18, 198n35, 201nn1–2
Studio Sounds, 73
Styles Beyond Compare, 27, 97, 106, 107, 123, 150
Sugarhill Gang, the, 146
Sugitan, Peter, 149

"Tacky into the Wind," 37
Templeton High School, 130
Thornton, Sarah, 14, 187n27, 191n1
3-Style Attractions, 21, 47
Thudrumble, 155–56
Tintiangco-Cubales, Allyson, 21, 62, 75, 109–10, 180n17, 181n23, 182n27, 182n29

Tiongson, Antonio, 74, 121–22, 160, 173–74n1, 176–77n19
Tommy Boy, 146, 197–98n31
Tongson, Karen, 45, 200–201n18
"Tribute 2 Bay Area Mobile DJs," 154, 199n7
Triple Threat (DJs), 152–55, 199nn2–3, 199n5
Tumakay, Paul, 35, 114, 116, 164, 165, 192n13, 201nn1–2
Tydings-McDuffie Act (1934), 37

Ultimate Creations, 18, 58, 73, 96, 98, 100, 105, 140
Union City, 21, 36, 42, 62, 75, 103, 106–8, 109–10, 183n30, 191–92n7
Unique Musique, 19, 42, 100–101, 106, 155
Universal Beats, 98
Universal Sounds, 35
Unlimited Play, 97–98
Unlimited Sounds, 11, 13, 56, 101, 106, 131, 132
urban (re)development and renewal, 40–41, 46–47

Vallejo, 36, 42, 59, 110, 132
Vargas, Liza, 72
Velocity Records, 146
Vergara, Benito, 41, 180n17
Villenueva, Noel, 72
violence, 83, 102, 121, 141–42, 169, 201n1
Viray, Ray, 33, 42, 86, 101, 142

Wang, Gary "V-Nutz," 195n16
Weber, Paul John, 33, 178n4
Westmoor High School, 2, 105, 132, 184n10
Wilson High School, 73, 164
Wolfe, George C., 11

Ycmat, Daisy, 74
Yoga Frog (DJ), 194n9
Young 'N' Tough (YNT), 73, 102, 186n24

218 / Index

www.ingramcontent.com/pod-product-compliance
Lightning Source LLC
Chambersburg PA
CBHW071818230426
43670CB00013B/2491